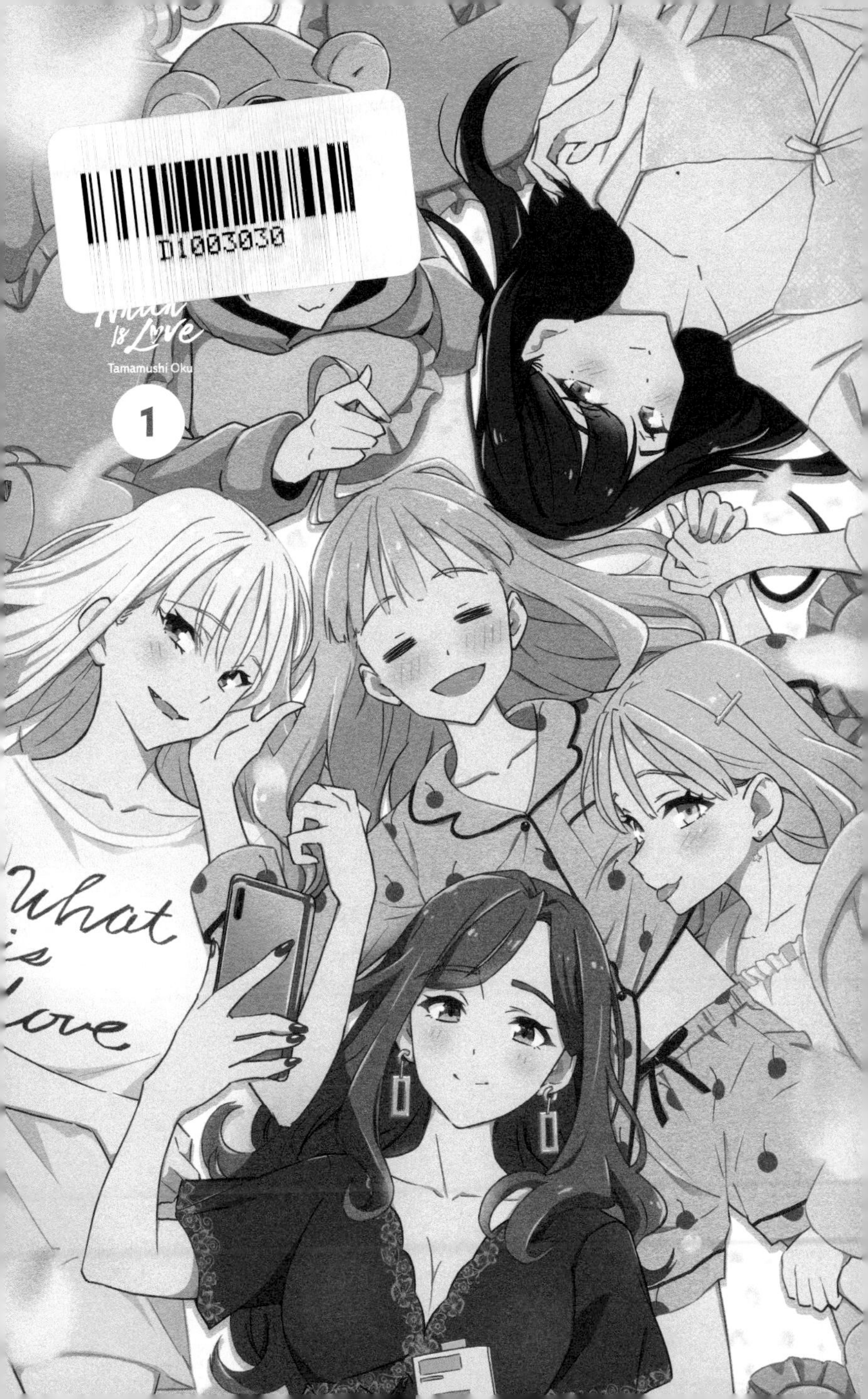
is Love
Tamamushi Oku
1

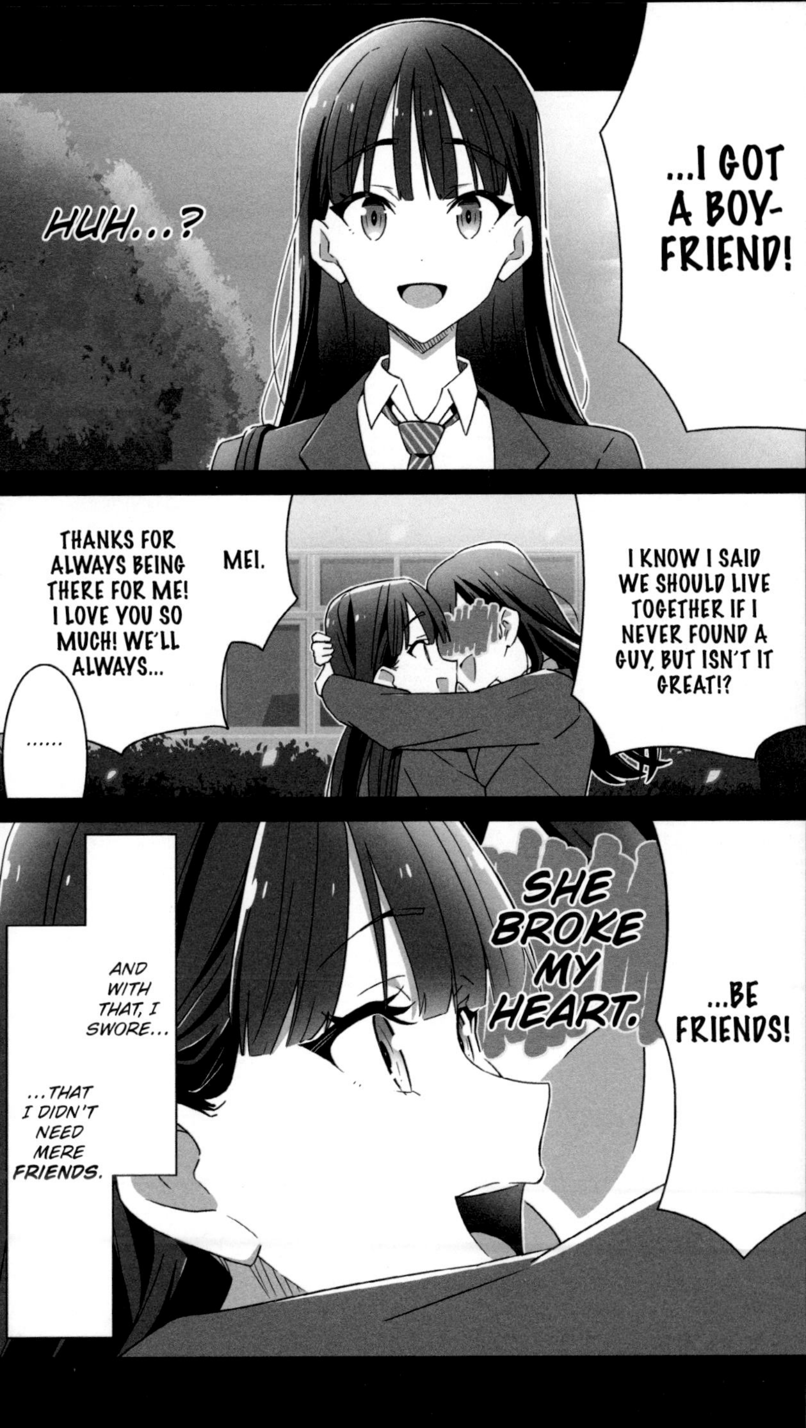
...I GOT A BOY-FRIEND!
HUH...?
I KNOW I SAID WE SHOULD LIVE TOGETHER IF I NEVER FOUND A GUY, BUT ISN'T IT GREAT!?
MEI.
THANKS FOR ALWAYS BEING THERE FOR ME! I LOVE YOU SO MUCH! WE'LL ALWAYS...
......
...BE FRIENDS!
SHE BROKE MY HEART.
AND WITH THAT, I SWORE...
...THAT I DIDN'T NEED MERE FRIENDS.

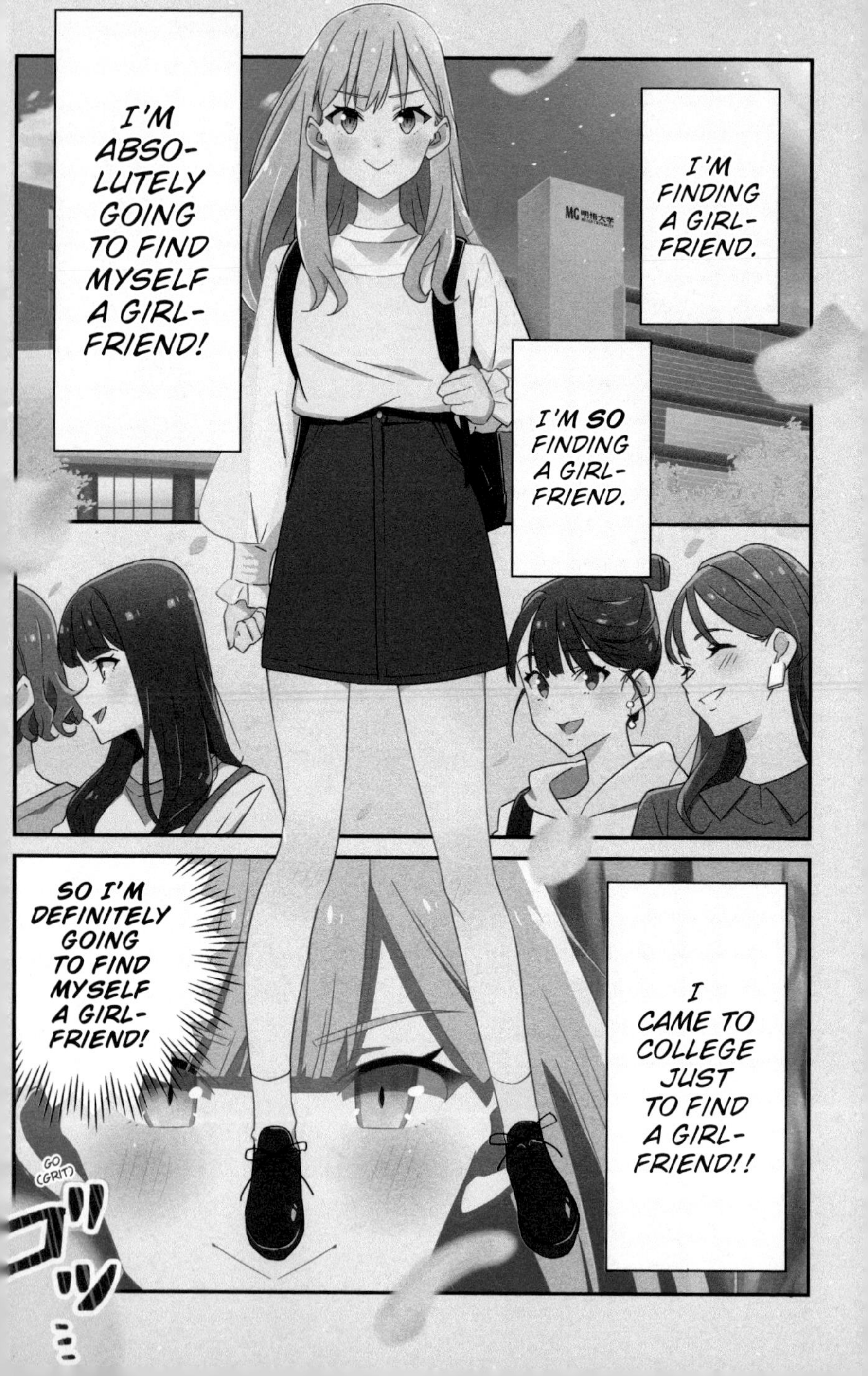
I'M FINDING A GIRL-FRIEND.
I'M SO FINDING A GIRL-FRIEND.
I'M ABSO-LUTELY GOING TO FIND MYSELF A GIRL-FRIEND!
I CAME TO COLLEGE JUST TO FIND A GIRL-FRIEND!!
SO I'M DEFINITELY GOING TO FIND MYSELF A GIRL-FRIEND!
GO (GRIT)
ゴッ

I Don't Know Which Is Love

1

Tamamushi Oku

contents

I Don't Know
Which
Is Love

Tamamushi Oku

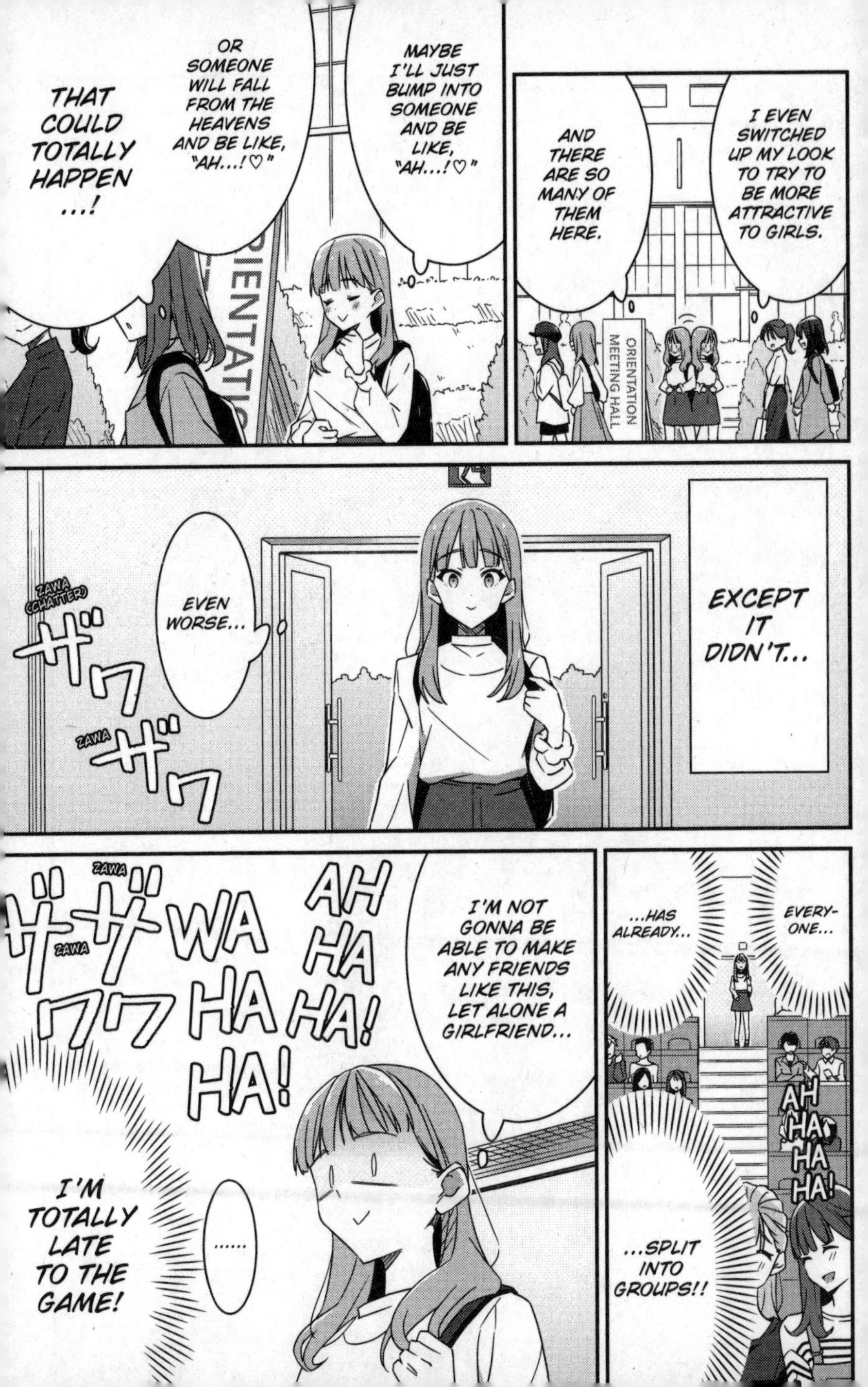
I EVEN SWITCHED UP MY LOOK TO TRY TO BE MORE ATTRACTIVE TO GIRLS.
AND THERE ARE SO MANY OF THEM HERE.
ORIENTATION MEETING HALL
MAYBE I'LL JUST BUMP INTO SOMEONE AND BE LIKE, "AH...!♡"
OR SOMEONE WILL FALL FROM THE HEAVENS AND BE LIKE, "AH...!♡"
THAT COULD TOTALLY HAPPEN...!
EXCEPT IT DIDN'T...
EVEN WORSE...
ZAWA (CHATTER)
ザワ
ZAWA
ザワ
EVERY-ONE...
...HAS ALREADY...
AH HA HA HA HA!
...SPLIT INTO GROUPS!!
I'M NOT GONNA BE ABLE TO MAKE ANY FRIENDS LIKE THIS, LET ALONE A GIRLFRIEND...
AH HA HA!
WA HA HA HA!
ZAWA
ザワ
ZAWA
ザワ
I'M TOTALLY LATE TO THE GAME!
......

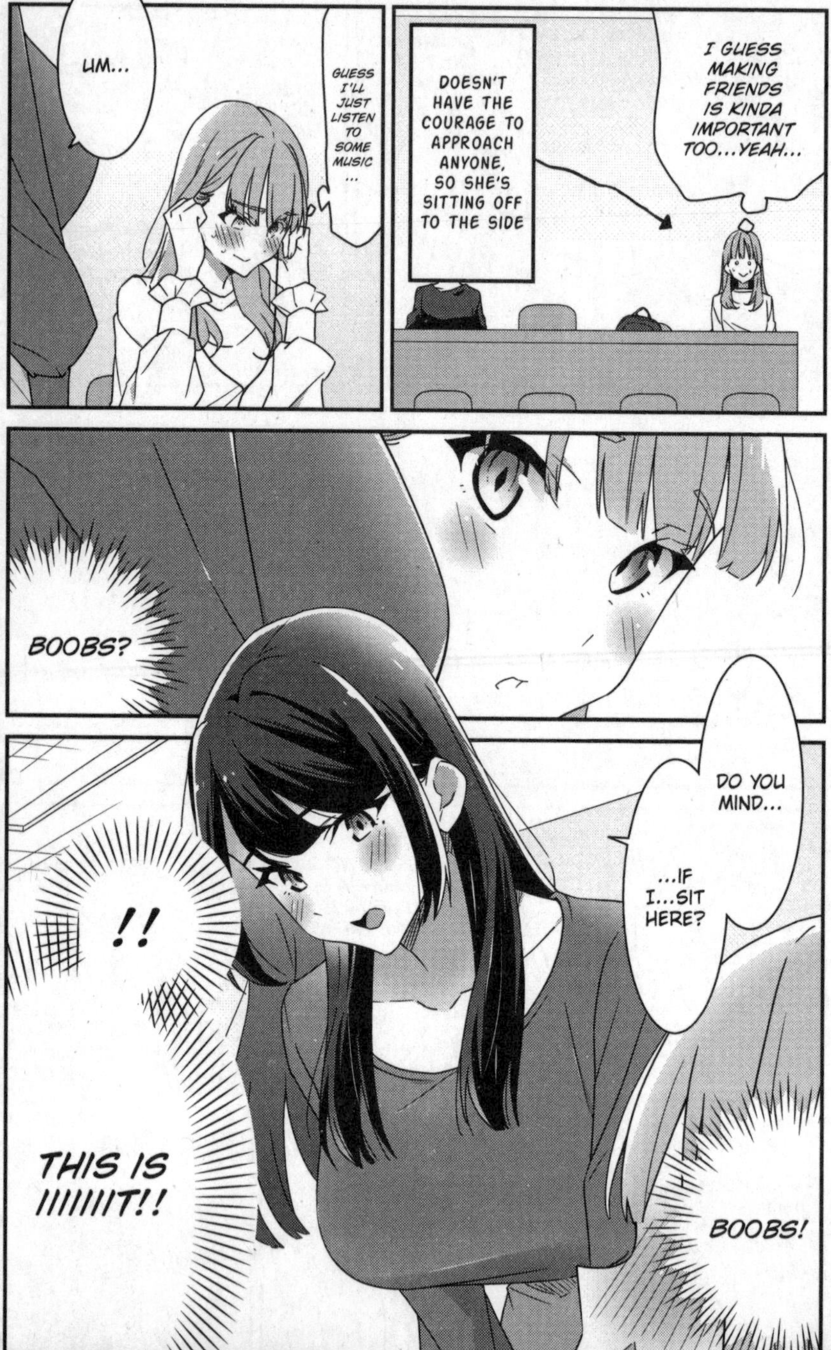
I GUESS MAKING FRIENDS IS KINDA IMPORTANT TOO...YEAH...
DOESN'T HAVE THE COURAGE TO APPROACH ANYONE, SO SHE'S SITTING OFF TO THE SIDE
GUESS I'LL JUST LISTEN TO SOME MUSIC...
UM...
BOOBS?
DO YOU MIND...
...IF I...SIT HERE?
!!
BOOBS!
THIS IS IIIIIIIT!!

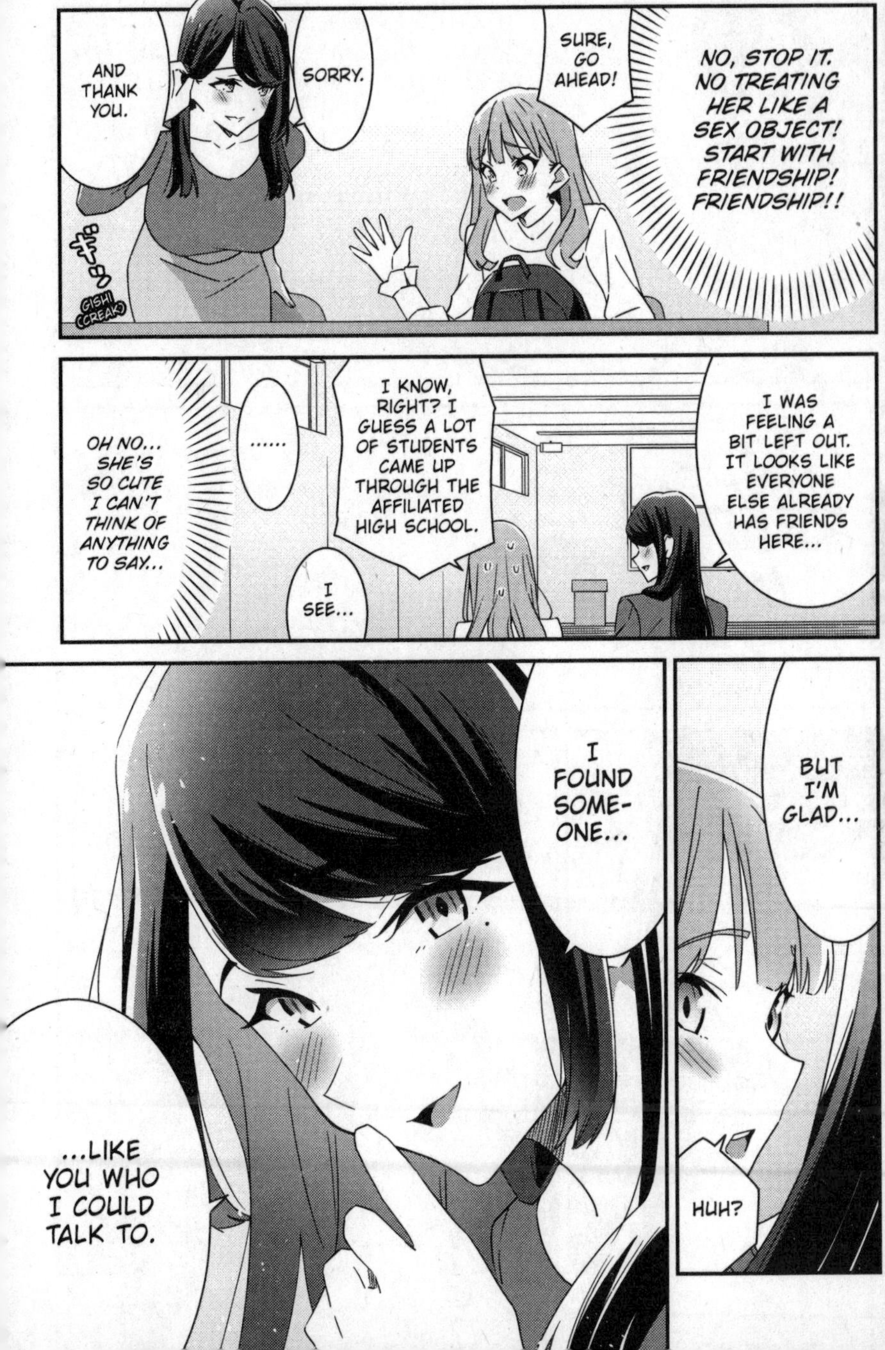
NO, STOP IT. NO TREATING HER LIKE A SEX OBJECT! START WITH FRIENDSHIP! FRIENDSHIP!!
SURE, GO AHEAD!
SORRY.
AND THANK YOU.
GISHI (CREAK)
I WAS FEELING A BIT LEFT OUT. IT LOOKS LIKE EVERYONE ELSE ALREADY HAS FRIENDS HERE...
I KNOW, RIGHT? I GUESS A LOT OF STUDENTS CAME UP THROUGH THE AFFILIATED HIGH SCHOOL.
I SEE...
......
OH NO... SHE'S SO CUTE I CAN'T THINK OF ANYTHING TO SAY...
BUT I'M GLAD...
HUH?
I FOUND SOME-ONE...
...LIKE YOU WHO I COULD TALK TO.

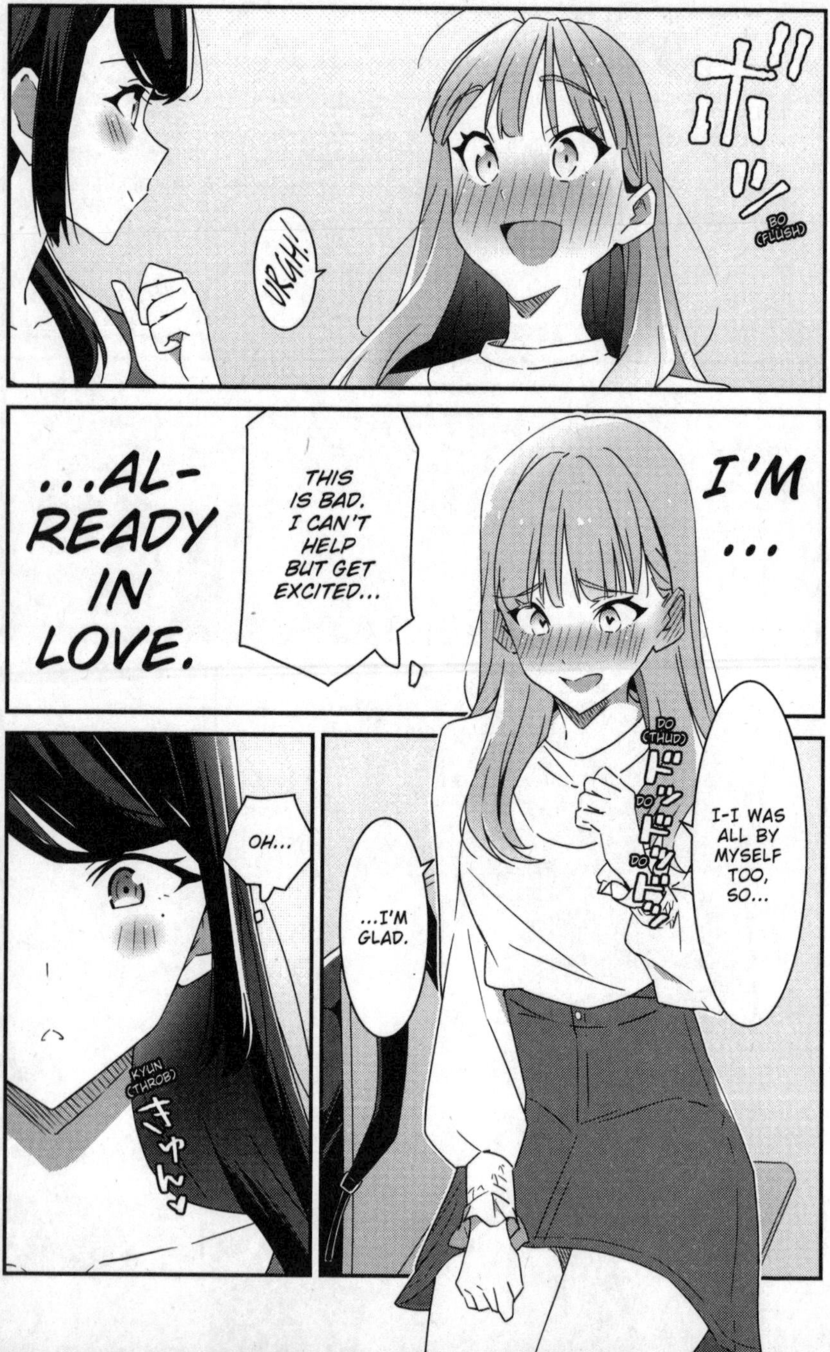
BO (FLUSH)
URGH!
I'M ...
THIS IS BAD. I CAN'T HELP BUT GET EXCITED...
...AL-READY IN LOVE.
DO (THUD) DO DO
I-I WAS ALL BY MYSELF TOO, SO...
...I'M GLAD.
OH...
KYUN (THROB)

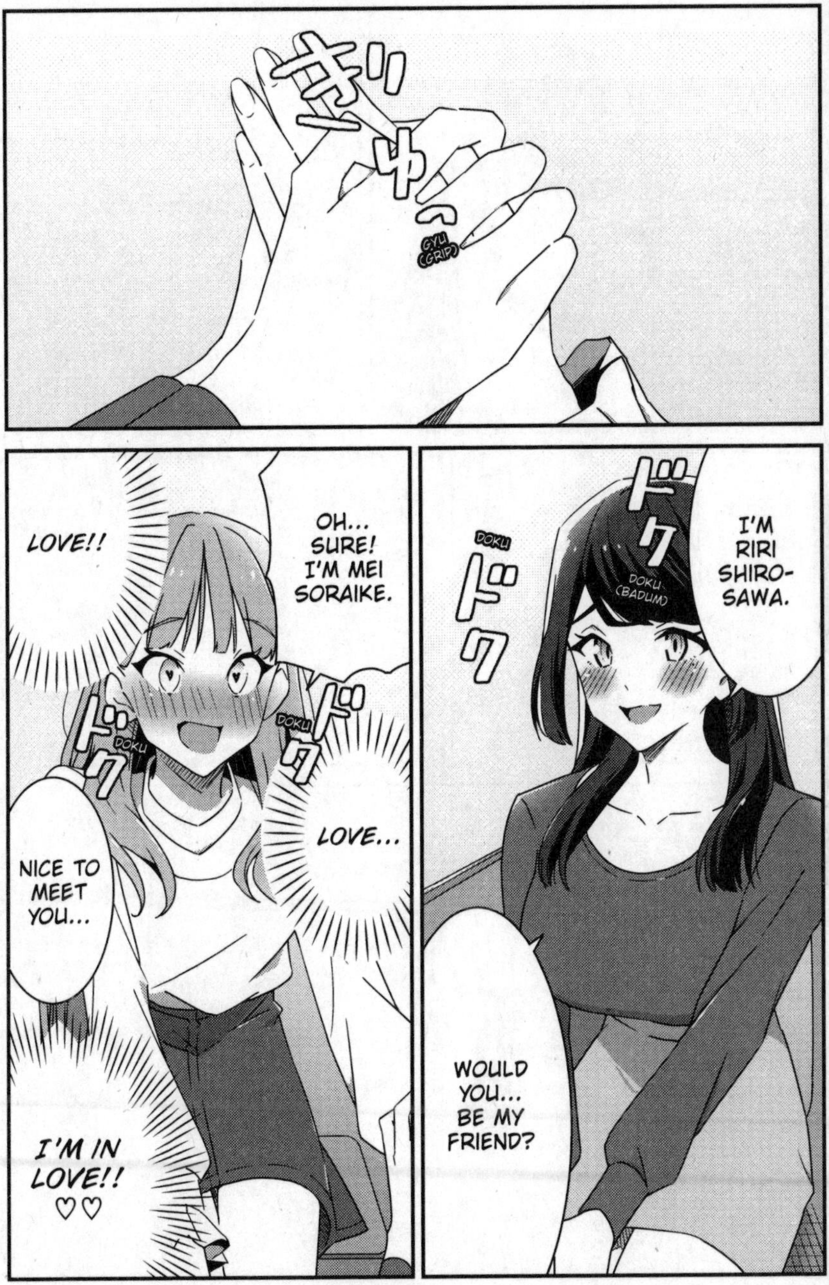
GYU
(GRIP)
I'M RIRI SHIRO-SAWA.
DOKU
DOKU
(BADUM)
WOULD YOU... BE MY FRIEND?
OH... SURE! I'M MEI SORAIKE.
LOVE!!
DOKU
DOKU
LOVE...
NICE TO MEET YOU...
I'M IN LOVE!! ♡♡

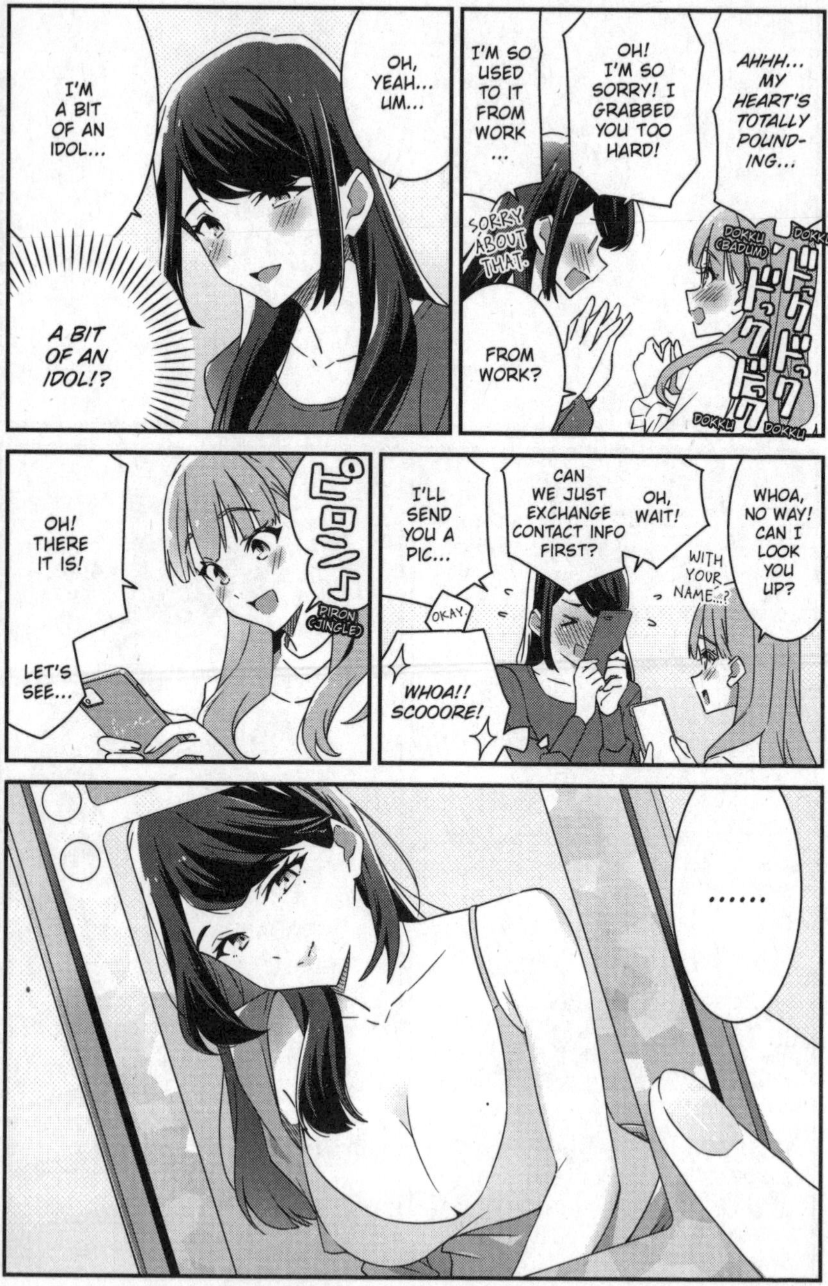

AHHH... MY HEART'S TOTALLY POUND-ING...
OH! I'M SO SORRY! I GRABBED YOU TOO HARD!
I'M SO USED TO IT FROM WORK ...
DOKKU (BADUMP) DOKKU
DOKKU DOKKU
SORRY ABOUT THAT.
FROM WORK?
OH, YEAH... UM...
I'M A BIT OF AN IDOL...
A BIT OF AN IDOL!?
WHOA, NO WAY! CAN I LOOK YOU UP?
WITH YOUR NAME...?
OH, WAIT!
CAN WE JUST EXCHANGE CONTACT INFO FIRST?
I'LL SEND YOU A PIC...
OKAY.
WHOA!! SCOOORE!
ピロン♪
PIRON (JINGLE)
OH! THERE IT IS!
LET'S SEE...
......

...!

ヒ°
PIIII
(BEEEEP)

...SO I WANTED YOU TO SEE SOMETHING DIFFERENT FIRST...

THE RACY ONES ALWAYS COME UP FIRST WHEN YOU SEARCH MY NAME...

RACY !?

AH! OH!

T-TOO...

.... CUTE...

I LOVE YOU!! MARRY ME!!

...MEI-CHAN?

......

WHAT DO YOU THINK...

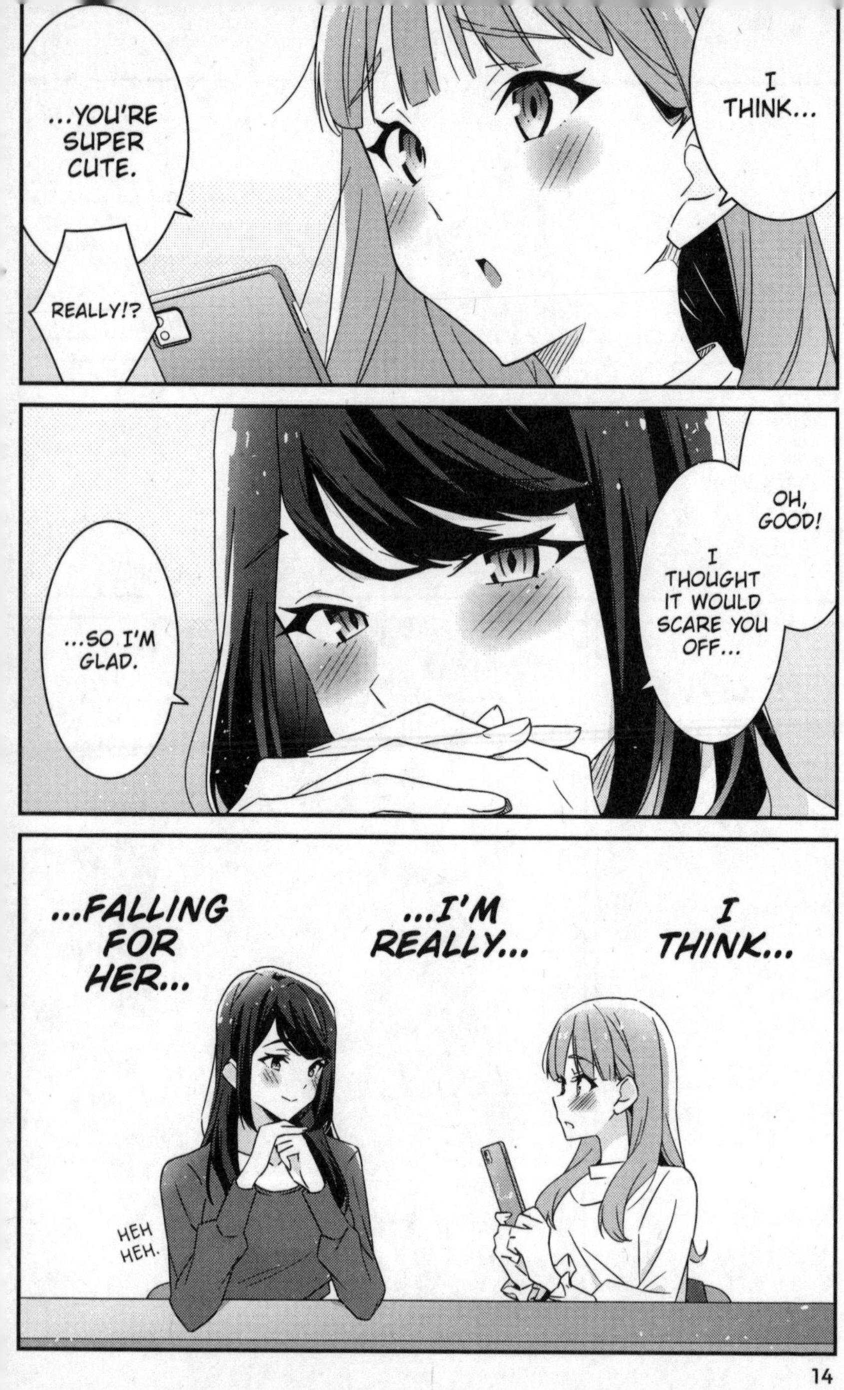
I THINK...
...YOU'RE SUPER CUTE.
REALLY!?
OH, GOOD!
I THOUGHT IT WOULD SCARE YOU OFF...
...SO I'M GLAD.
I THINK...
...I'M REALLY...
...FALLING FOR HER...
HEH HEH.

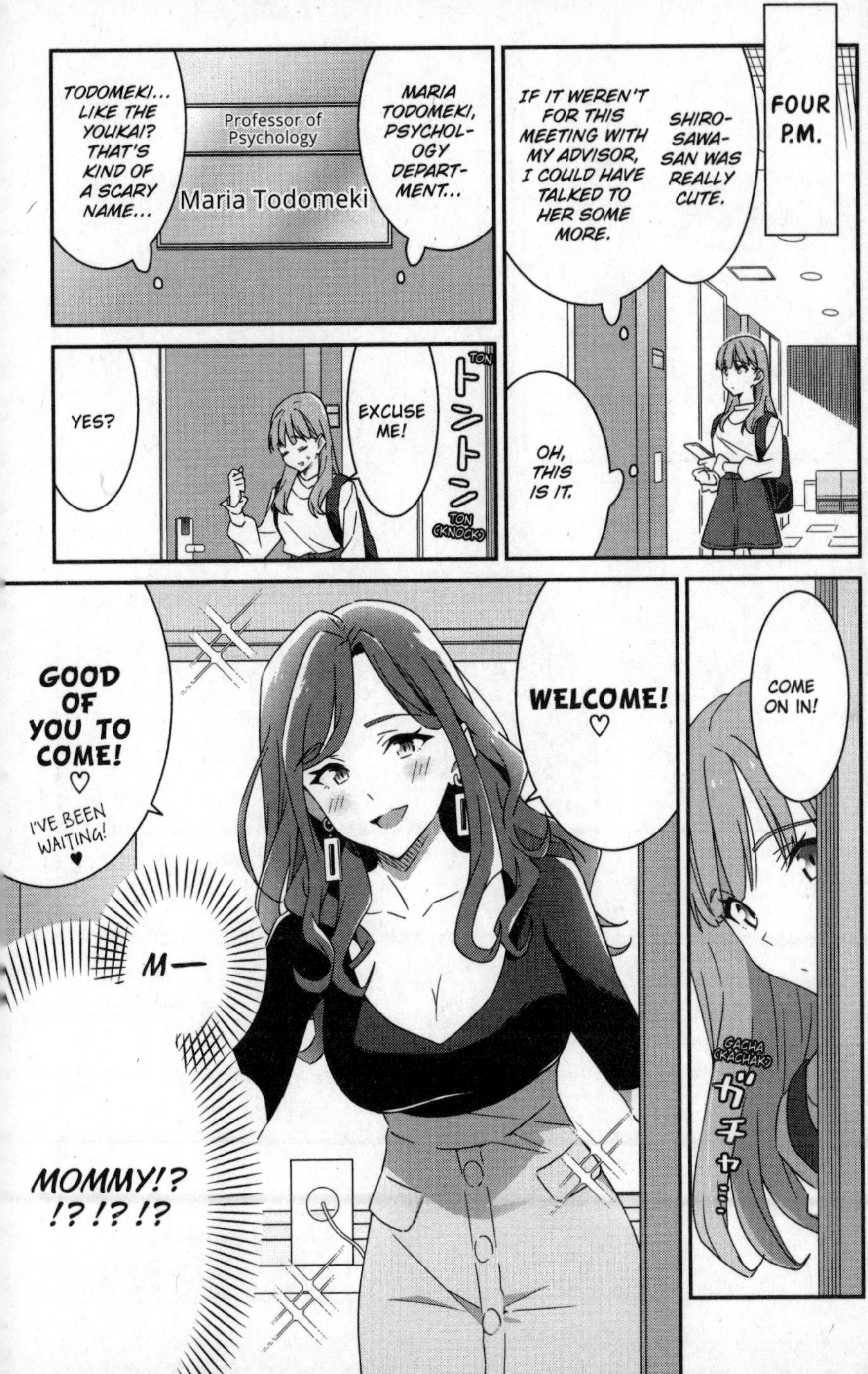
FOUR P.M.
IF IT WEREN'T FOR THIS MEETING WITH MY ADVISOR, I COULD HAVE TALKED TO HER SOME MORE.
SHIRO-SAWA-SAN WAS REALLY CUTE.
OH, THIS IS IT.
MARIA TODOMEKI, PSYCHOL-OGY DEPART-MENT...
Professor of Psychology
Maria Todomeki
TODOMEKI... LIKE THE YOUKAI? THAT'S KIND OF A SCARY NAME...
TON TON (KNOCK)
EXCUSE ME!
YES?
COME ON IN!
GACHA (KACHAK)
WELCOME! ♡
GOOD OF YOU TO COME! ♡
I'VE BEEN WAITING! ♥
M—
MOMMY!?!?!?!?

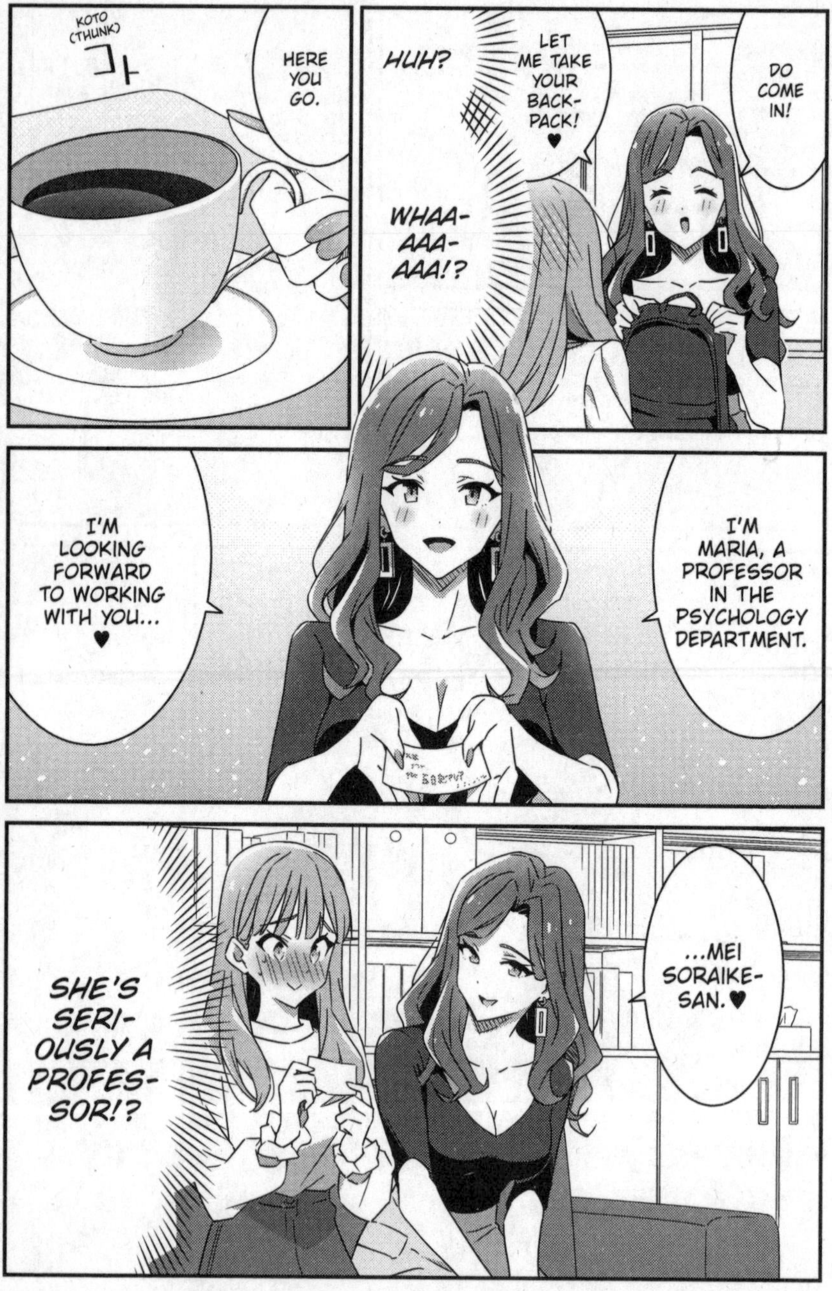
DO COME IN!
LET ME TAKE YOUR BACKPACK! ♥
HUH?
WHAAAAAAAA!?
HERE YOU GO.
KOTO (THUNK)
I'M MARIA, A PROFESSOR IN THE PSYCHOLOGY DEPARTMENT.
I'M LOOKING FORWARD TO WORKING WITH YOU... ♥
...MEI SORAIKE-SAN. ♥
SHE'S SERIOUSLY A PROFESSOR!?

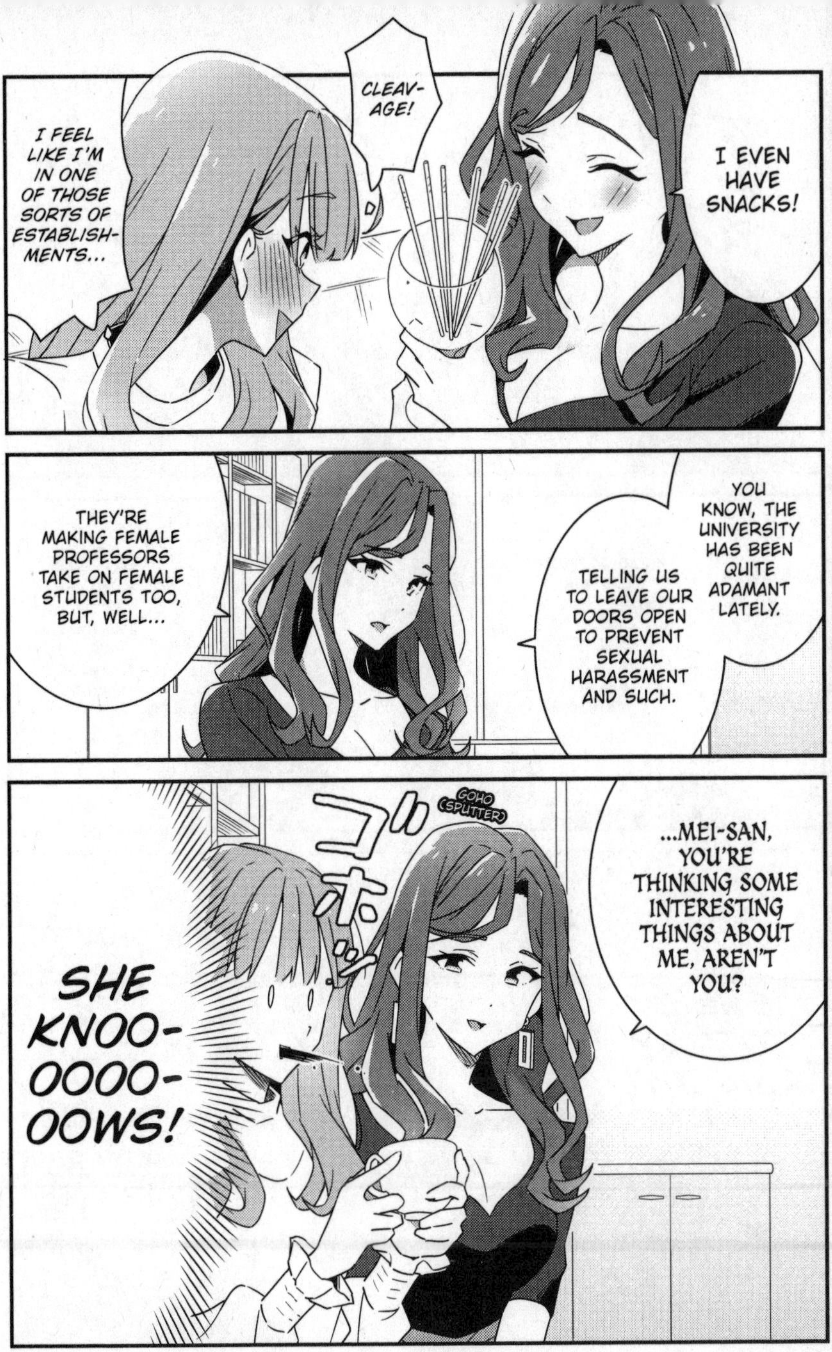
I EVEN HAVE SNACKS!
CLEAV-AGE!
I FEEL LIKE I'M IN ONE OF THOSE SORTS OF ESTABLISH-MENTS...
YOU KNOW, THE UNIVERSITY HAS BEEN QUITE ADAMANT LATELY.
TELLING US TO LEAVE OUR DOORS OPEN TO PREVENT SEXUAL HARASSMENT AND SUCH.
THEY'RE MAKING FEMALE PROFESSORS TAKE ON FEMALE STUDENTS TOO, BUT, WELL...
...MEI-SAN, YOU'RE THINKING SOME INTERESTING THINGS ABOUT ME, AREN'T YOU?
GOHO (SPUTTER)
ゴホッ
SHE KNOO-OOOO-OOWS!

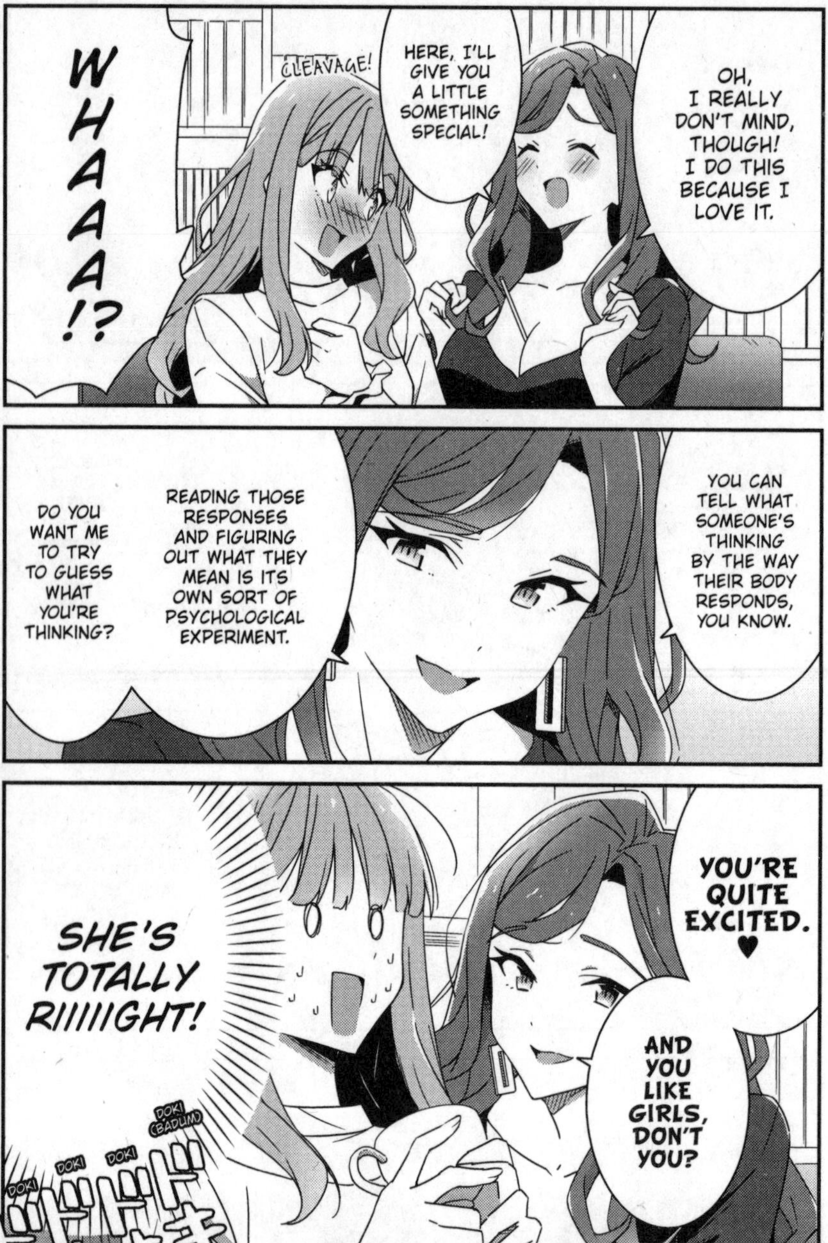
OH, I REALLY DON'T MIND, THOUGH! I DO THIS BECAUSE I LOVE IT.
HERE, I'LL GIVE YOU A LITTLE SOMETHING SPECIAL!
CLEAVAGE!
WHAAAA!?
YOU CAN TELL WHAT SOMEONE'S THINKING BY THE WAY THEIR BODY RESPONDS, YOU KNOW.
READING THOSE RESPONSES AND FIGURING OUT WHAT THEY MEAN IS ITS OWN SORT OF PSYCHOLOGICAL EXPERIMENT.
DO YOU WANT ME TO TRY TO GUESS WHAT YOU'RE THINKING?
YOU'RE QUITE EXCITED. ♥
AND YOU LIKE GIRLS, DON'T YOU?
SHE'S TOTALLY RIIIIIGHT!
DOKI (BADUM)
DOKI
DOKI
DOKI
ドキドキドキドキ

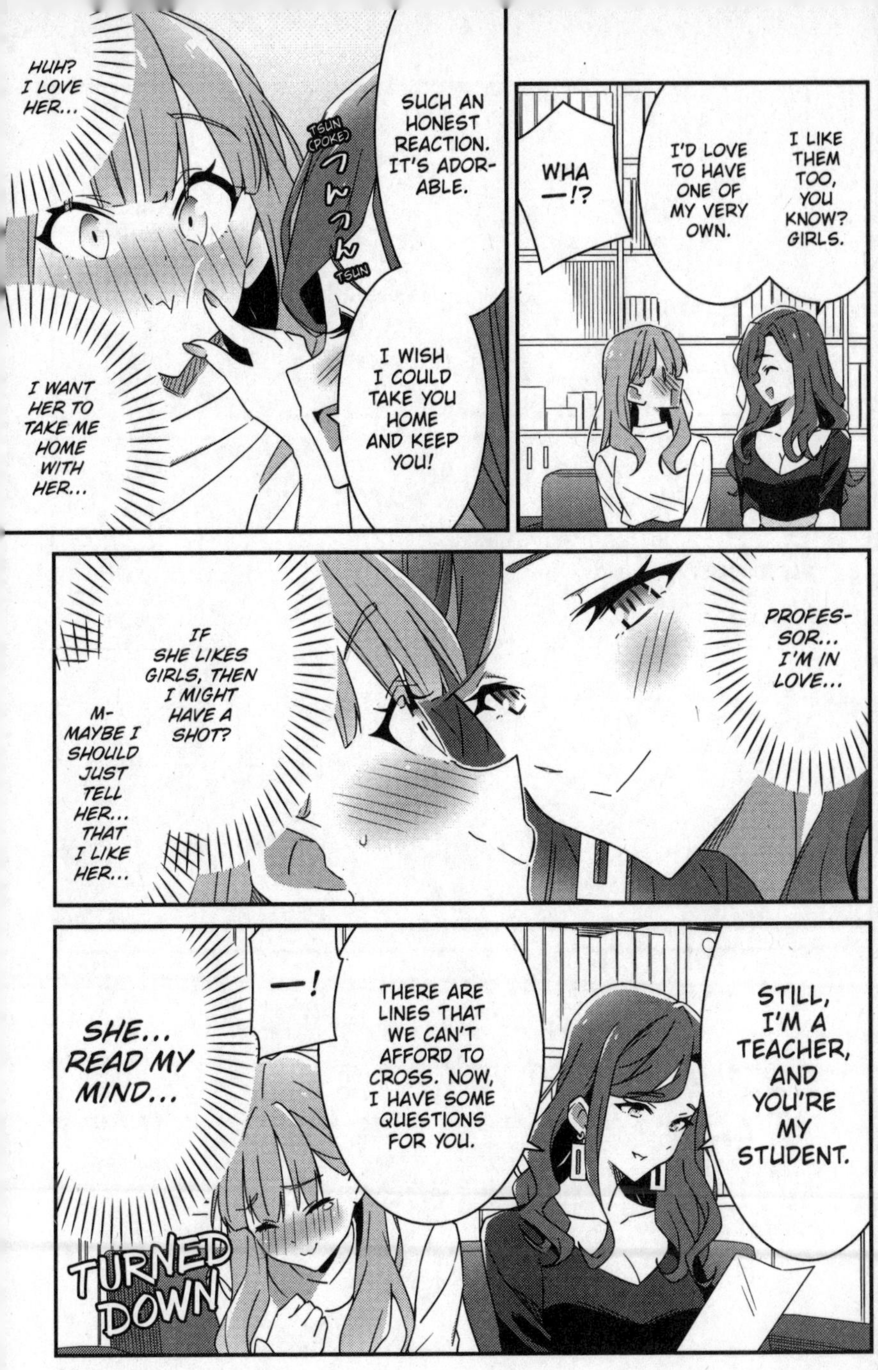
I LIKE THEM TOO, YOU KNOW? GIRLS.
I'D LOVE TO HAVE ONE OF MY VERY OWN.
WHA—!?
SUCH AN HONEST REACTION. IT'S ADORABLE.
TSUN (POKE) つんつん TSUN
HUH? I LOVE HER...
I WISH I COULD TAKE YOU HOME AND KEEP YOU!
I WANT HER TO TAKE ME HOME WITH HER...
PROFESSOR... I'M IN LOVE...
IF SHE LIKES GIRLS, THEN I MIGHT HAVE A SHOT?
M-MAYBE I SHOULD JUST TELL HER... THAT I LIKE HER...
STILL, I'M A TEACHER, AND YOU'RE MY STUDENT.
THERE ARE LINES THAT WE CAN'T AFFORD TO CROSS. NOW, I HAVE SOME QUESTIONS FOR YOU.
—!
SHE... READ MY MIND...
TURNED DOWN

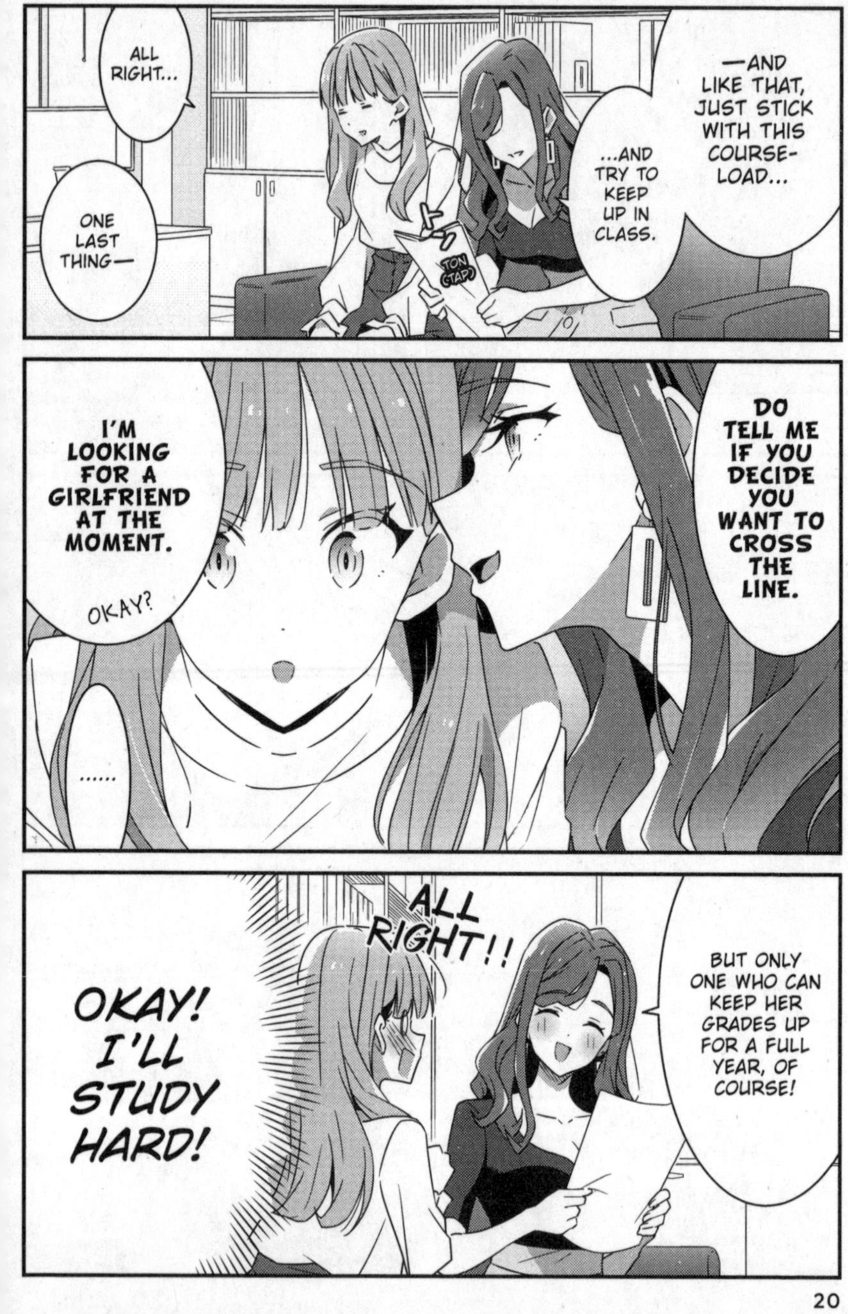
—AND LIKE THAT, JUST STICK WITH THIS COURSE-LOAD...
...AND TRY TO KEEP UP IN CLASS.
TON (TAP)
ALL RIGHT...
ONE LAST THING—
DO TELL ME IF YOU DECIDE YOU WANT TO CROSS THE LINE.
I'M LOOKING FOR A GIRLFRIEND AT THE MOMENT.
OKAY?
......
BUT ONLY ONE WHO CAN KEEP HER GRADES UP FOR A FULL YEAR, OF COURSE!
ALL RIGHT!!
OKAY! I'LL STUDY HARD!

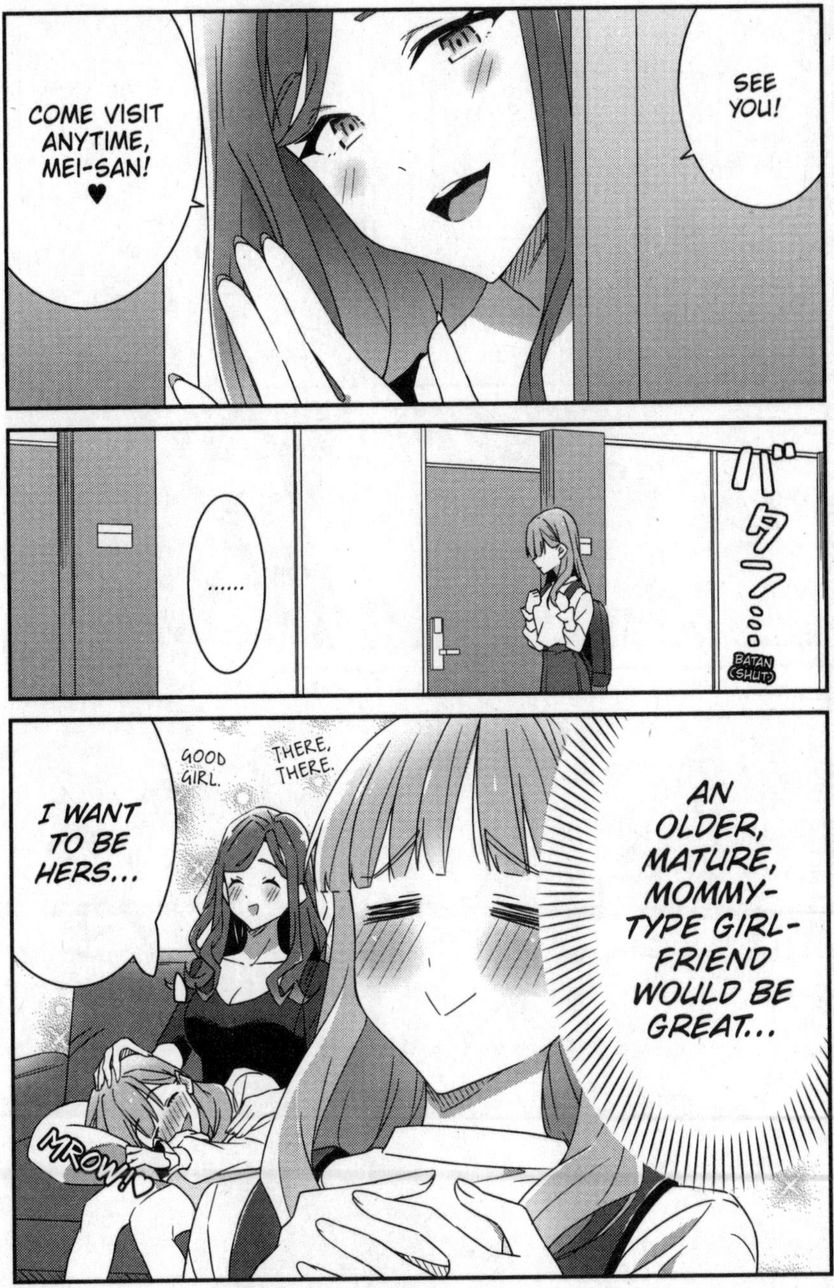
SEE YOU!
COME VISIT ANYTIME, MEI-SAN! ♥
バタン…
BATAN (SHUT)
......
AN OLDER, MATURE, MOMMY-TYPE GIRL-FRIEND WOULD BE GREAT...
THERE, THERE.
GOOD GIRL.
I WANT TO BE HERS...
MROW! ♥

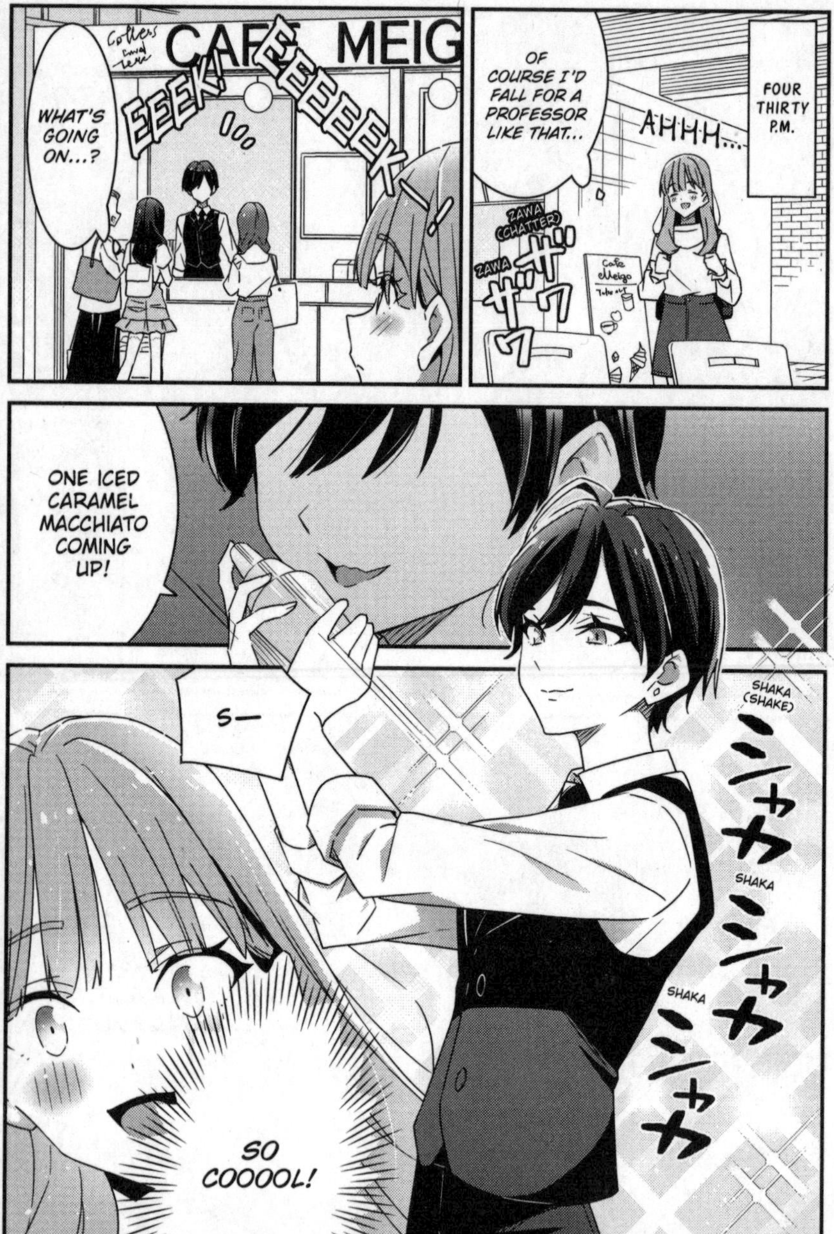
FOUR THIRTY P.M.
AHHHH...
OF COURSE I'D FALL FOR A PROFESSOR LIKE THAT...
ZAWA (CHATTER)
ZAWA
CAFE MEIG
EEEK!
EEEEEEK
WHAT'S GOING ON...?
ONE ICED CARAMEL MACCHIATO COMING UP!
S—
SHAKA (SHAKE)
SHAKA
SHAKA
SO COOOOL!

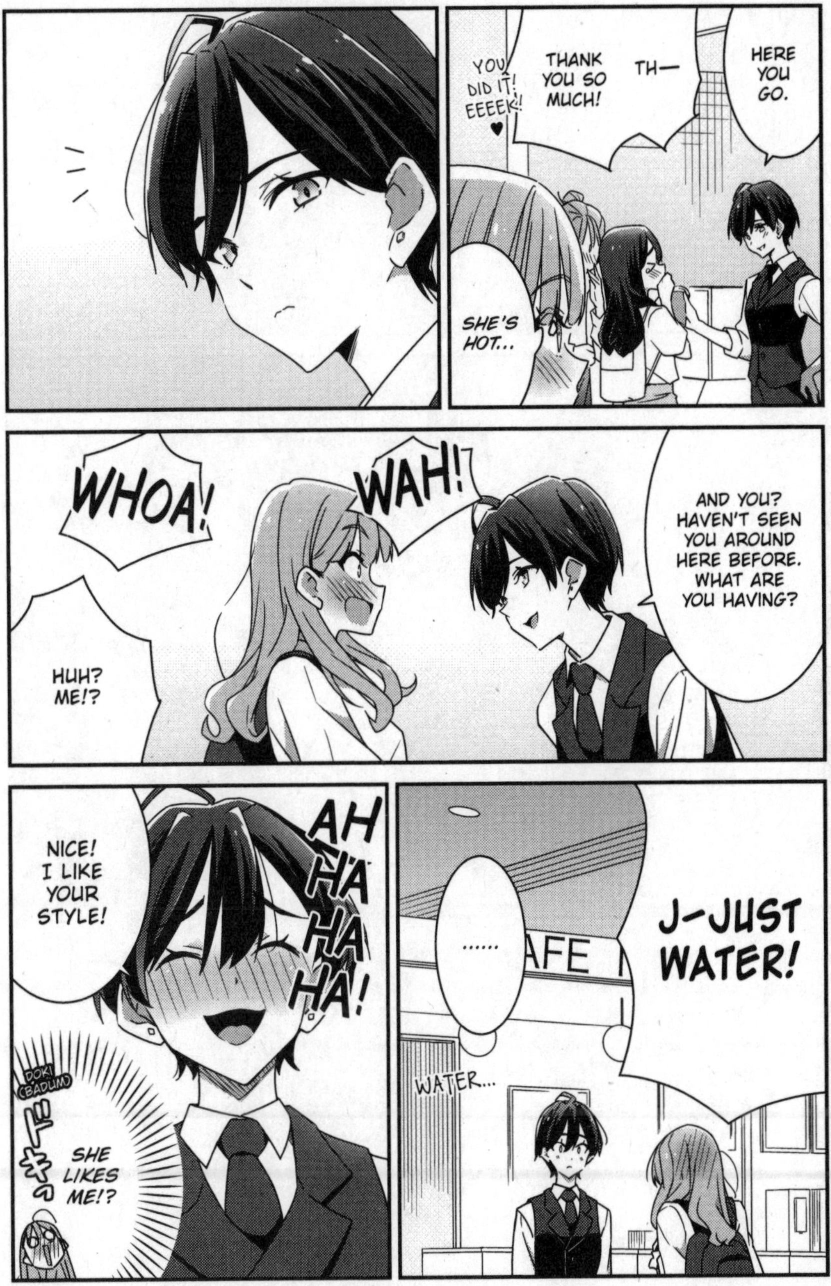
HERE YOU GO.
TH—
THANK YOU SO MUCH!
YOU DID IT! EEEEK!! ♥
SHE'S HOT...
AND YOU? HAVEN'T SEEN YOU AROUND HERE BEFORE. WHAT ARE YOU HAVING?
WAH!
WHOA!
HUH? ME!?
J-JUST WATER!
......
AFE
WATER...
AH HA HA HA HA!
NICE! I LIKE YOUR STYLE!
DOKI (BADUM)
SHE LIKES ME!?

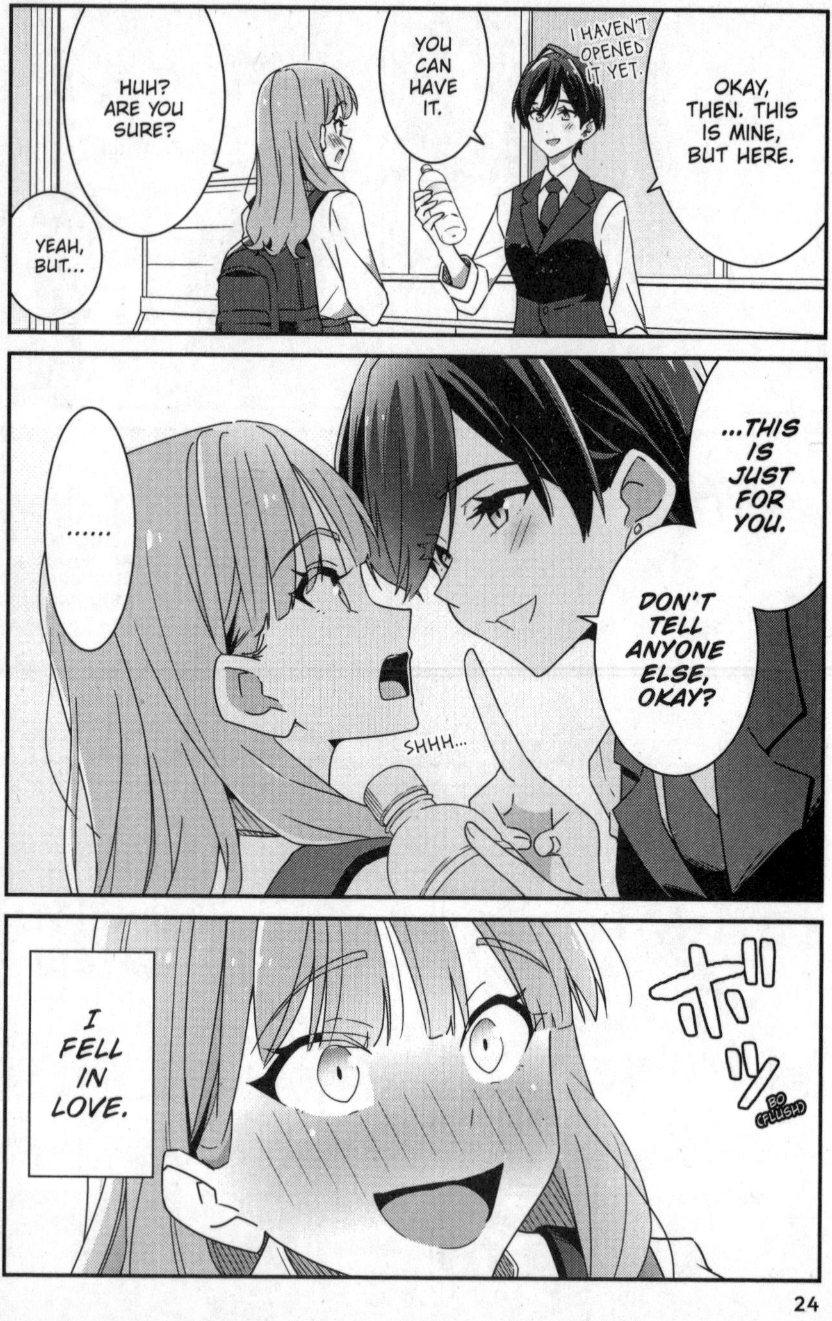
OKAY, THEN. THIS IS MINE, BUT HERE.
I HAVEN'T OPENED IT YET.
YOU CAN HAVE IT.
HUH? ARE YOU SURE?
YEAH, BUT...
...THIS IS JUST FOR YOU.
DON'T TELL ANYONE ELSE, OKAY?
SHHH...
......
BO (FLUSH)
I FELL IN LOVE.

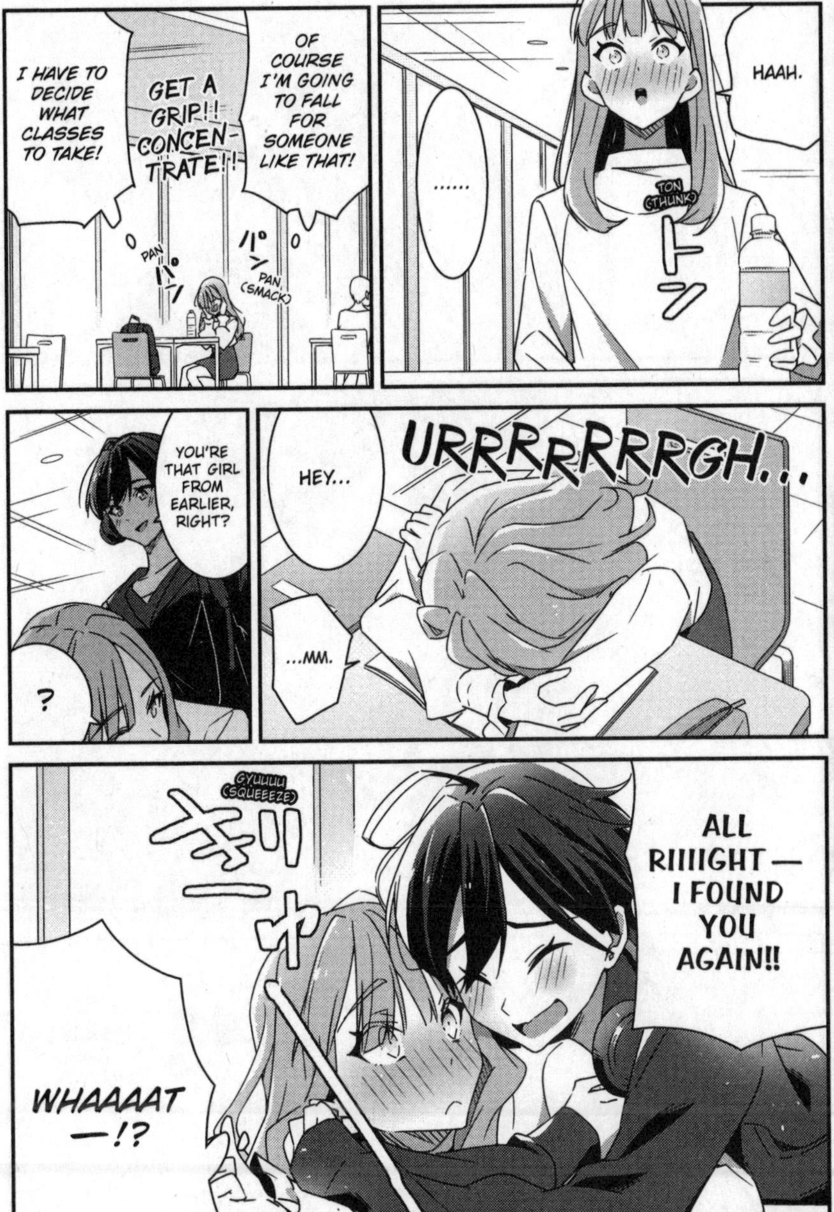
HAAH.
......
TON (THUNK)
トン
OF COURSE I'M GOING TO FALL FOR SOMEONE LIKE THAT!
GET A GRIP!! CONCENTRATE!!
I HAVE TO DECIDE WHAT CLASSES TO TAKE!
PAN (SMACK)
パン
PAN
パン
URRRRRRRGH...
HEY...
...MM.
YOU'RE THAT GIRL FROM EARLIER, RIGHT?
?
ALL RIIIIGHT— I FOUND YOU AGAIN!!
GYUUUU (SQUEEEZE)
ぎゅーッ
WHAAAAT—!?

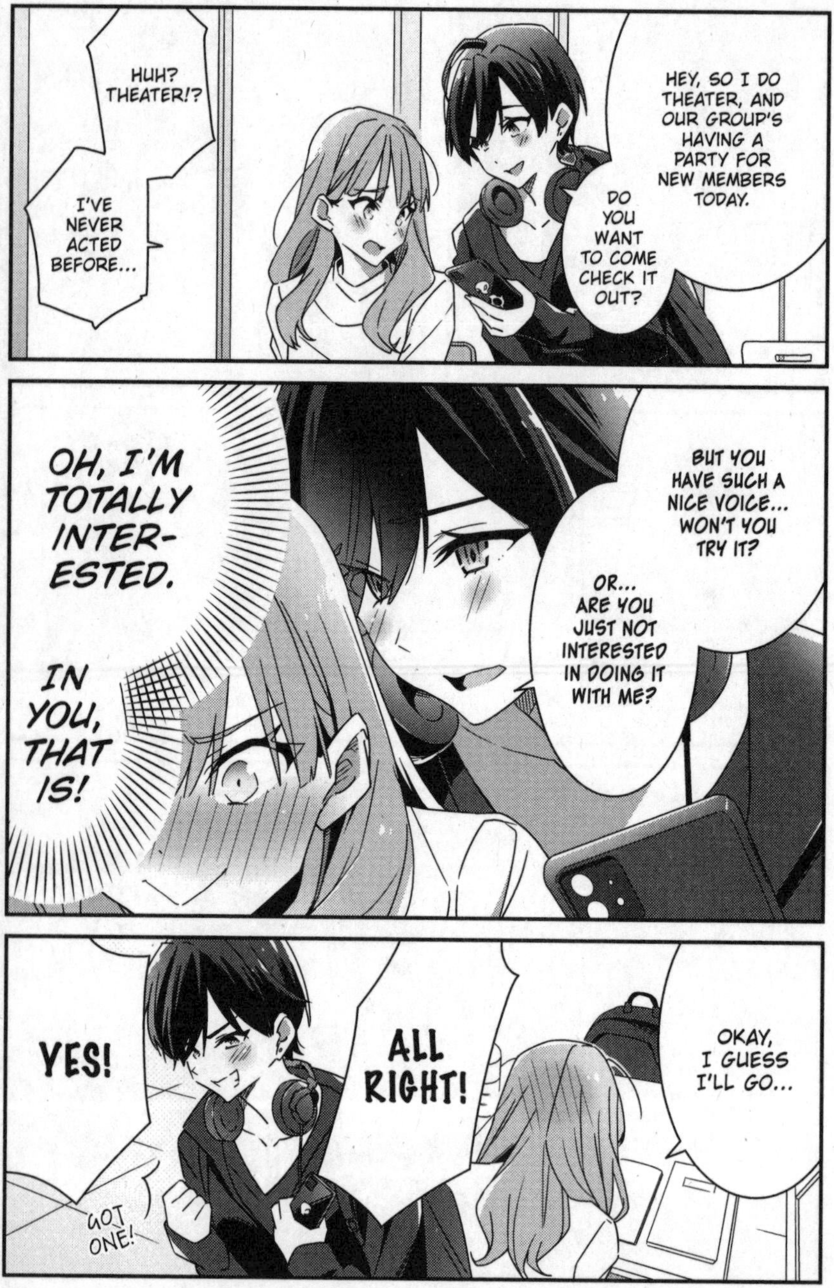
HEY, SO I DO THEATER, AND OUR GROUP'S HAVING A PARTY FOR NEW MEMBERS TODAY.
DO YOU WANT TO COME CHECK IT OUT?
HUH? THEATER!?
I'VE NEVER ACTED BEFORE...
BUT YOU HAVE SUCH A NICE VOICE... WON'T YOU TRY IT?
OR... ARE YOU JUST NOT INTERESTED IN DOING IT WITH ME?
OH, I'M TOTALLY INTER-ESTED.
IN YOU, THAT IS!
OKAY, I GUESS I'LL GO...
ALL RIGHT!
YES!
GOT ONE!

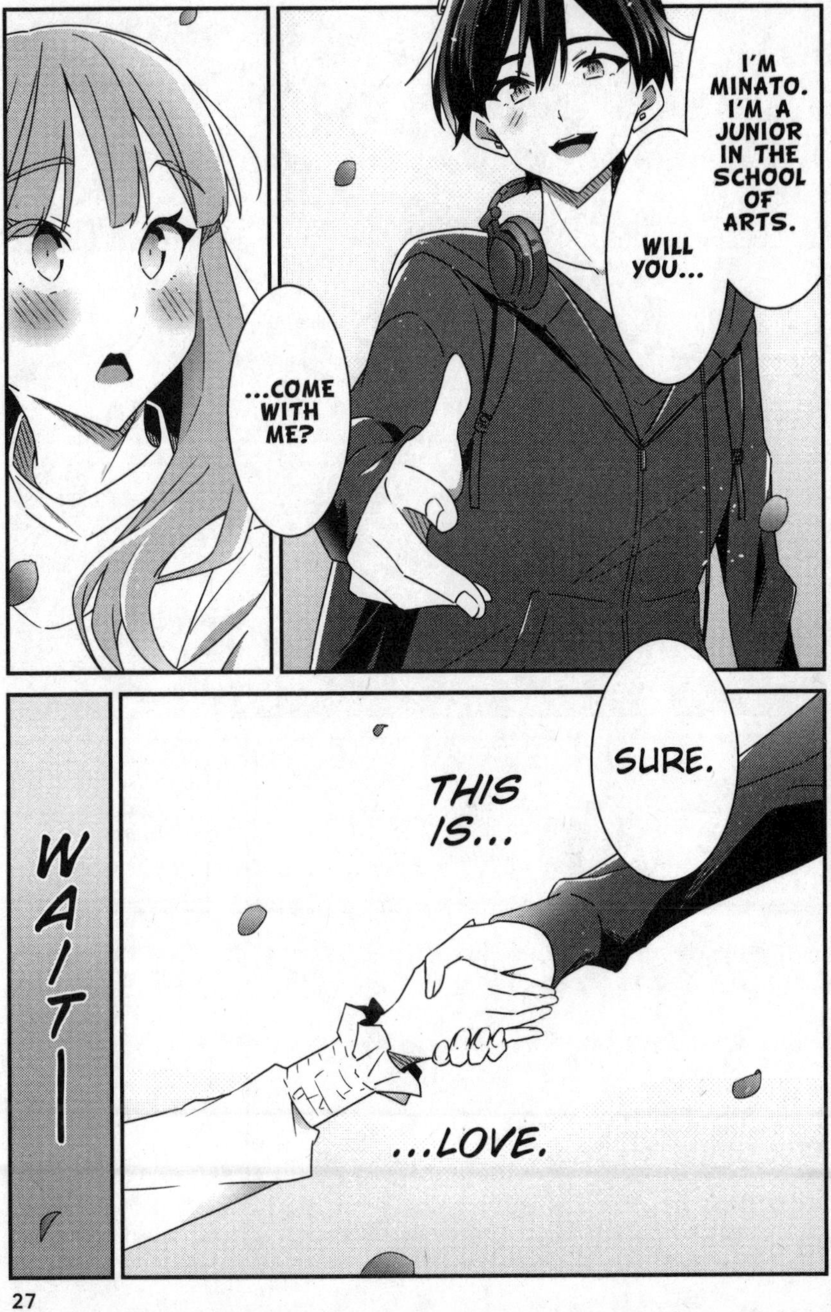
I'M MINATO. I'M A JUNIOR IN THE SCHOOL OF ARTS.
WILL YOU...
...COME WITH ME?
SURE.
THIS IS...
...LOVE.
WAIT—

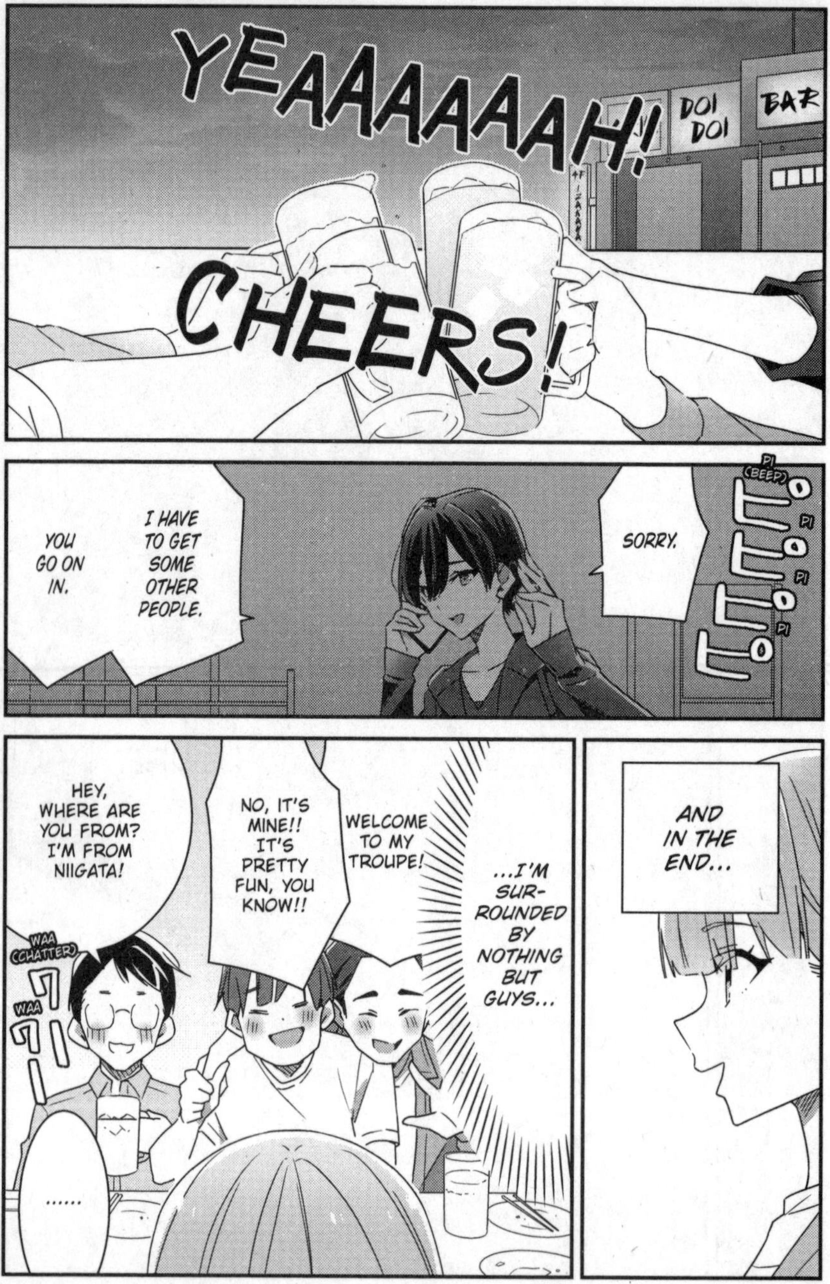
YEAAAAAAAH!
DOI DOI
BAR
CHEERS!
PI (BEEP) PI PI PI
SORRY.
I HAVE TO GET SOME OTHER PEOPLE.
YOU GO ON IN.
AND IN THE END...
...I'M SUR-ROUNDED BY NOTHING BUT GUYS...
WELCOME TO MY TROUPE!
NO, IT'S MINE!! IT'S PRETTY FUN, YOU KNOW!!
HEY, WHERE ARE YOU FROM? I'M FROM NIIGATA!
WAA (CHATTER) WAA
......

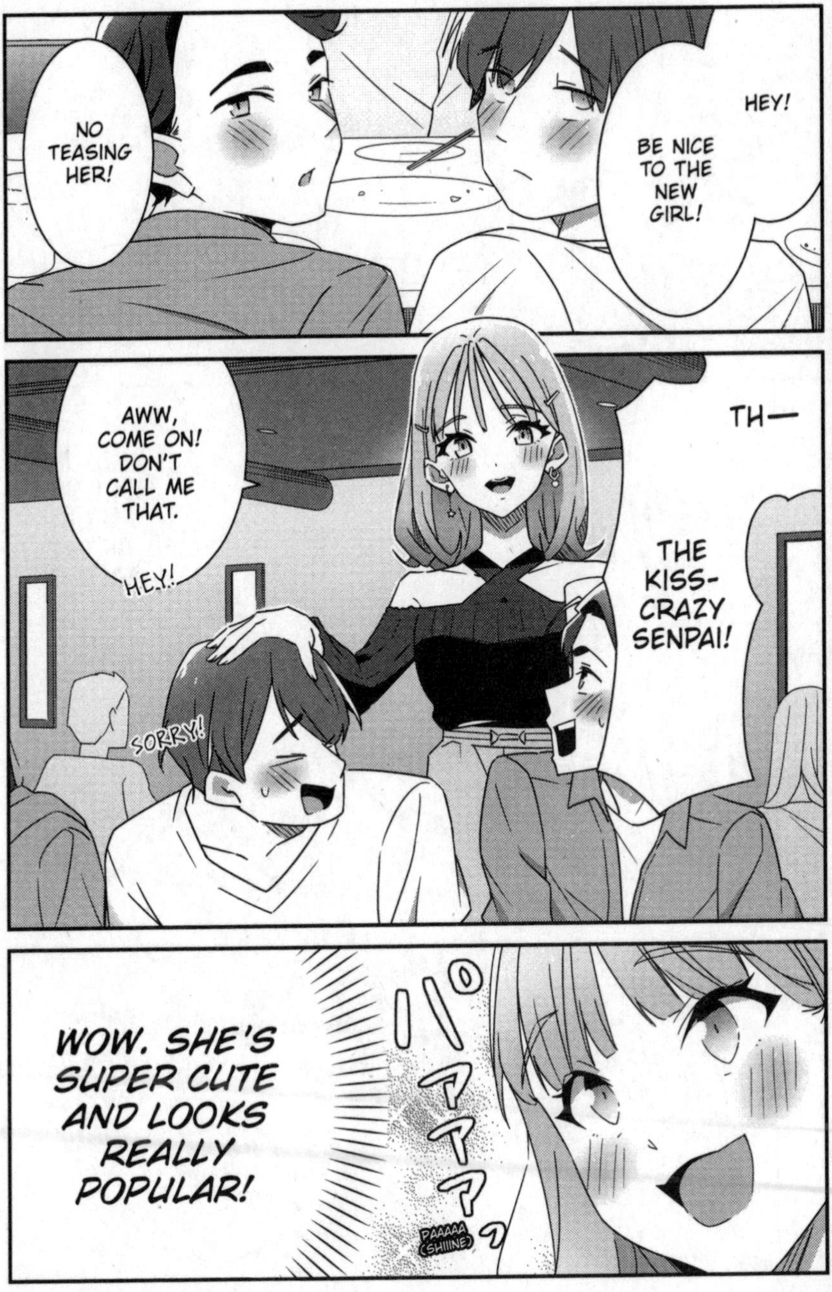
HEY!
BE NICE TO THE NEW GIRL!
NO TEASING HER!
TH—
THE KISS-CRAZY SENPAI!
AWW, COME ON! DON'T CALL ME THAT.
HEY!
SORRY!
PAAAAA (SHIIINE)
WOW. SHE'S SUPER CUTE AND LOOKS REALLY POPULAR!

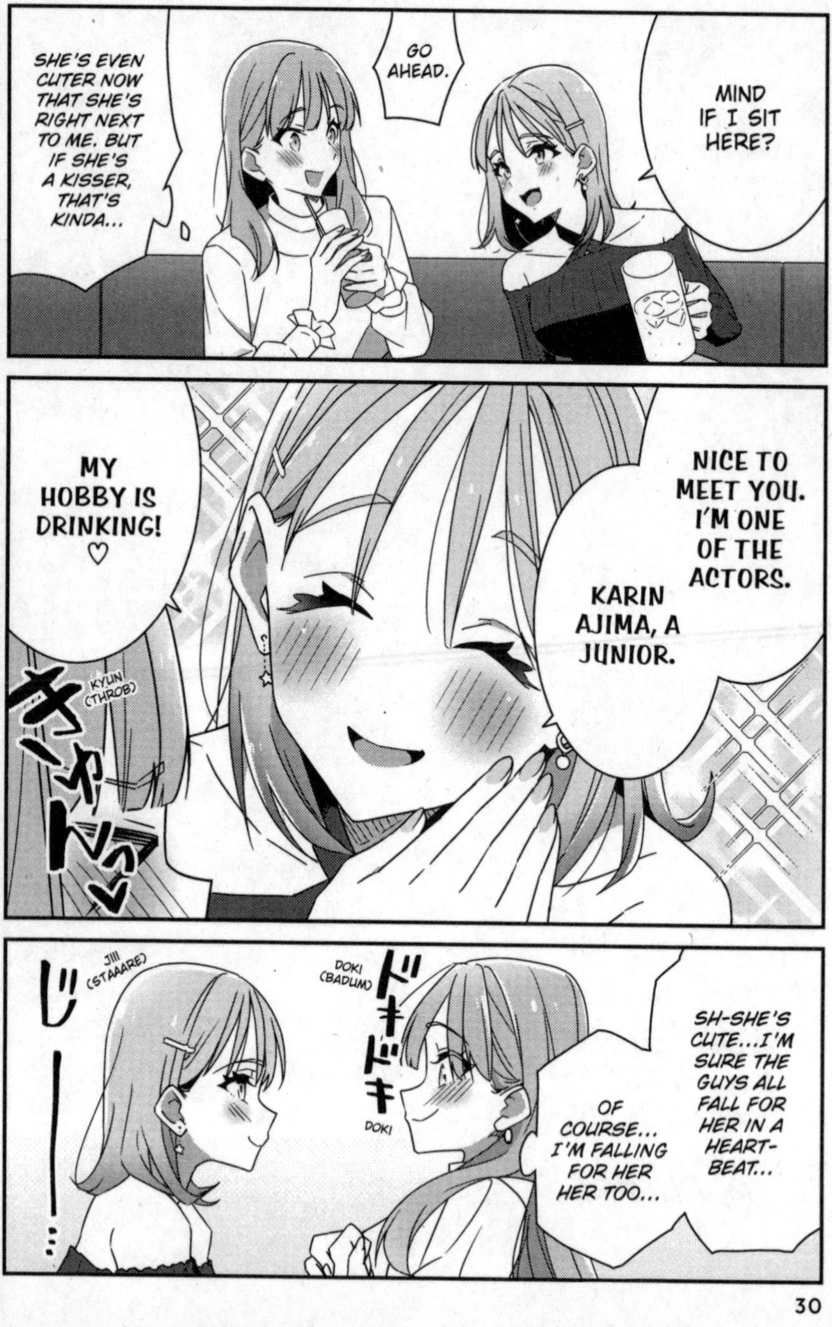
MIND IF I SIT HERE?
GO AHEAD.
SHE'S EVEN CUTER NOW THAT SHE'S RIGHT NEXT TO ME. BUT IF SHE'S A KISSER, THAT'S KINDA...
NICE TO MEET YOU. I'M ONE OF THE ACTORS.
KARIN AJIMA, A JUNIOR.
MY HOBBY IS DRINKING! ♡
KYUN (THROB)
DOKI (BADUM)
DOKI
SH-SHE'S CUTE...I'M SURE THE GUYS ALL FALL FOR HER IN A HEART-BEAT...
OF COURSE... I'M FALLING FOR HER HER TOO...
JIII (STAAARE)

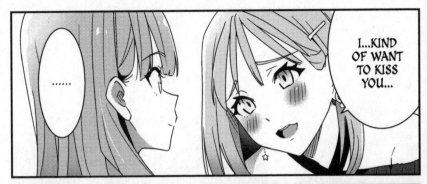

I...KIND OF WANT TO KISS YOU...
......
HUH?
KISS?
FRIENDS
GIRL-FRIENDS
BYUN (FWOOSH)
KISSING AND OTHER STUFF...
ZOOM!!
UHHHH...!
...SERIOUS-LY!? BUT WE'RE NOT EVEN DATING!!
HUH? WHAT ABOUT ME? WHAT DO I WANT?
I WANT TO KISS HER!!
IT ONLY TOOK 0.3 SECONDS FOR CURIOSITY TO WIN OUT.

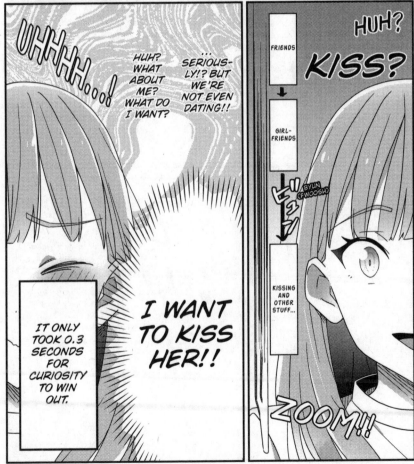

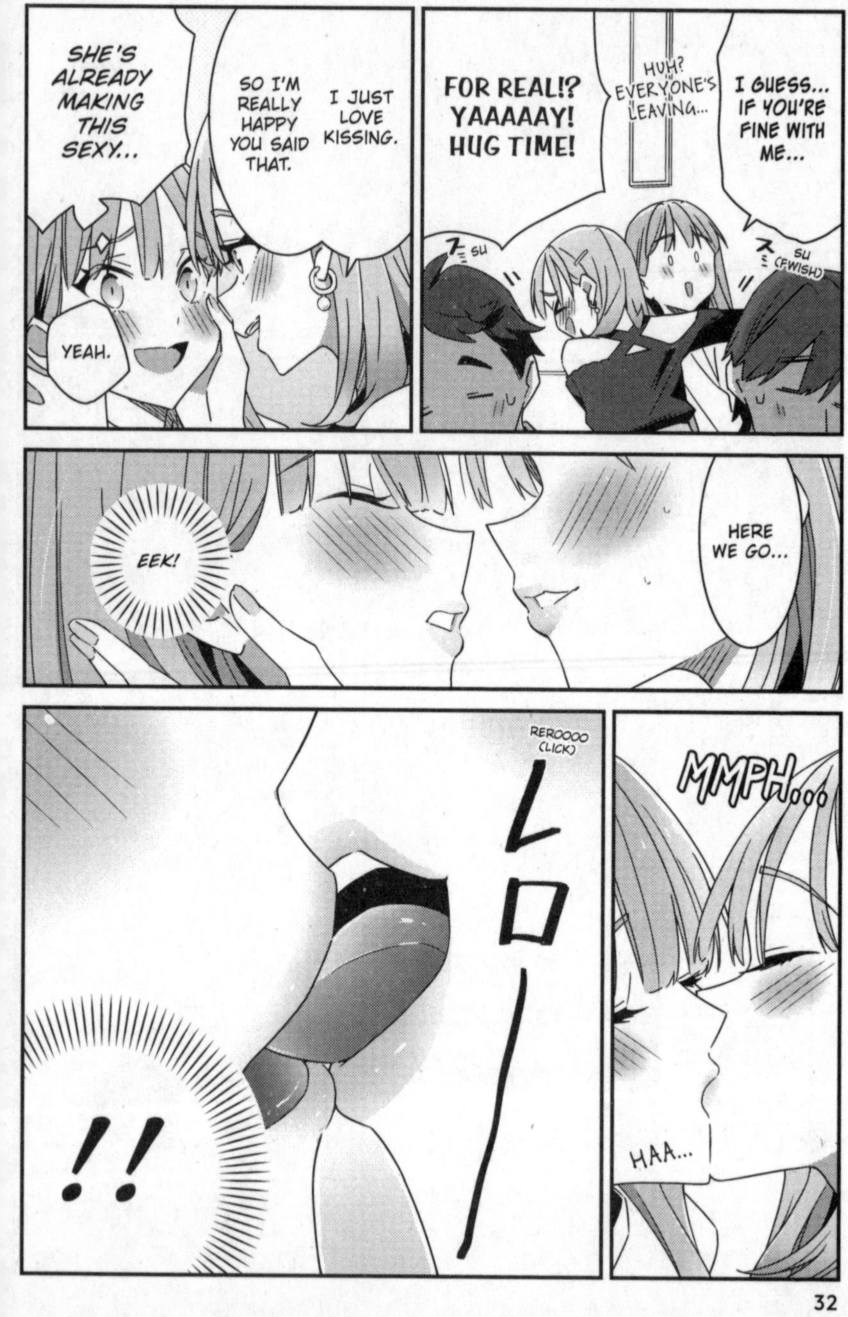
I GUESS... IF YOU'RE FINE WITH ME...
HUH? EVERYONE'S LEAVING...
FOR REAL!? YAAAAAY! HUG TIME!
SU
SU (FWISH)
I JUST LOVE KISSING.
SO I'M REALLY HAPPY YOU SAID THAT.
SHE'S ALREADY MAKING THIS SEXY...
YEAH.
HERE WE GO...
EEK!
MMPH...
HAA...
REROOOO (CLICK)
!!

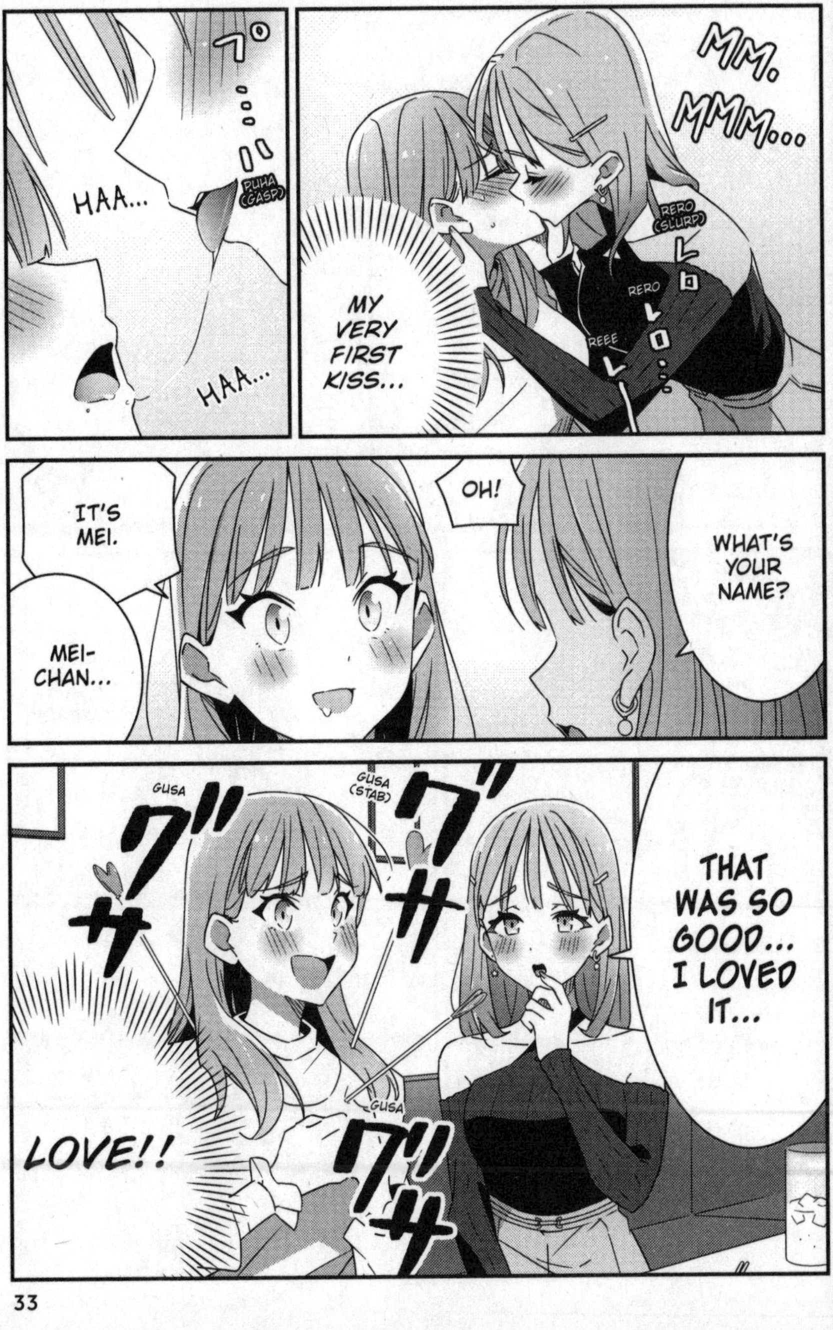
MM. MMM...
RERO (SLURP)
RERO
REEE
MY VERY FIRST KISS...
PUHA (GASP)
HAA...
HAA...
WHAT'S YOUR NAME?
OH!
IT'S MEI.
MEI-CHAN...
THAT WAS SO GOOD... I LOVED IT...
GUSA (STAB)
GUSA
GUSA
LOVE!!

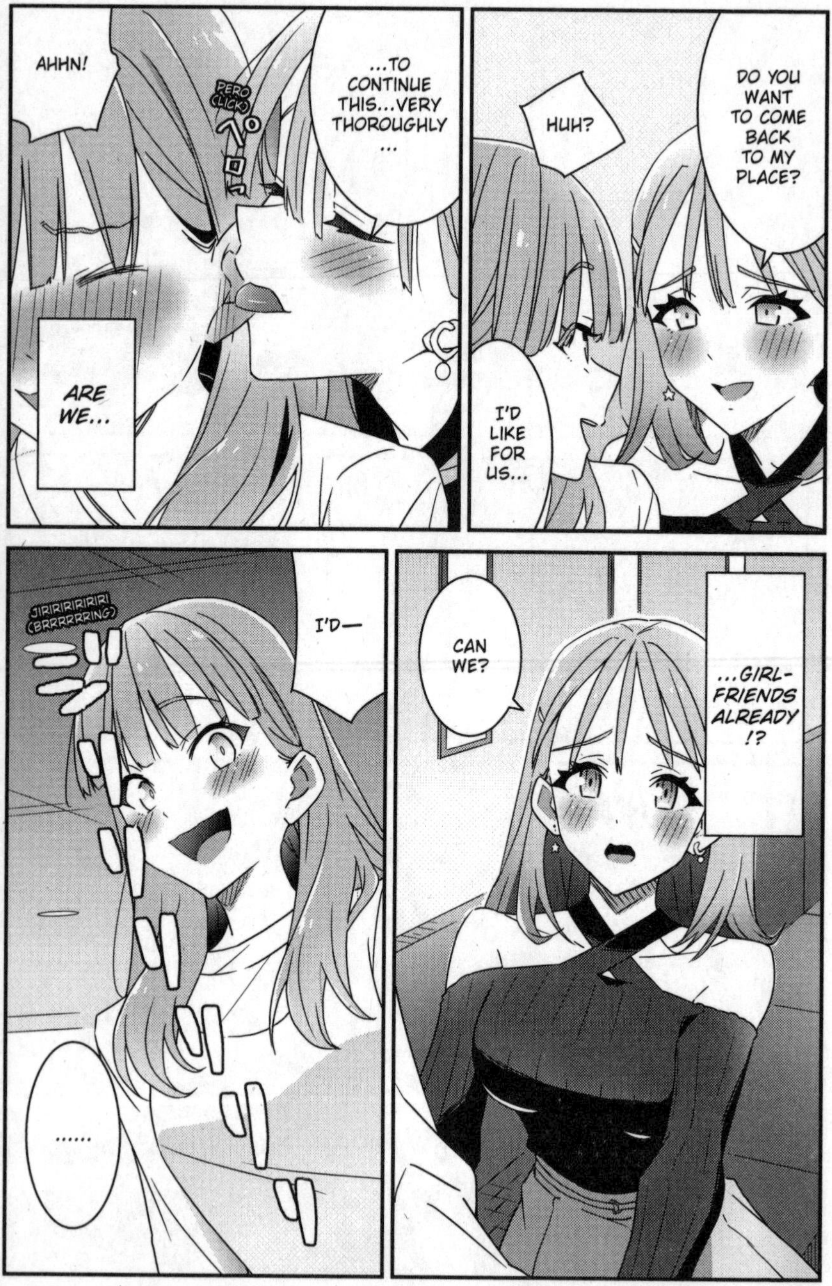
DO YOU WANT TO COME BACK TO MY PLACE?
HUH?
I'D LIKE FOR US...
...TO CONTINUE THIS...VERY THOROUGHLY...
PERO (LICK)
AHHN!
ARE WE...
...GIRL-FRIENDS ALREADY!?
CAN WE?
I'D—
JIRIRIRIRIRIRI (BRRRRRRING)
......

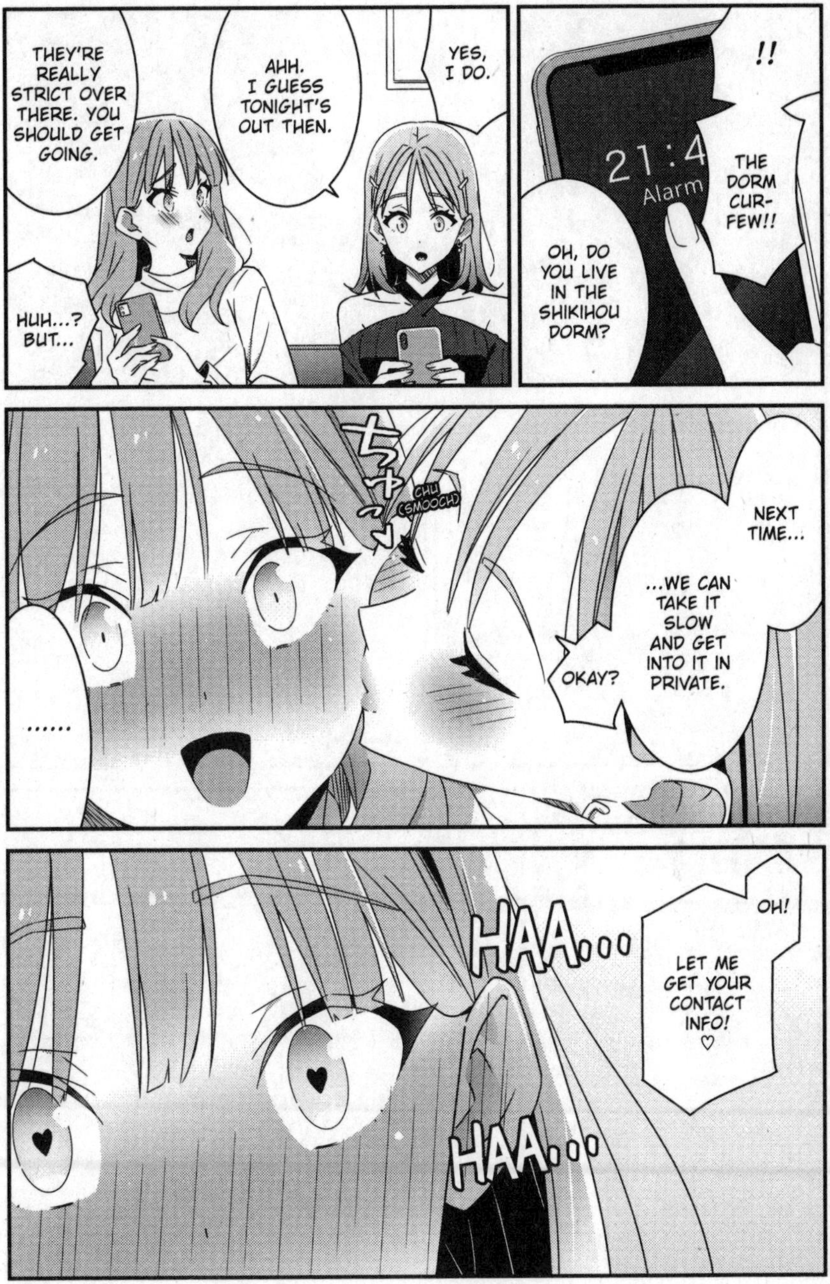
!!
THE DORM CURFEW!!
21:4
Alarm
OH, DO YOU LIVE IN THE SHIKIHOU DORM?
YES, I DO.
AHH. I GUESS TONIGHT'S OUT THEN.
THEY'RE REALLY STRICT OVER THERE. YOU SHOULD GET GOING.
HUH...? BUT...
NEXT TIME...
...WE CAN TAKE IT SLOW AND GET INTO IT IN PRIVATE.
OKAY?
ちゅっ
CHU (SMOOCH)
......
OH!
LET ME GET YOUR CONTACT INFO! ♡
HAA...
HAA...

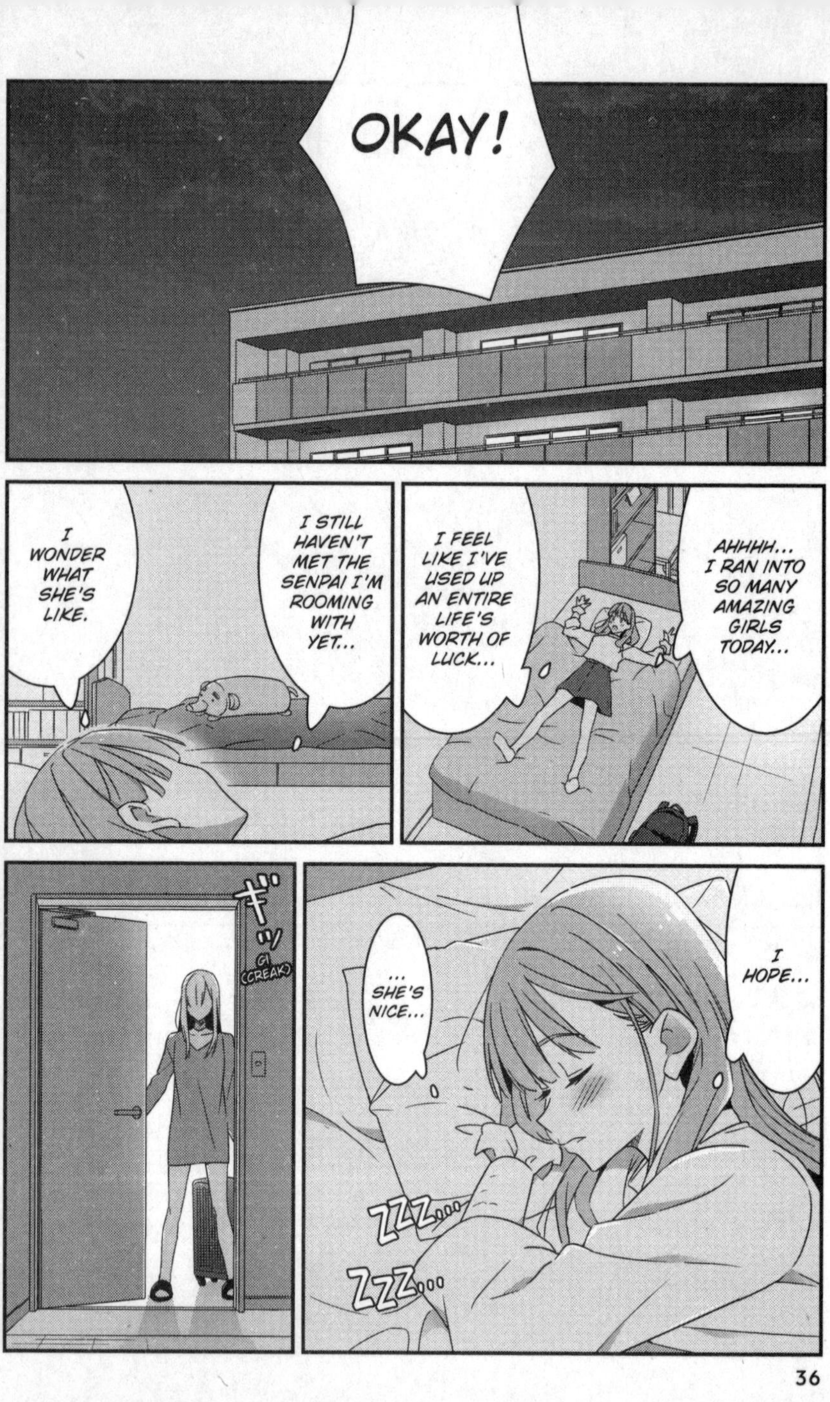
OKAY!
AHHHH... I RAN INTO SO MANY AMAZING GIRLS TODAY...
I FEEL LIKE I'VE USED UP AN ENTIRE LIFE'S WORTH OF LUCK...
I STILL HAVEN'T MET THE SENPAI I'M ROOMING WITH YET...
I WONDER WHAT SHE'S LIKE.
I HOPE...
...SHE'S NICE...
ZZZ...
ZZZ...
ギッ
GI (CREAK)

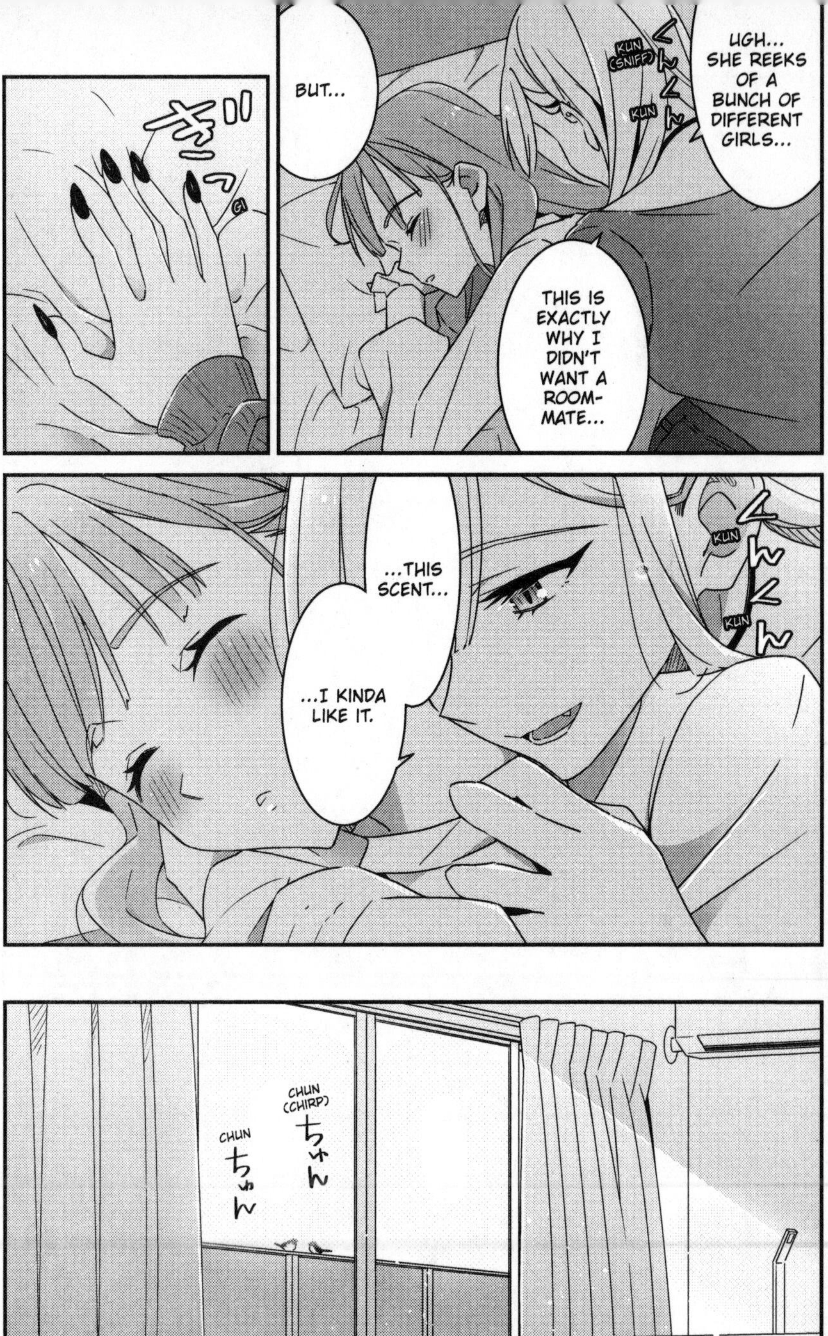

KUN (SNIFF)
KUN
UGH... SHE REEKS OF A BUNCH OF DIFFERENT GIRLS...
BUT...
THIS IS EXACTLY WHY I DIDN'T WANT A ROOM-MATE...
GI
KUN
KUN
...THIS SCENT...
...I KINDA LIKE IT.
CHUN (CHIRP)
CHUN

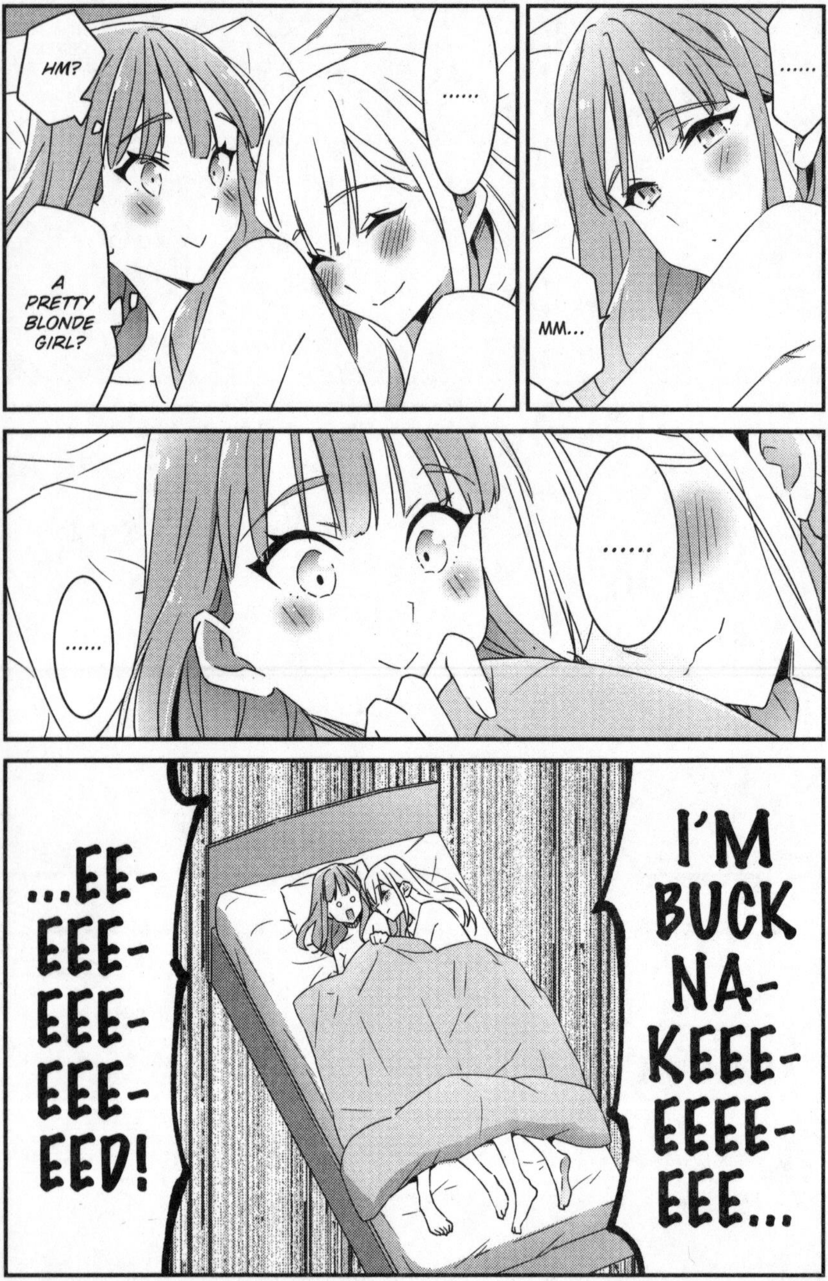
......
MM...
......
HM?
A PRETTY BLONDE GIRL?
......
......
I'M BUCK NA-KEEEE-EEEE-EEE...
...EE-EEE-EEE-EEE-EEE-EED!

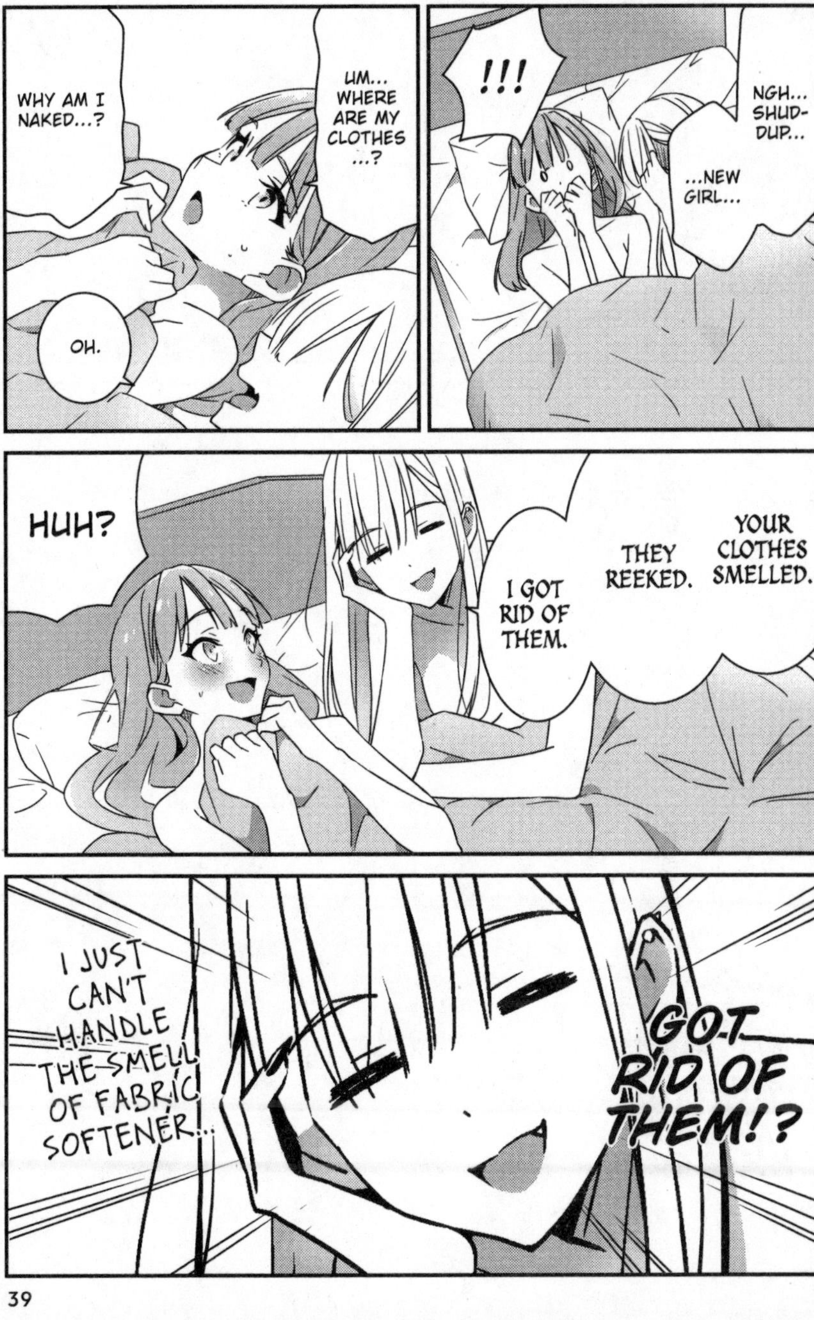
NGH... SHUD-DUP...
!!!
...NEW GIRL...
UM... WHERE ARE MY CLOTHES ...?
WHY AM I NAKED...?
OH.
YOUR CLOTHES SMELLED.
THEY REEKED.
I GOT RID OF THEM.
HUH?
GOT RID OF THEM!?
I JUST CAN'T HANDLE THE SMELL OF FABRIC SOFTENER...

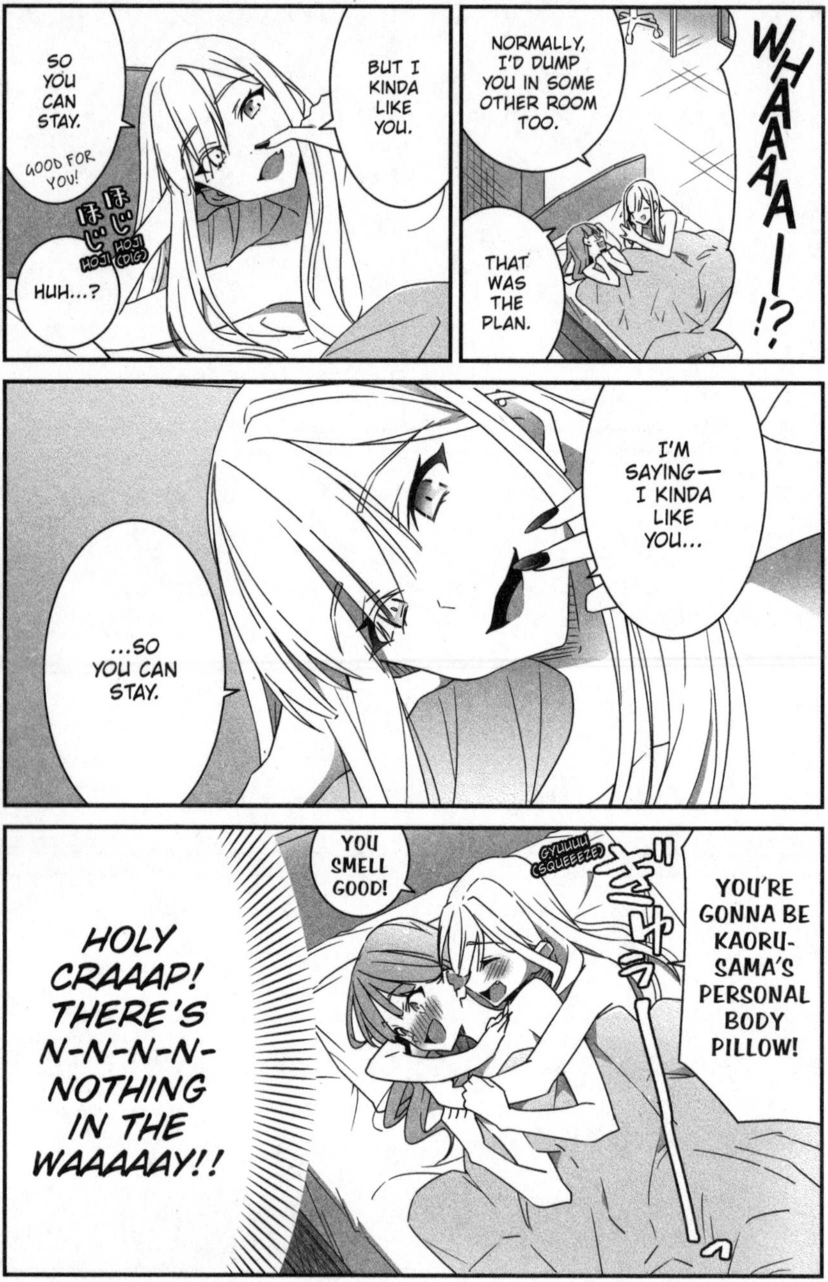
WHAAAAI!?
NORMALLY, I'D DUMP YOU IN SOME OTHER ROOM TOO.
THAT WAS THE PLAN.
BUT I KINDA LIKE YOU.
SO YOU CAN STAY.
GOOD FOR YOU!
ほじほじ HOJI HOJI (DIG)
HUH...?
I'M SAYING— I KINDA LIKE YOU...
...SO YOU CAN STAY.
YOU'RE GONNA BE KAORU-SAMA'S PERSONAL BODY PILLOW!
ぎゅう GYUUUU (SQUEEEZE)
YOU SMELL GOOD!
HOLY CRAAAP! THERE'S N-N-N-N-NOTHING IN THE WAAAAAY!!

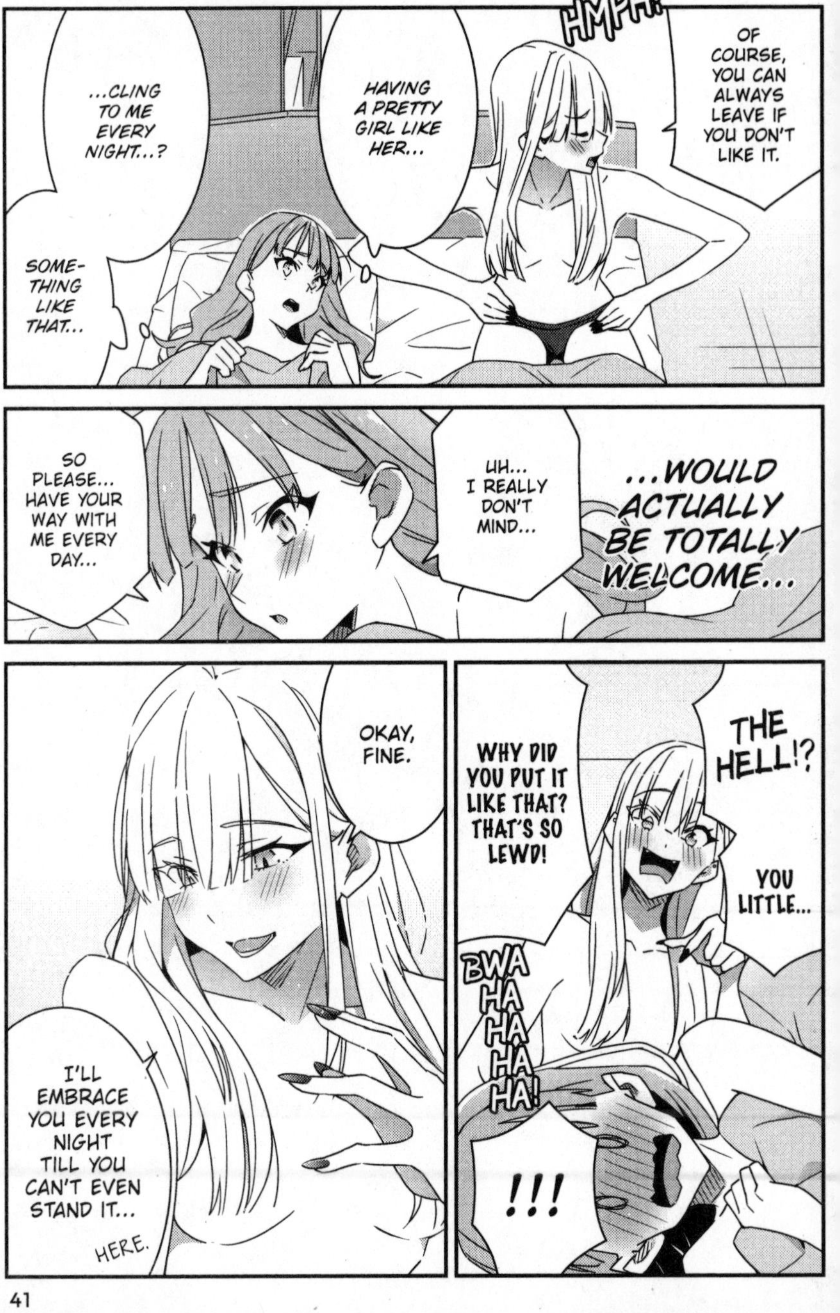
HMPH!
OF COURSE, YOU CAN ALWAYS LEAVE IF YOU DON'T LIKE IT.
HAVING A PRETTY GIRL LIKE HER...
...CLING TO ME EVERY NIGHT...?
SOME-THING LIKE THAT...
...WOULD ACTUALLY BE TOTALLY WELCOME...
UH... I REALLY DON'T MIND...
SO PLEASE... HAVE YOUR WAY WITH ME EVERY DAY...
THE HELL!?
WHY DID YOU PUT IT LIKE THAT? THAT'S SO LEWD!
YOU LITTLE...
BWA HA HA HA HA HA!
!!!
OKAY, FINE.
I'LL EMBRACE YOU EVERY NIGHT TILL YOU CAN'T EVEN STAND IT...
HERE.

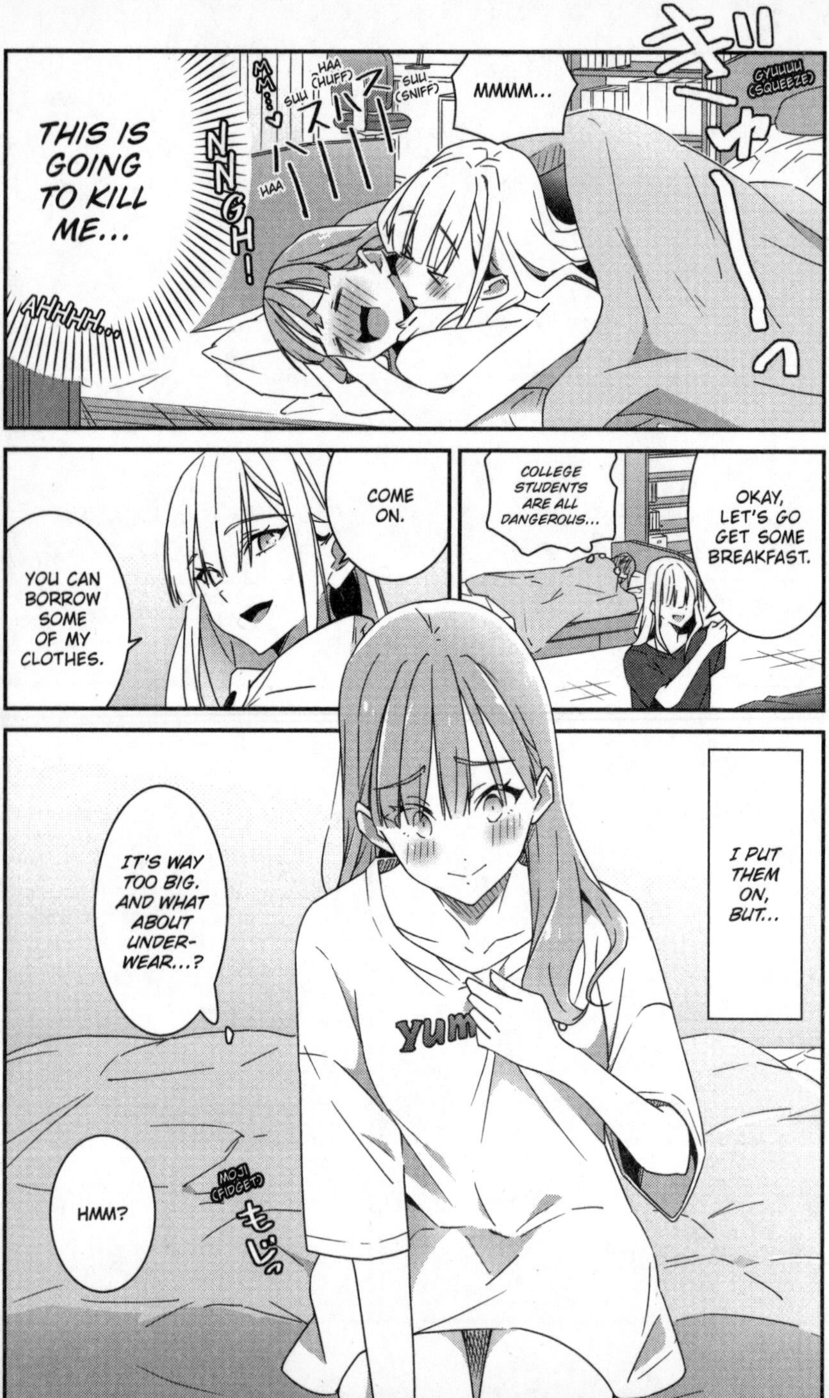
GYUUUU (SQUEEZE)
MMMM...
SUU (SNIFF)
HAA (HUFF)
SUU
HAA
MM...♥
NNNGH!
THIS IS GOING TO KILL ME...
AHHHH...
OKAY, LET'S GO GET SOME BREAKFAST.
COLLEGE STUDENTS ARE ALL DANGEROUS...
COME ON.
YOU CAN BORROW SOME OF MY CLOTHES.
I PUT THEM ON, BUT...
IT'S WAY TOO BIG. AND WHAT ABOUT UNDER-WEAR...?
MOJI (FIDGET)
HMM?

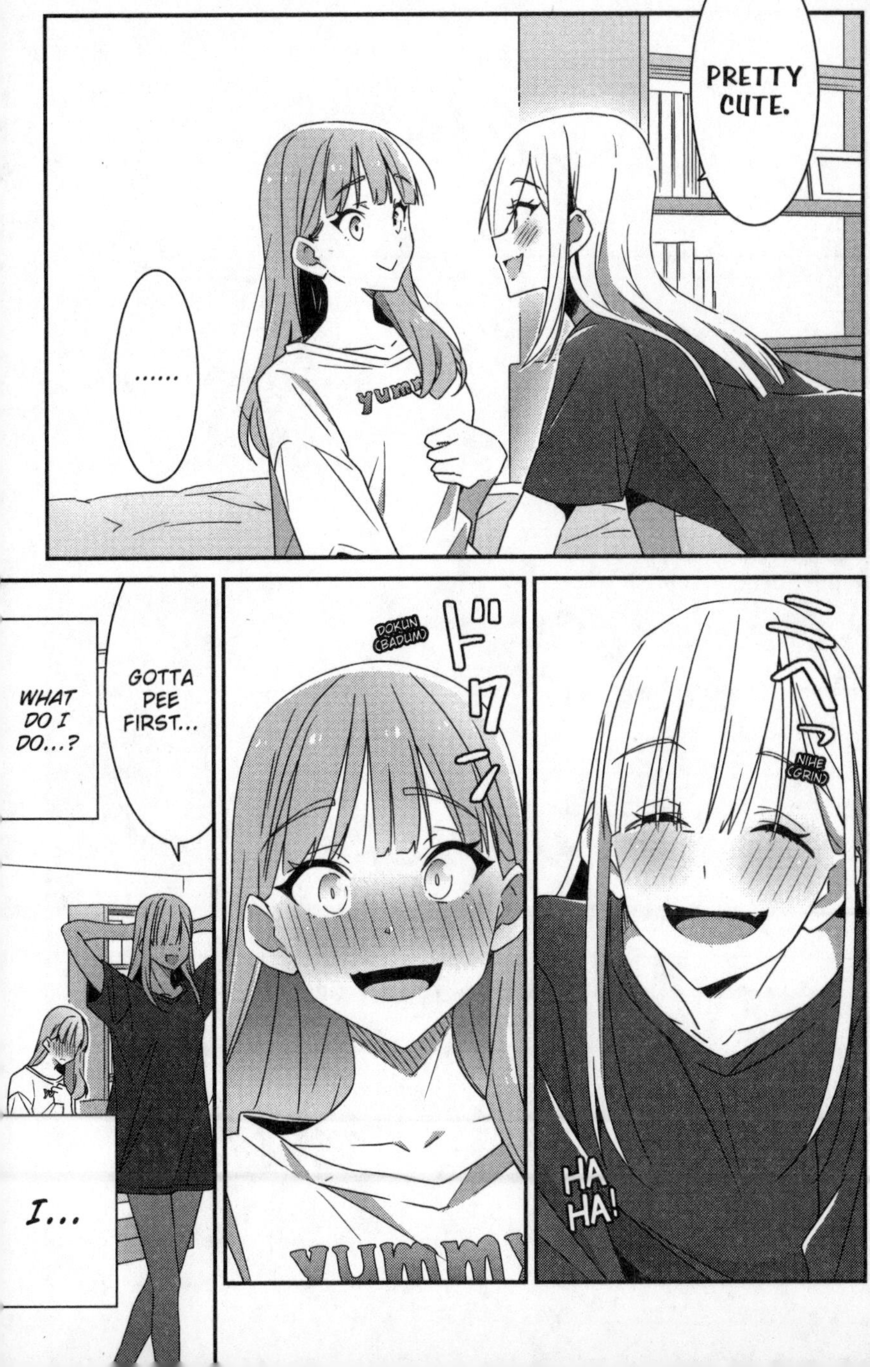
PRETTY CUTE.
......
NIHE (GRIN)
HA HA!
DOKUN (BADUM)
GOTTA PEE FIRST...
WHAT DO I DO...?
I...

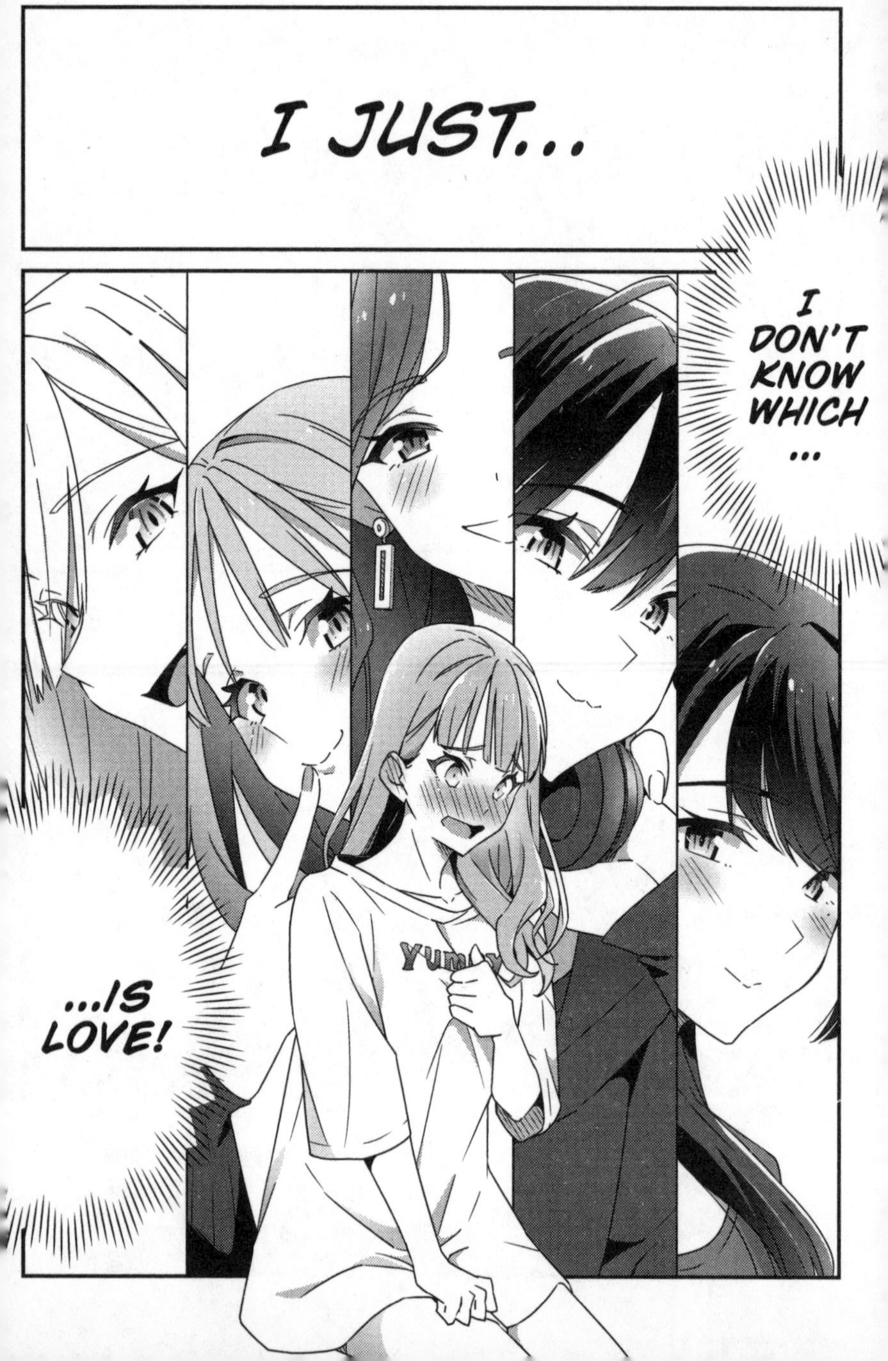
I JUST...
I DON'T KNOW WHICH ...
...IS LOVE!

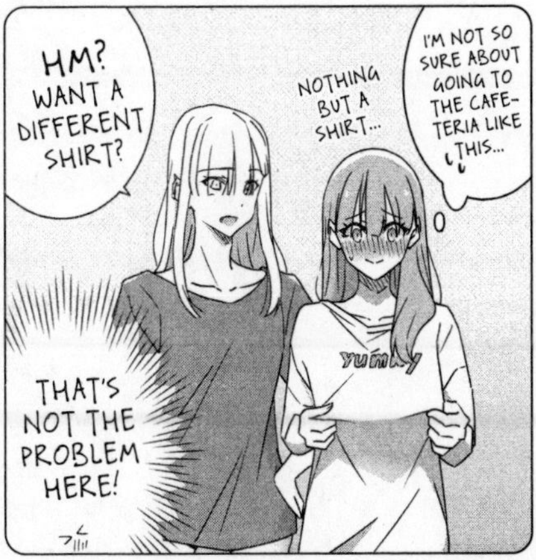
I'M NOT SO SURE ABOUT GOING TO THE CAFE-TERIA LIKE THIS...
NOTHING BUT A SHIRT...
HM? WANT A DIFFERENT SHIRT?
THAT'S NOT THE PROBLEM HERE!

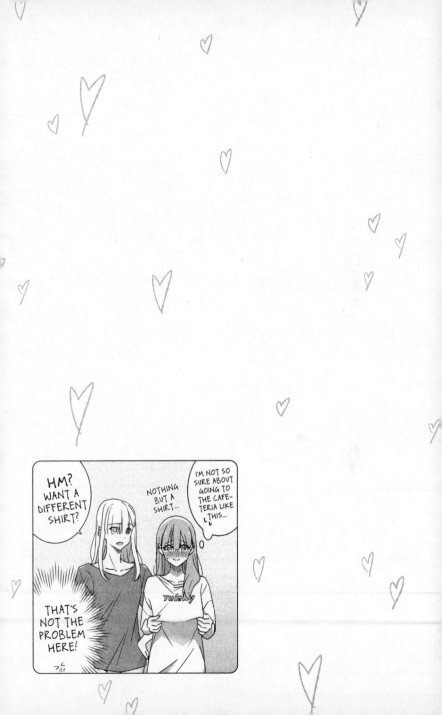

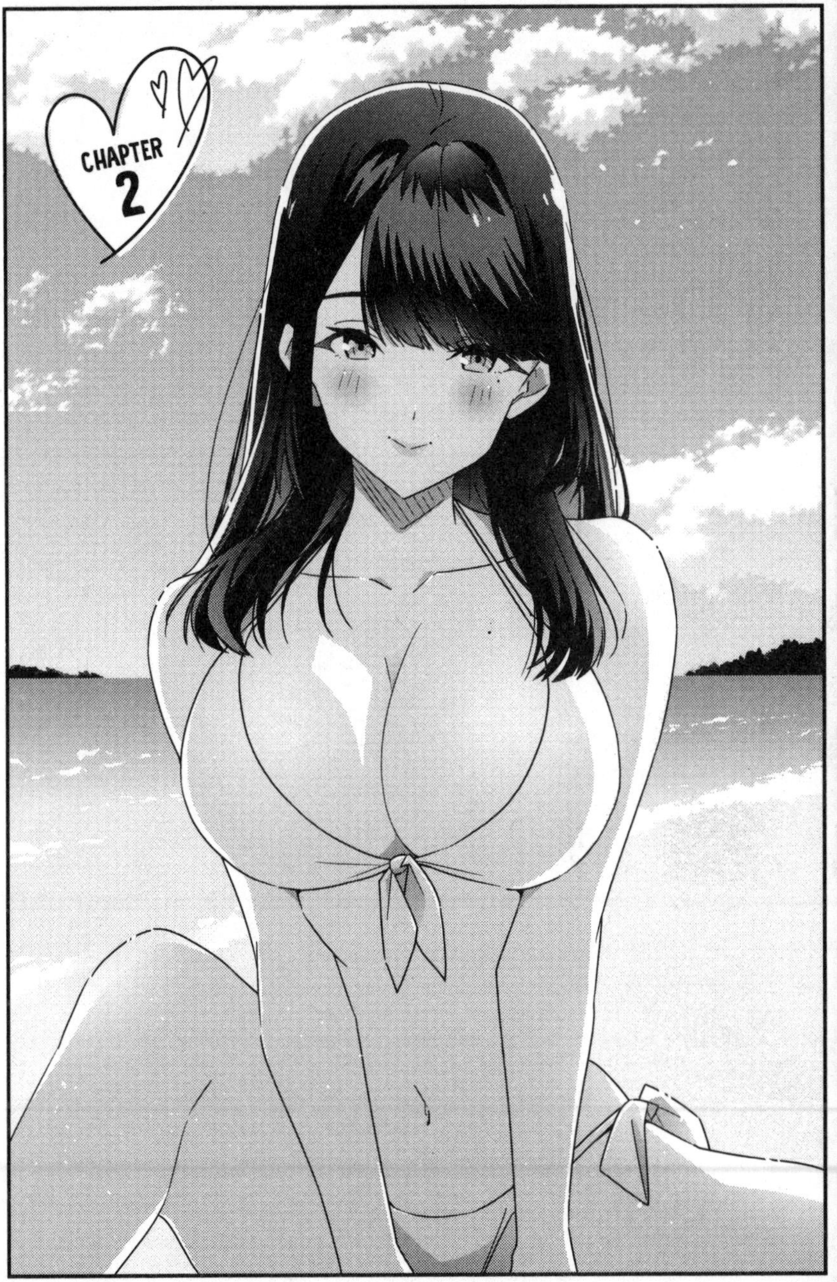
CHAPTER
2

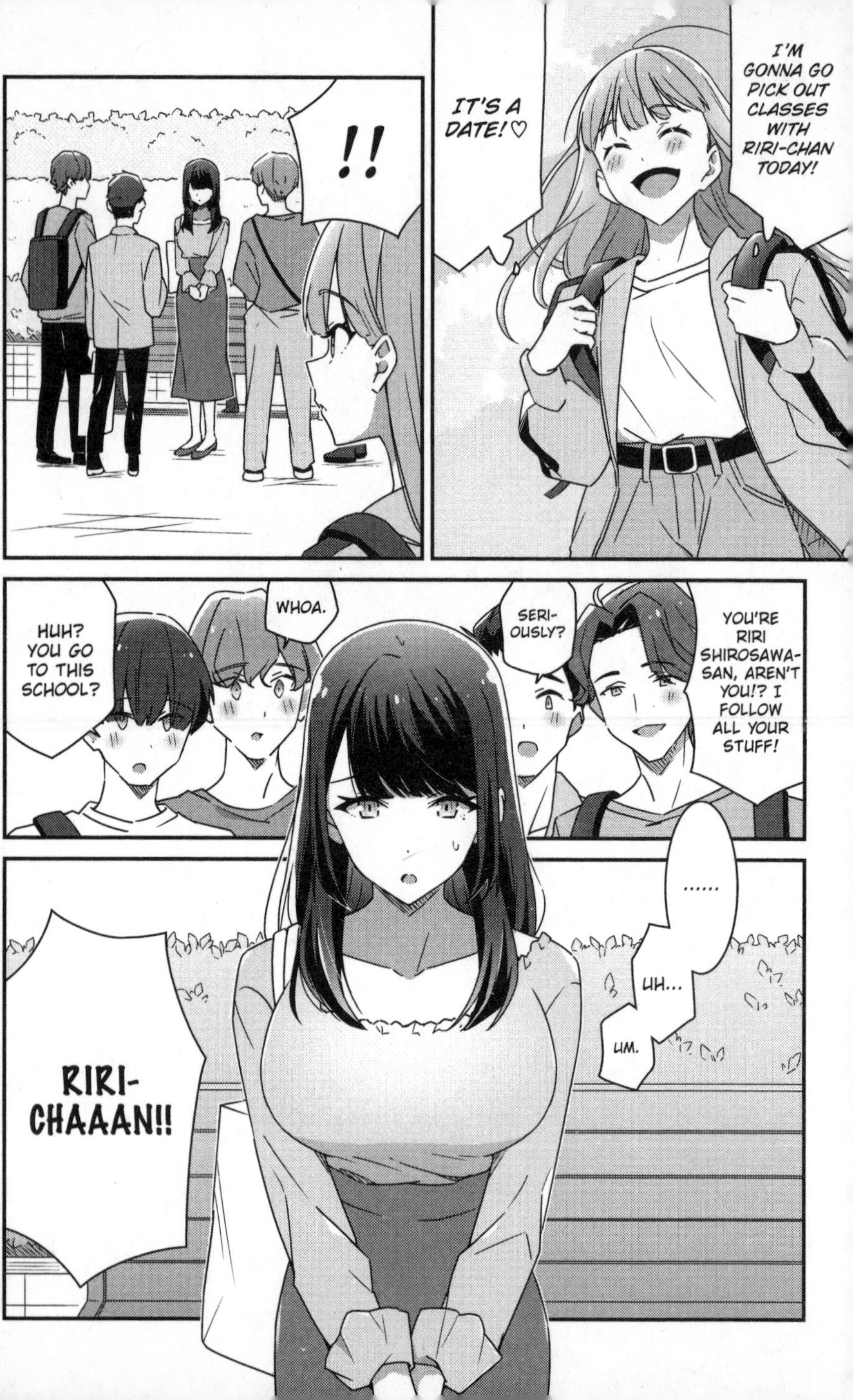
I'M GONNA GO PICK OUT CLASSES WITH RIRI-CHAN TODAY!
IT'S A DATE!♡
!!
YOU'RE RIRI SHIROSAWA-SAN, AREN'T YOU!? I FOLLOW ALL YOUR STUFF!
SERI-OUSLY?
WHOA.
HUH? YOU GO TO THIS SCHOOL?
......
UH...
UM.
RIRI-CHAAAN!!

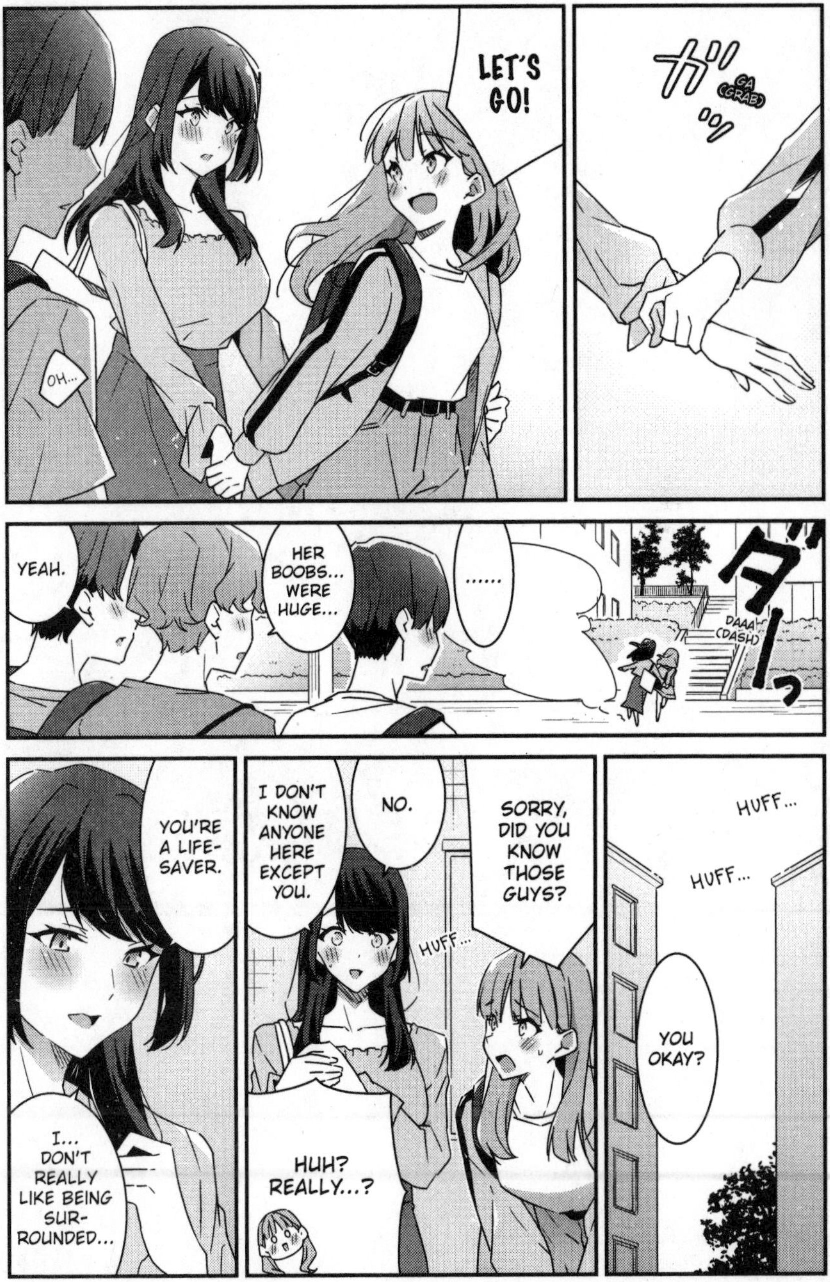
GA (GRAB)
LET'S GO!
OH...
DAAA (DASH)
......
HER BOOBS... WERE HUGE...
YEAH.
HUFF...
HUFF...
YOU OKAY?
SORRY, DID YOU KNOW THOSE GUYS?
NO.
I DON'T KNOW ANYONE HERE EXCEPT YOU.
HUFF...
HUH? REALLY...?
YOU'RE A LIFE-SAVER.
I... DON'T REALLY LIKE BEING SUR-ROUNDED...

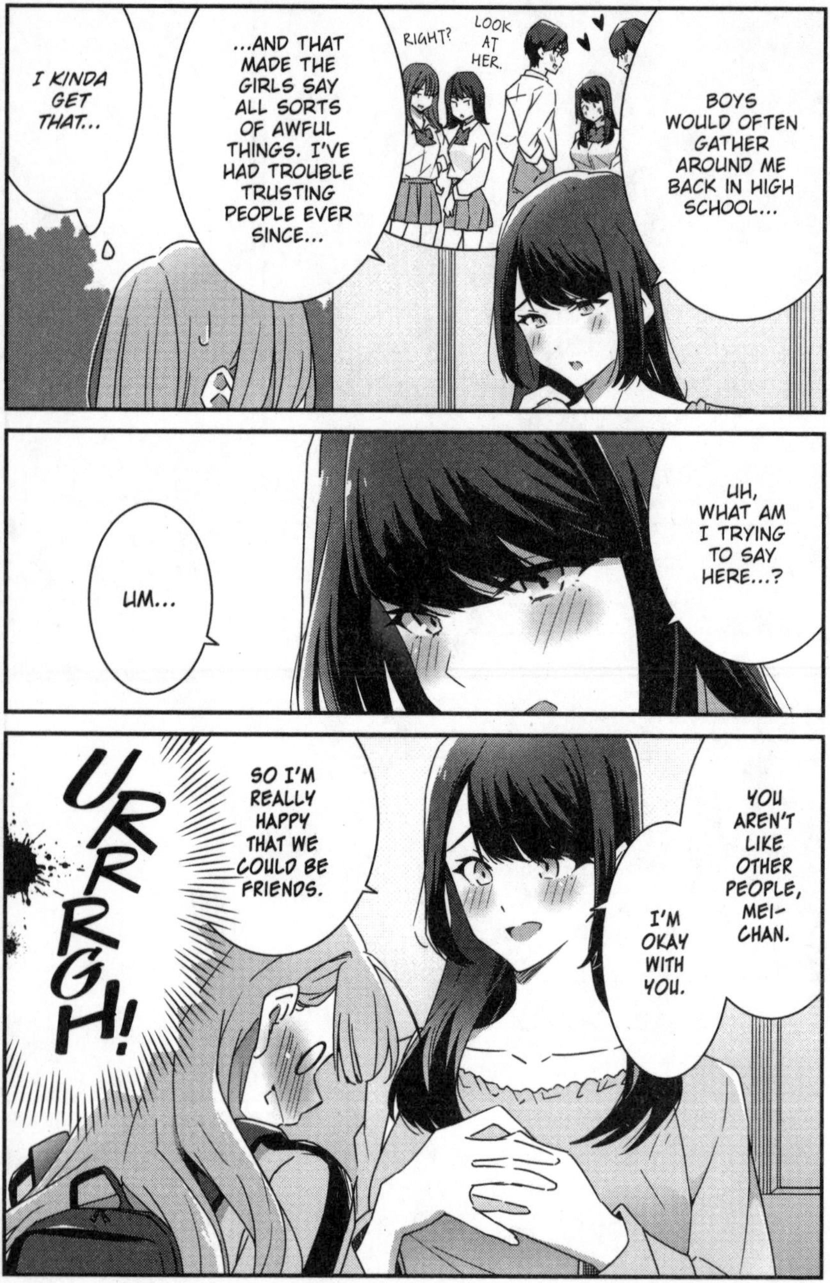
BOYS WOULD OFTEN GATHER AROUND ME BACK IN HIGH SCHOOL...
LOOK AT HER.
RIGHT?
...AND THAT MADE THE GIRLS SAY ALL SORTS OF AWFUL THINGS. I'VE HAD TROUBLE TRUSTING PEOPLE EVER SINCE...
I KINDA GET THAT...
UH, WHAT AM I TRYING TO SAY HERE...?
UM...
YOU AREN'T LIKE OTHER PEOPLE, MEI-CHAN.
I'M OKAY WITH YOU.
SO I'M REALLY HAPPY THAT WE COULD BE FRIENDS.
URRRGH!

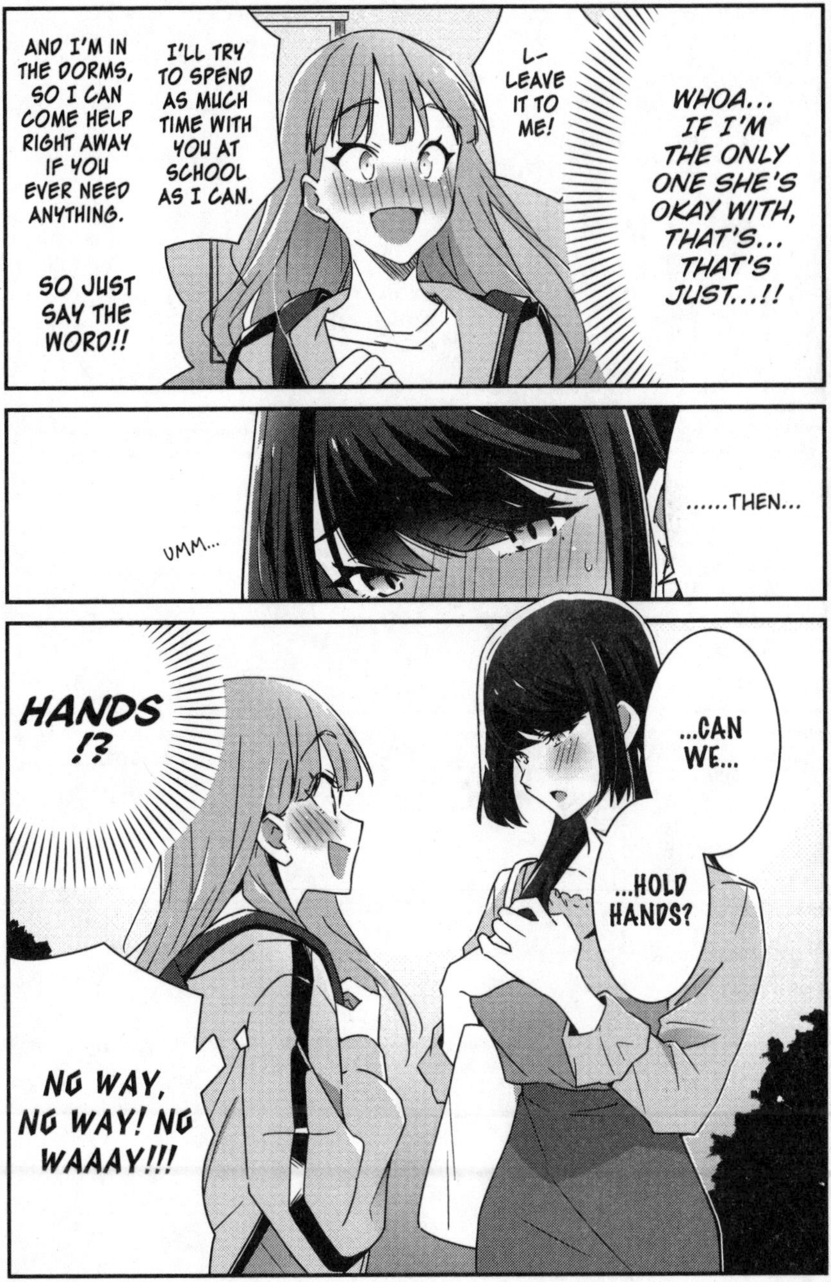
WHOA... IF I'M THE ONLY ONE SHE'S OKAY WITH, THAT'S... THAT'S JUST...!!
L-LEAVE IT TO ME!
I'LL TRY TO SPEND AS MUCH TIME WITH YOU AT SCHOOL AS I CAN.
AND I'M IN THE DORMS, SO I CAN COME HELP RIGHT AWAY IF YOU EVER NEED ANYTHING.
SO JUST SAY THE WORD!!
......THEN...
UMM...
...CAN WE...
...HOLD HANDS?
HANDS!?
NO WAY, NO WAY! NO WAAAY!!!

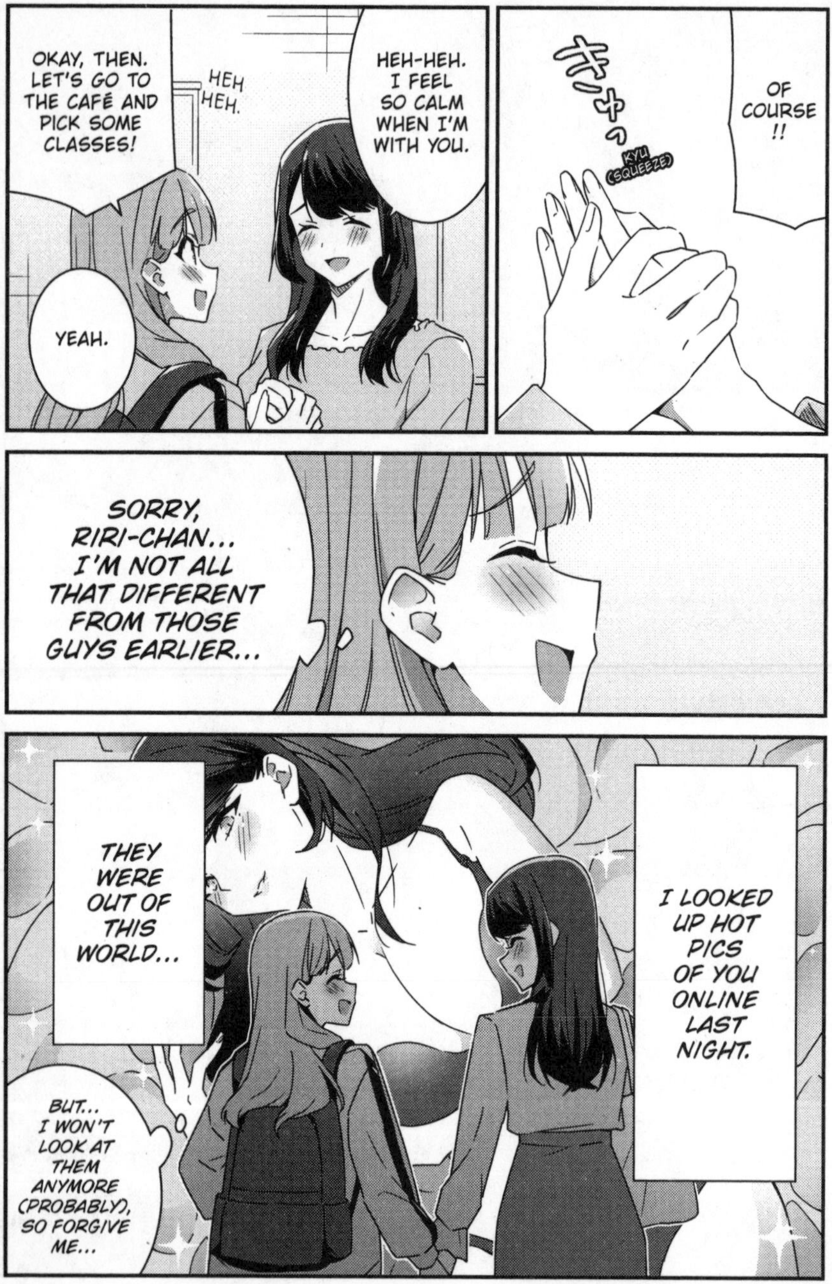
OKAY, THEN. LET'S GO TO THE CAFÉ AND PICK SOME CLASSES!
HEH HEH.
HEH-HEH. I FEEL SO CALM WHEN I'M WITH YOU.
YEAH.
OF COURSE !!
KYU (SQUEEZE)
SORRY, RIRI-CHAN... I'M NOT ALL THAT DIFFERENT FROM THOSE GUYS EARLIER...
I LOOKED UP HOT PICS OF YOU ONLINE LAST NIGHT.
THEY WERE OUT OF THIS WORLD...
BUT... I WON'T LOOK AT THEM ANYMORE (PROBABLY), SO FORGIVE ME...

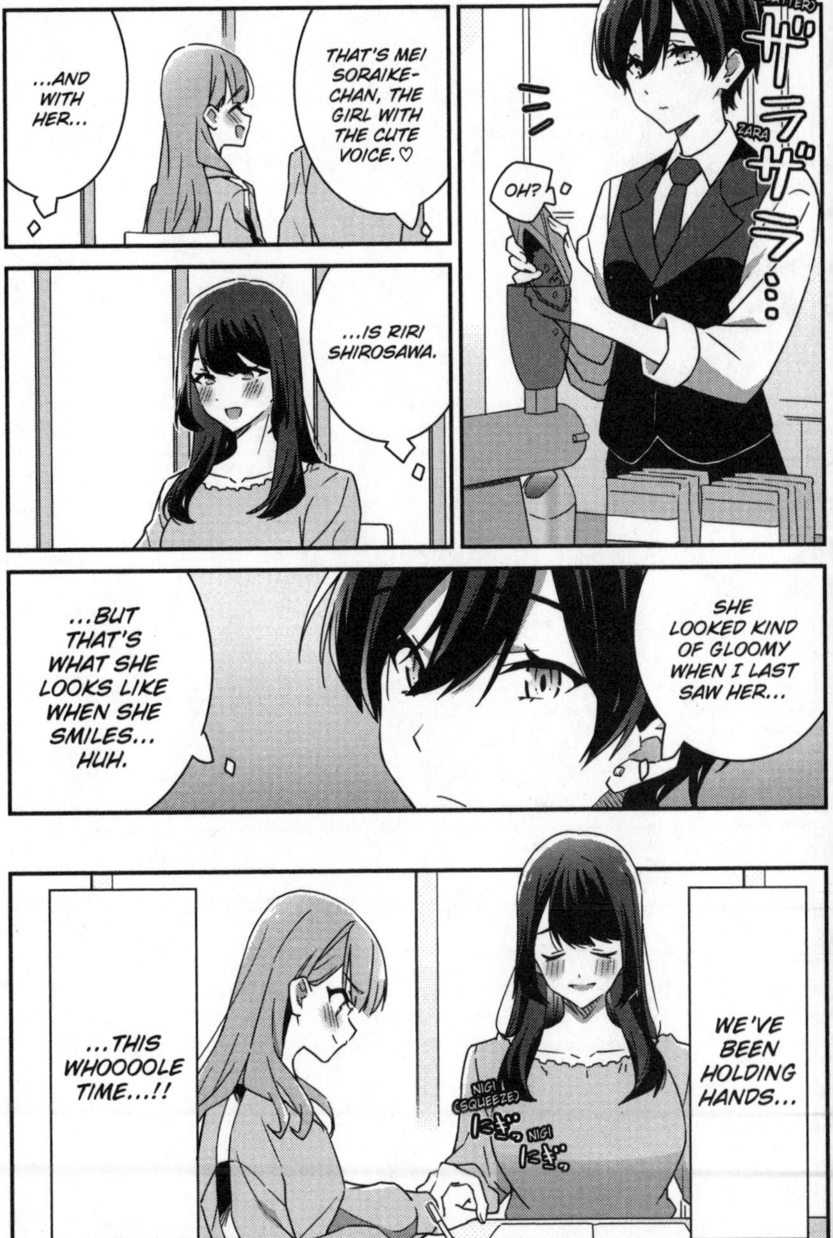
ZARA (CLATTER)
ザラ
ZARA
ザラ…
OH?
THAT'S MEI SORAIKE-CHAN, THE GIRL WITH THE CUTE VOICE.♡
...AND WITH HER...
...IS RIRI SHIROSAWA.
SHE LOOKED KIND OF GLOOMY WHEN I LAST SAW HER...
...BUT THAT'S WHAT SHE LOOKS LIKE WHEN SHE SMILES... HUH.
WE'VE BEEN HOLDING HANDS...
NIGI (SQUEEZE)
にぎっ
NIGI
にぎっ
...THIS WHOOOOLE TIME...!!

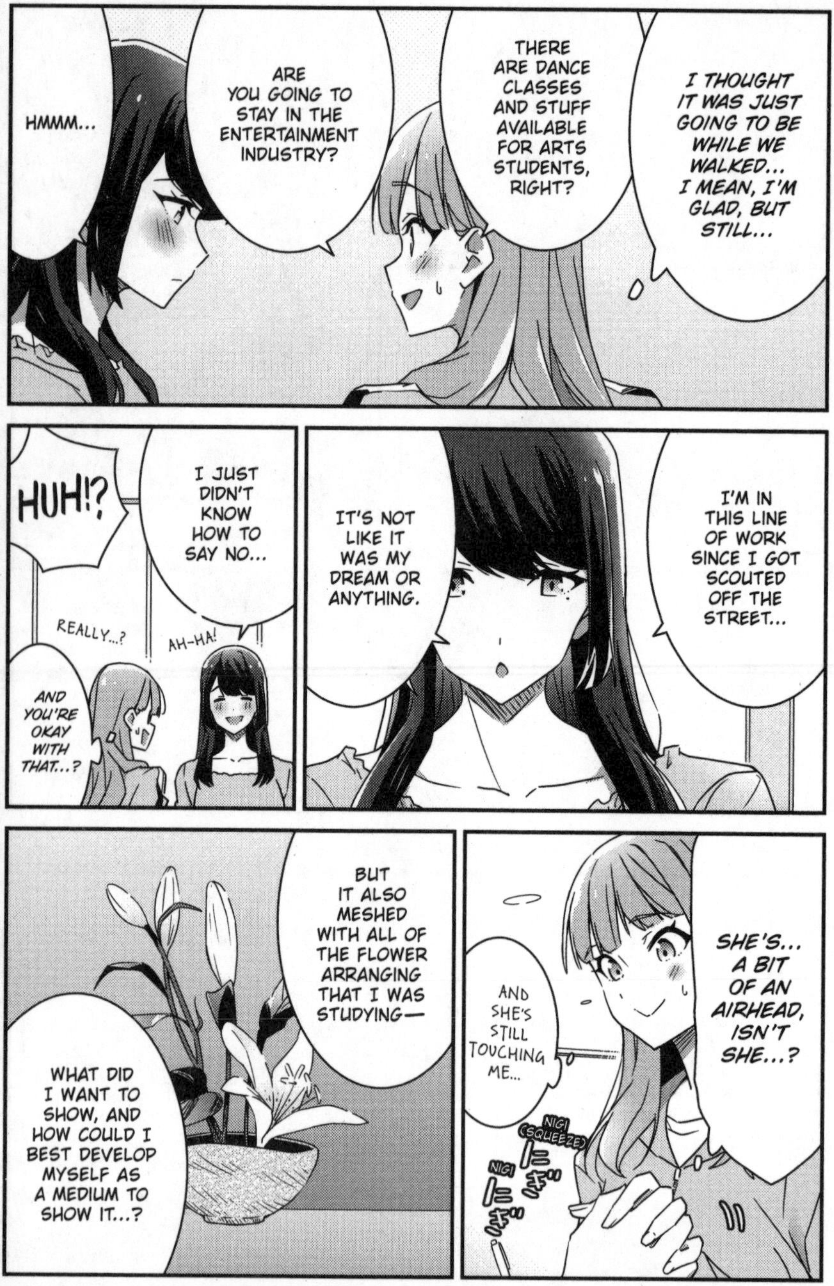
I THOUGHT IT WAS JUST GOING TO BE WHILE WE WALKED... I MEAN, I'M GLAD, BUT STILL...
THERE ARE DANCE CLASSES AND STUFF AVAILABLE FOR ARTS STUDENTS, RIGHT?
ARE YOU GOING TO STAY IN THE ENTERTAINMENT INDUSTRY?
HMMM...
I'M IN THIS LINE OF WORK SINCE I GOT SCOUTED OFF THE STREET...
IT'S NOT LIKE IT WAS MY DREAM OR ANYTHING.
I JUST DIDN'T KNOW HOW TO SAY NO...
HUH!?
AH-HA!
REALLY...?
AND YOU'RE OKAY WITH THAT...?
SHE'S... A BIT OF AN AIRHEAD, ISN'T SHE...?
AND SHE'S STILL TOUCHING ME...
NIGI (SQUEEZE)
NIGI
BUT IT ALSO MESHED WITH ALL OF THE FLOWER ARRANGING THAT I WAS STUDYING—
WHAT DID I WANT TO SHOW, AND HOW COULD I BEST DEVELOP MYSELF AS A MEDIUM TO SHOW IT...?

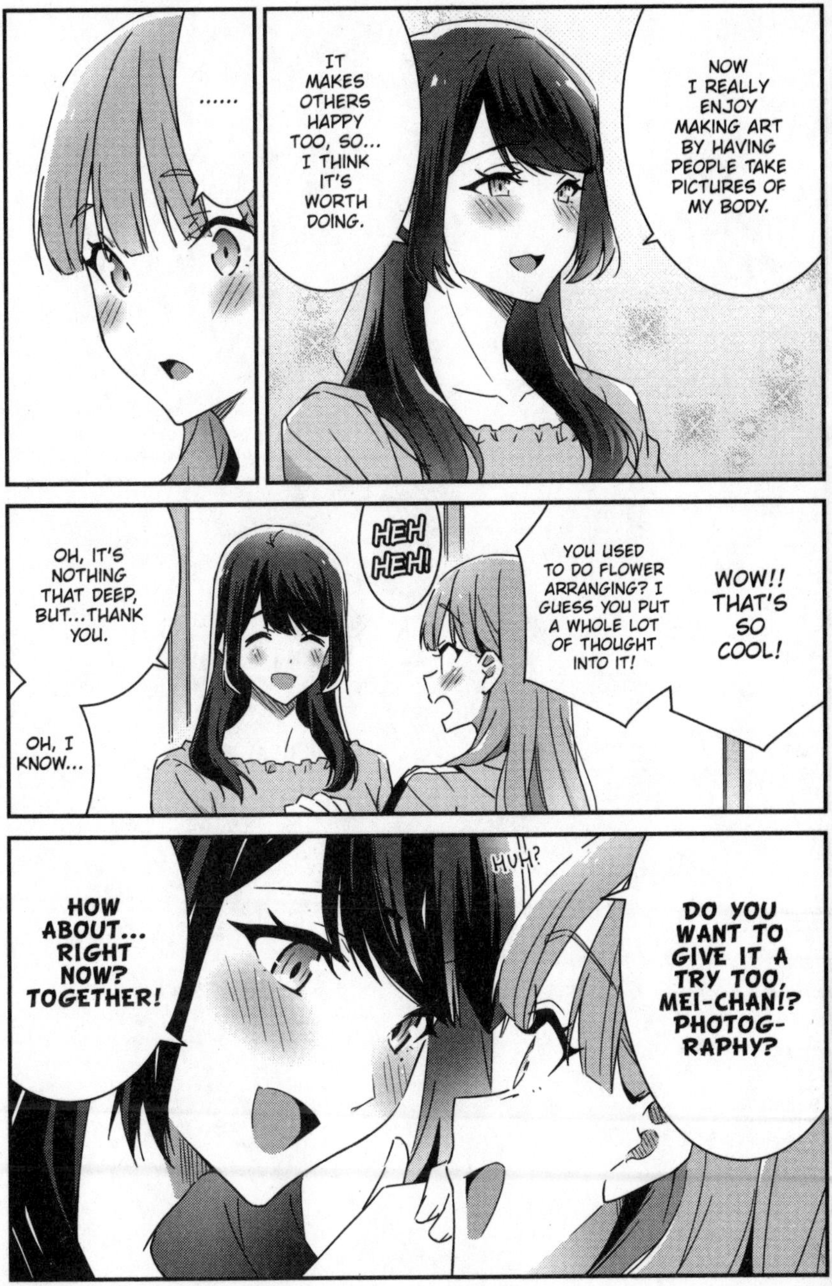
NOW I REALLY ENJOY MAKING ART BY HAVING PEOPLE TAKE PICTURES OF MY BODY.
IT MAKES OTHERS HAPPY TOO, SO... I THINK IT'S WORTH DOING.
......
WOW!! THAT'S SO COOL!
YOU USED TO DO FLOWER ARRANGING? I GUESS YOU PUT A WHOLE LOT OF THOUGHT INTO IT!
HEH HEH!
OH, IT'S NOTHING THAT DEEP, BUT...THANK YOU.
OH, I KNOW...
DO YOU WANT TO GIVE IT A TRY TOO, MEI-CHAN!? PHOTOG-RAPHY?
HUH?
HOW ABOUT... RIGHT NOW? TOGETHER!

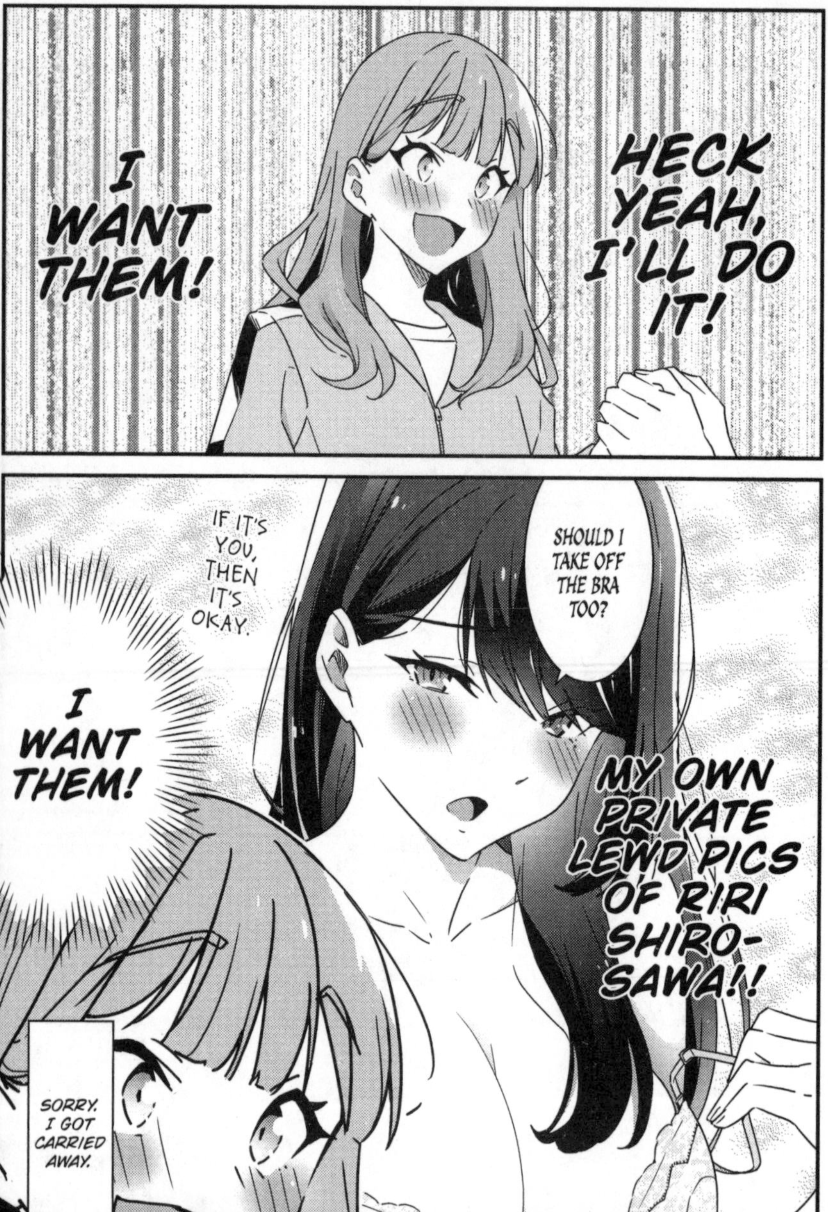
HECK YEAH, I'LL DO IT!
I WANT THEM!
SHOULD I TAKE OFF THE BRA TOO?
IF IT'S YOU, THEN IT'S OKAY.
MY OWN PRIVATE LEWD PICS OF RIRI SHIRO-SAWA!!
I WANT THEM!
SORRY. I GOT CARRIED AWAY.

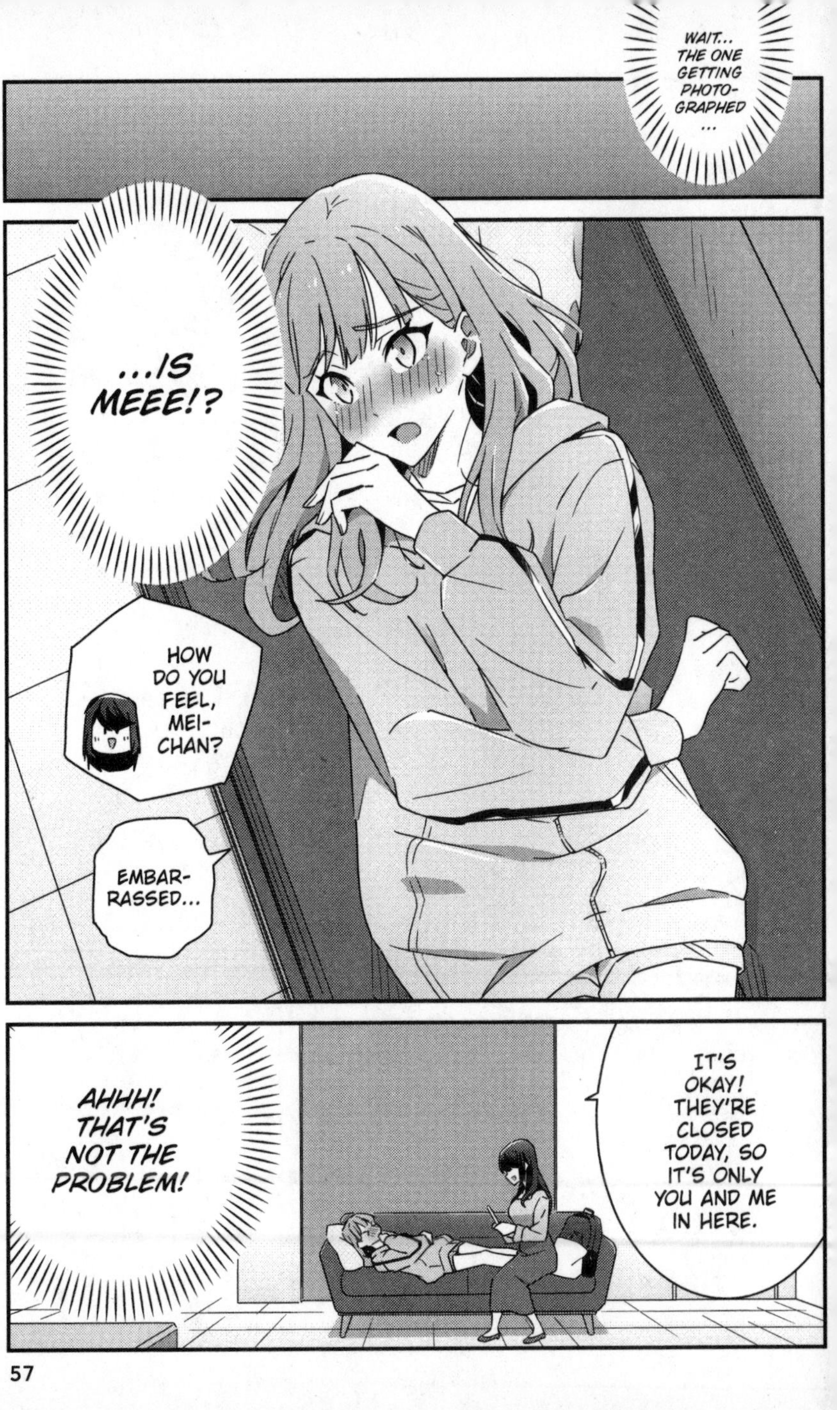
WAIT... THE ONE GETTING PHOTO-GRAPHED...
...IS MEEE!?
HOW DO YOU FEEL, MEI-CHAN?
EMBAR-RASSED...
IT'S OKAY! THEY'RE CLOSED TODAY, SO IT'S ONLY YOU AND ME IN HERE.
AHHH! THAT'S NOT THE PROBLEM!

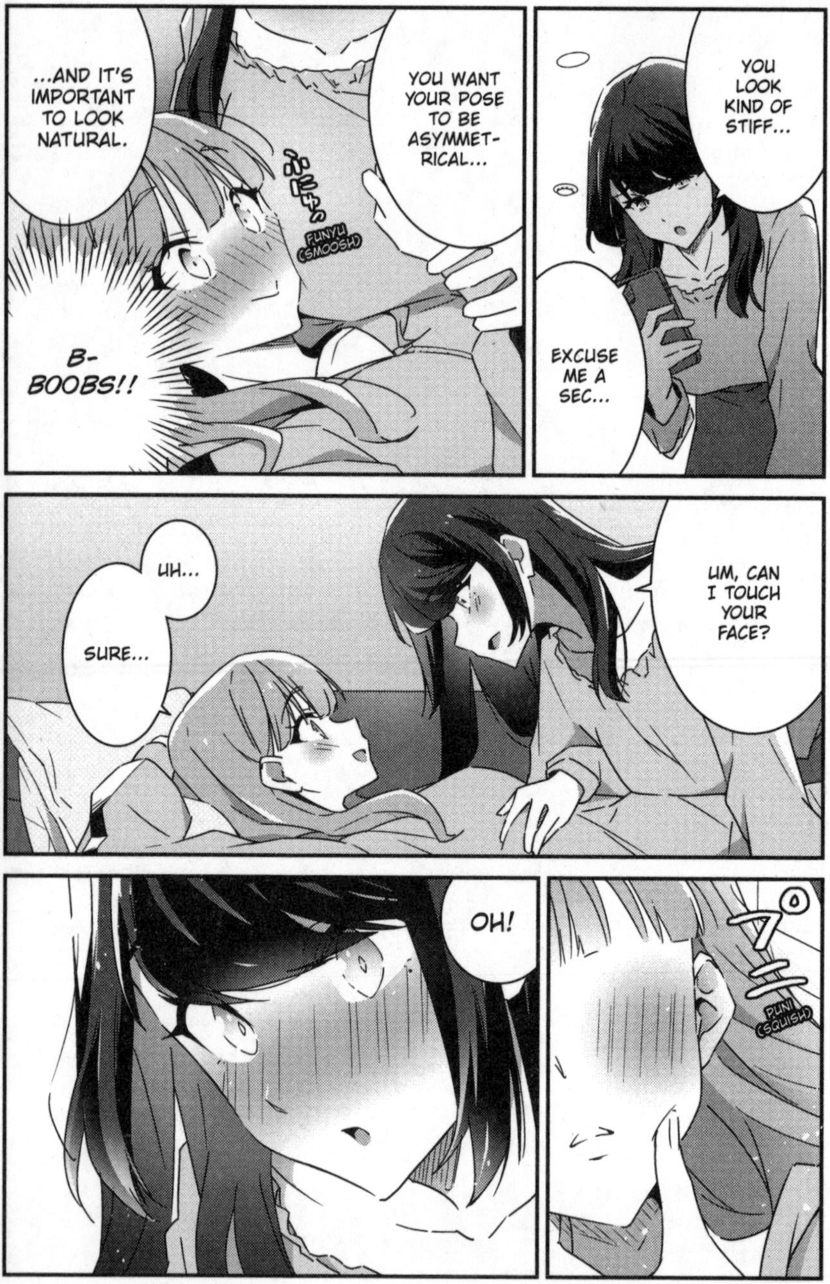
YOU LOOK KIND OF STIFF...
EXCUSE ME A SEC...
YOU WANT YOUR POSE TO BE ASYMMETRICAL...
...AND IT'S IMPORTANT TO LOOK NATURAL.
ふにゅ
FUNYU (SMOOSH)
B-BOOBS!!
UM, CAN I TOUCH YOUR FACE?
UH...
SURE...
PUNI (SQUISH)
OH!

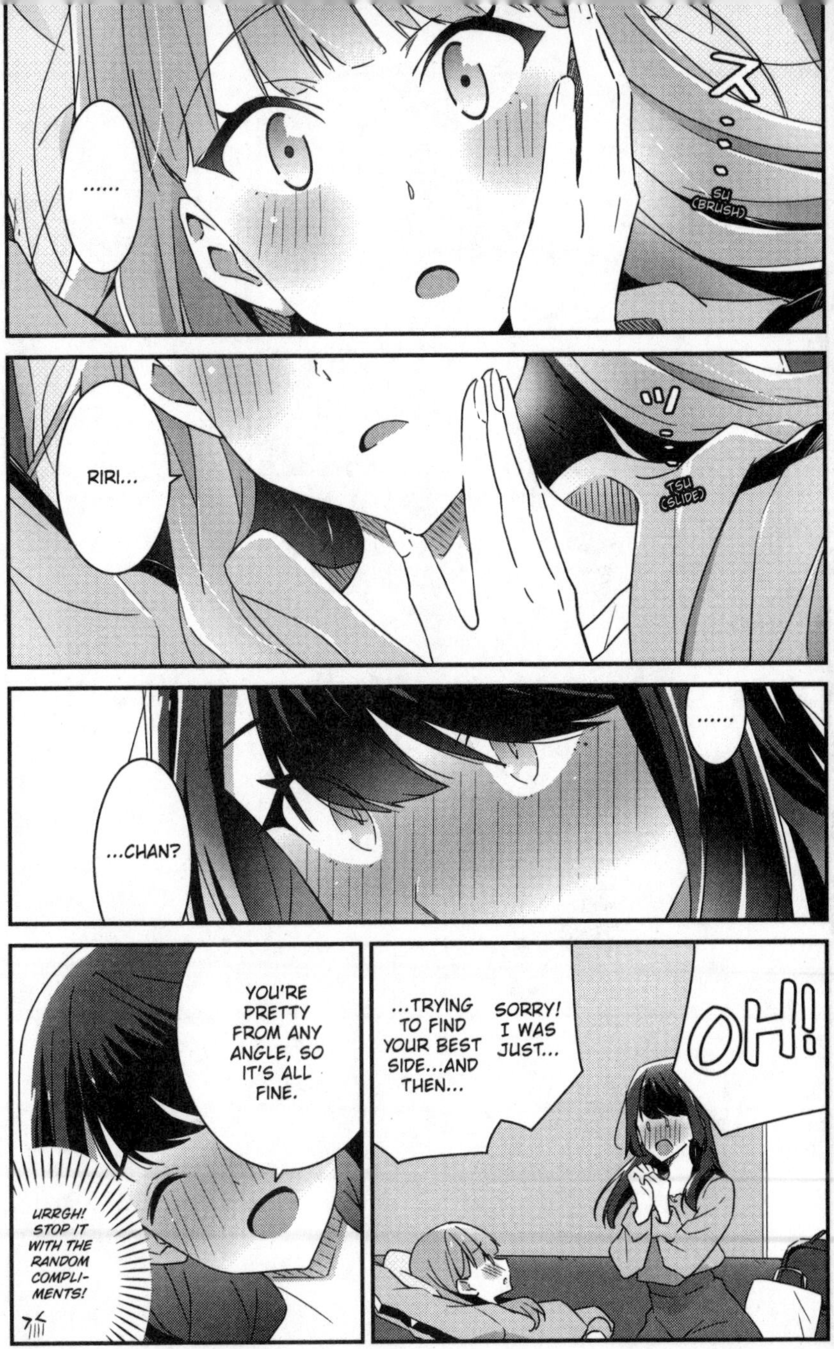
......
SU (BRUSH)
RIRI...
TSU (SLIDE)
......
...CHAN?
OH!
SORRY! I WAS JUST...
...TRYING TO FIND YOUR BEST SIDE...AND THEN...
YOU'RE PRETTY FROM ANY ANGLE, SO IT'S ALL FINE.
URRGH! STOP IT WITH THE RANDOM COMPLIMENTS!

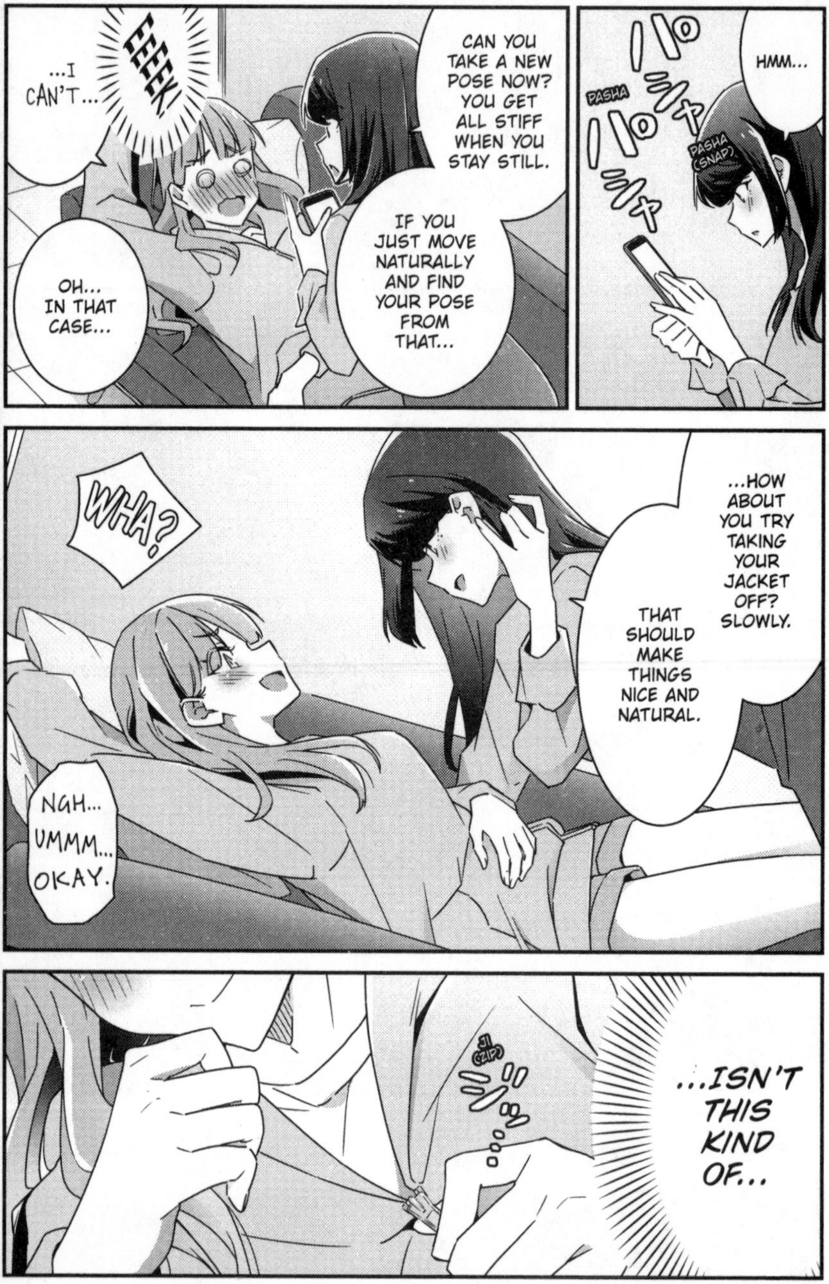
HMM...
PASHA
PASHA (SNAP)
CAN YOU TAKE A NEW POSE NOW? YOU GET ALL STIFF WHEN YOU STAY STILL.
EEEEK
...I CAN'T...
IF YOU JUST MOVE NATURALLY AND FIND YOUR POSE FROM THAT...
OH... IN THAT CASE...
...HOW ABOUT YOU TRY TAKING YOUR JACKET OFF? SLOWLY.
THAT SHOULD MAKE THINGS NICE AND NATURAL.
WHA?
NGH... UMMM... OKAY.
...ISN'T THIS KIND OF...
JI (ZIP)

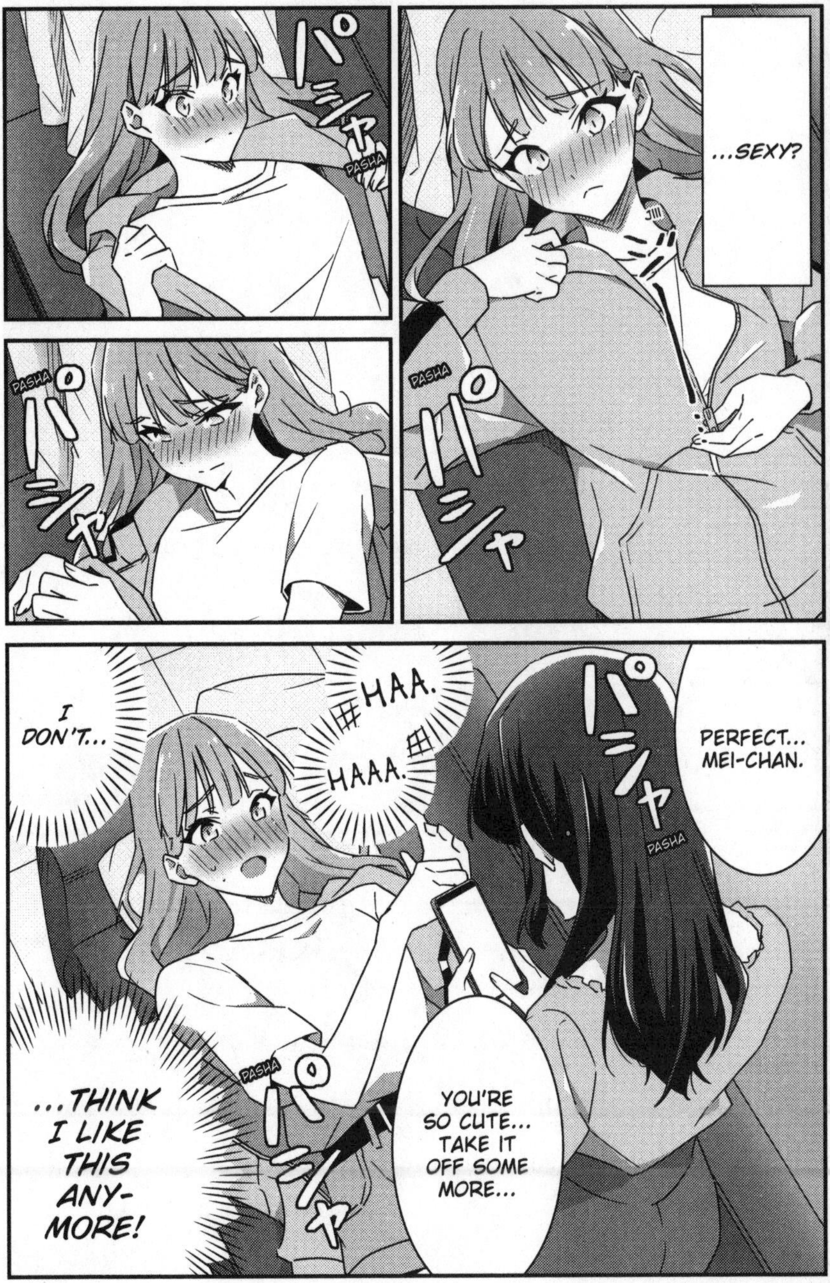
...SEXY?
JIII
ジー
PASHA
パシャ
パシャ
PASHA
PASHA
パシャ
PERFECT... MEI-CHAN.
パシャ
PASHA
HAA.
HAAA.
I DON'T...
YOU'RE SO CUTE... TAKE IT OFF SOME MORE...
PASHA
パシャ
...THINK I LIKE THIS ANY-MORE!

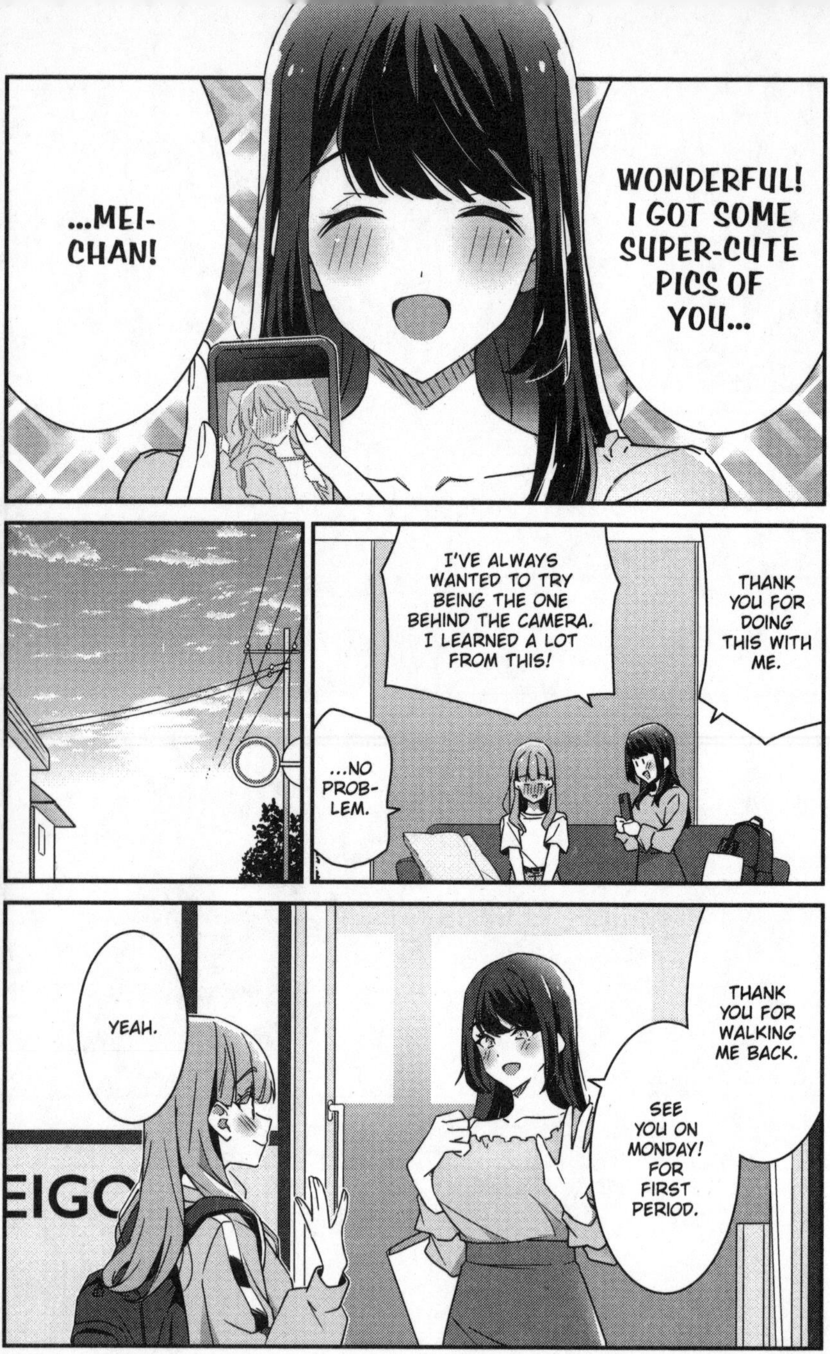
WONDERFUL! I GOT SOME SUPER-CUTE PICS OF YOU...
...MEI-CHAN!
THANK YOU FOR DOING THIS WITH ME.
I'VE ALWAYS WANTED TO TRY BEING THE ONE BEHIND THE CAMERA. I LEARNED A LOT FROM THIS!
...NO PROB-LEM.
THANK YOU FOR WALKING ME BACK.
SEE YOU ON MONDAY! FOR FIRST PERIOD.
YEAH.

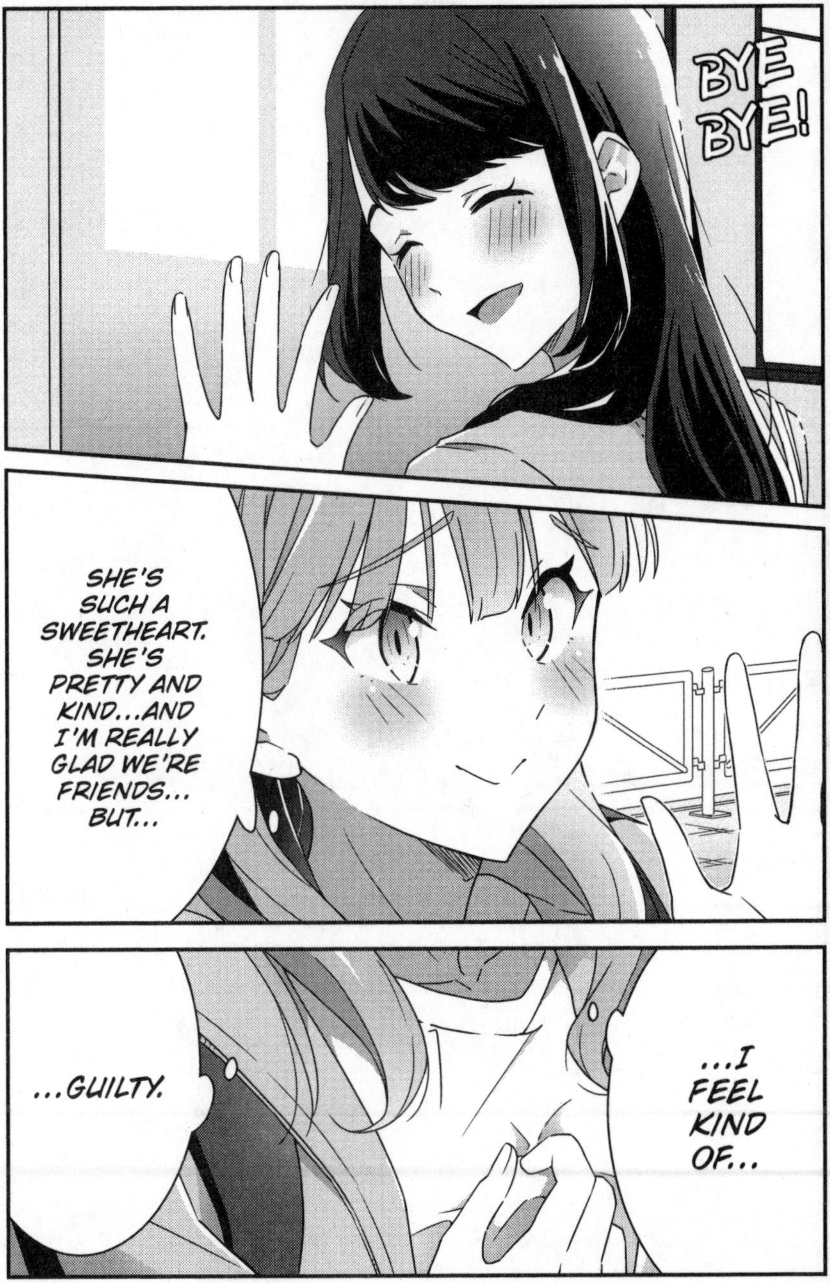
BYE BYE!
SHE'S SUCH A SWEETHEART. SHE'S PRETTY AND KIND...AND I'M REALLY GLAD WE'RE FRIENDS... BUT...
...I FEEL KIND OF...
...GUILTY.

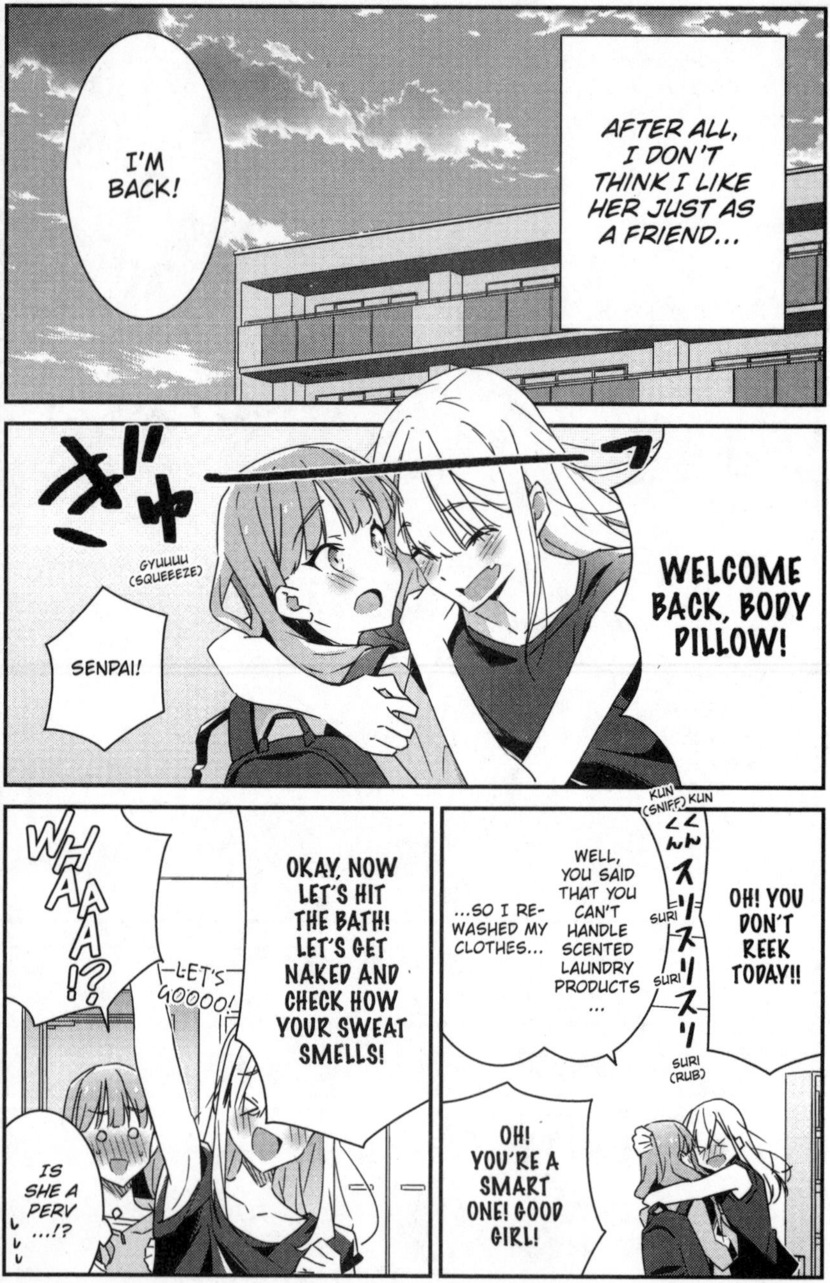
AFTER ALL, I DON'T THINK I LIKE HER JUST AS A FRIEND...
I'M BACK!
ぎゅーっ
GYUUUU (SQUEEEZE)
WELCOME BACK, BODY PILLOW!
SENPAI!
KUN (SNIFF) KUN
くんくん
OH! YOU DON'T REEK TODAY!!
スリスリスリ
SURI SURI SURI (RUB)
WELL, YOU SAID THAT YOU CAN'T HANDLE SCENTED LAUNDRY PRODUCTS ...
...SO I RE-WASHED MY CLOTHES...
OH! YOU'RE A SMART ONE! GOOD GIRL!
OKAY, NOW LET'S HIT THE BATH! LET'S GET NAKED AND CHECK HOW YOUR SWEAT SMELLS!
LET'S GOOOO!
WHAAA!?
IS SHE A PERV ...!?

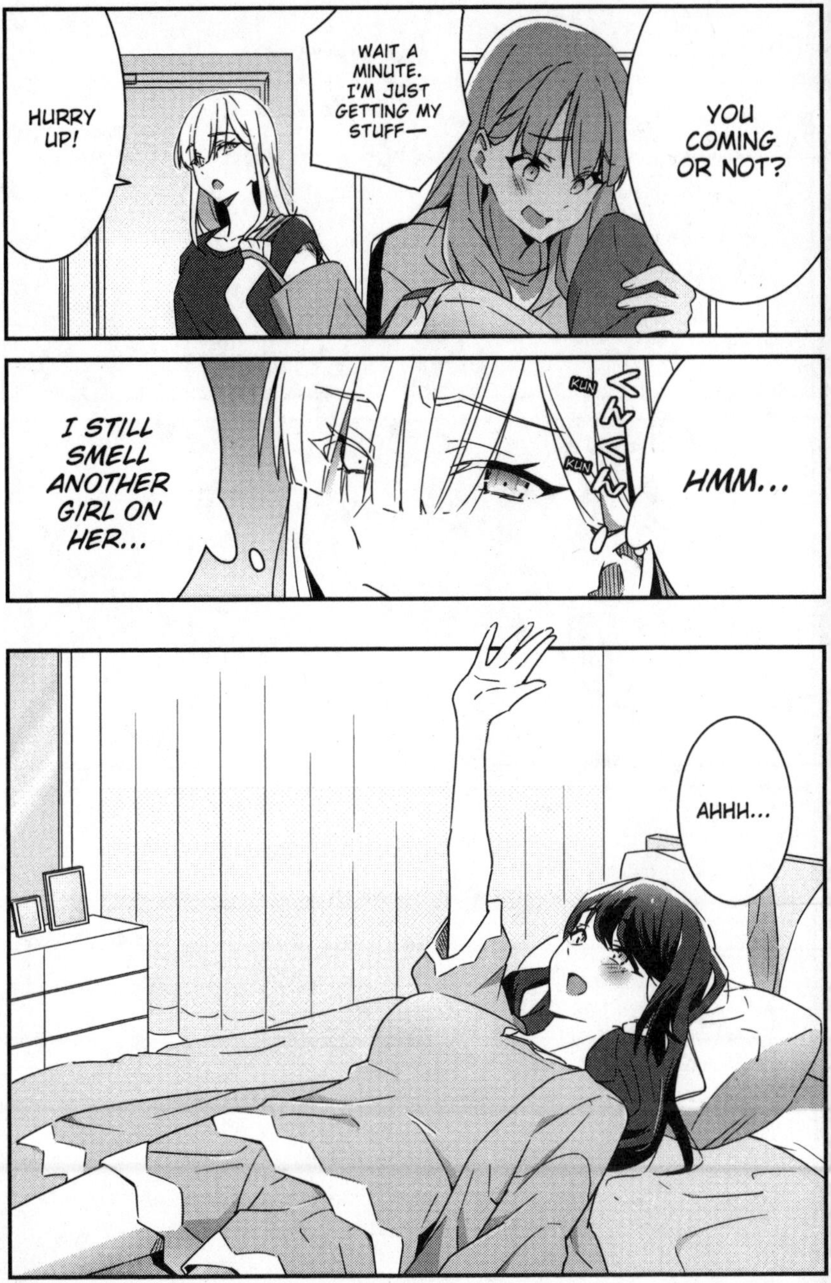
YOU COMING OR NOT?
WAIT A MINUTE. I'M JUST GETTING MY STUFF—
HURRY UP!
HMM...
KUN
KUN
I STILL SMELL ANOTHER GIRL ON HER...
AHHH...

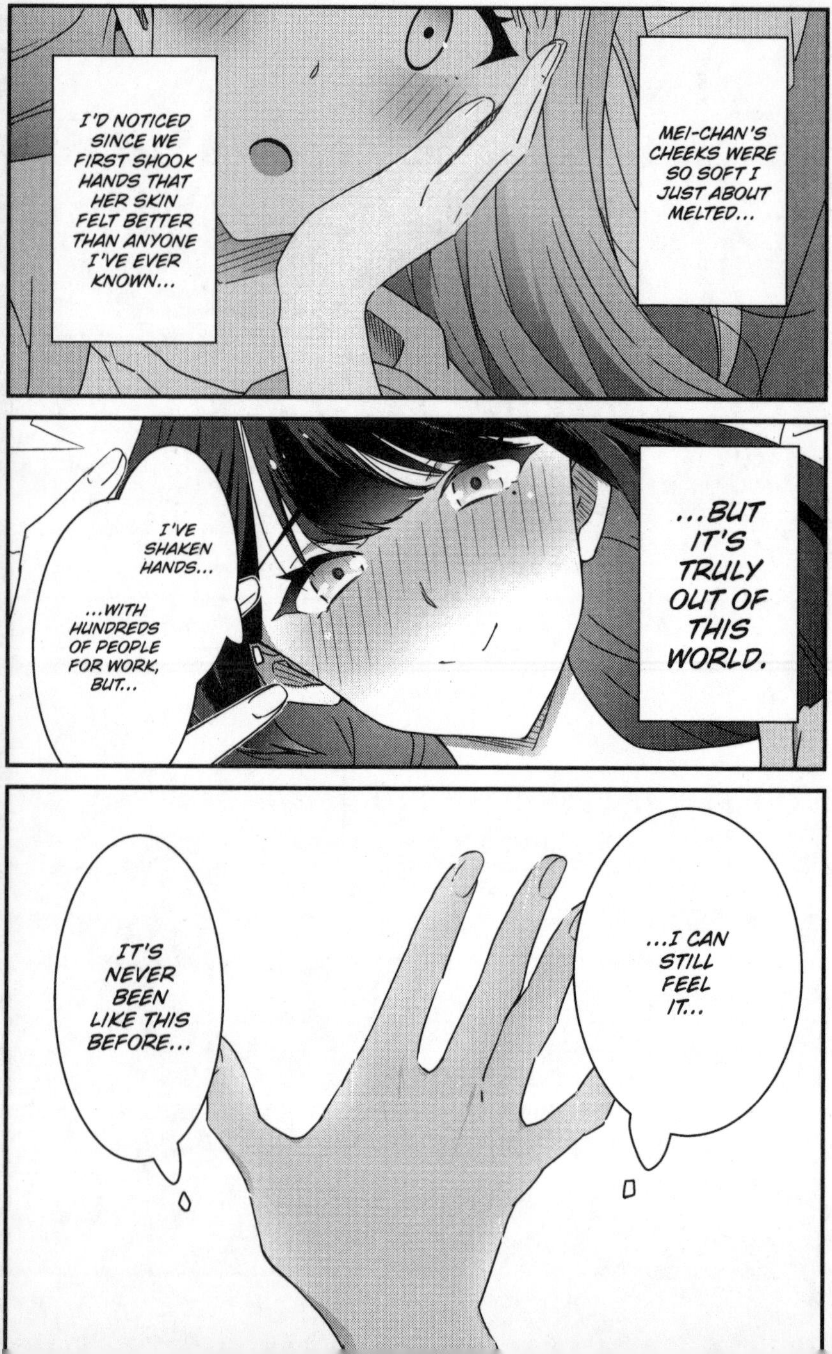
MEI-CHAN'S CHEEKS WERE SO SOFT I JUST ABOUT MELTED...
I'D NOTICED SINCE WE FIRST SHOOK HANDS THAT HER SKIN FELT BETTER THAN ANYONE I'VE EVER KNOWN...
I'VE SHAKEN HANDS... ...WITH HUNDREDS OF PEOPLE FOR WORK, BUT...
...BUT IT'S TRULY OUT OF THIS WORLD.
...I CAN STILL FEEL IT...
IT'S NEVER BEEN LIKE THIS BEFORE...

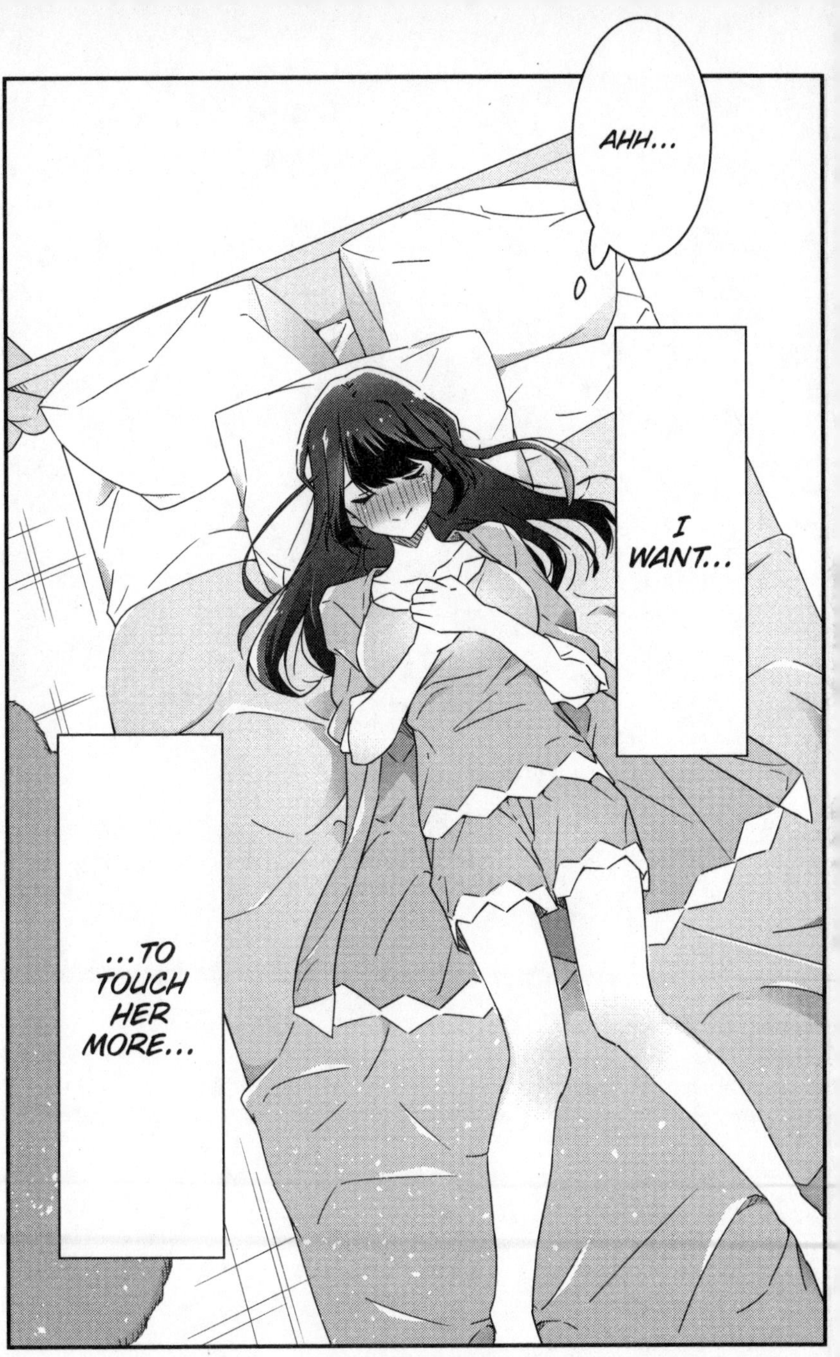
AHH...
I WANT...
...TO TOUCH HER MORE...

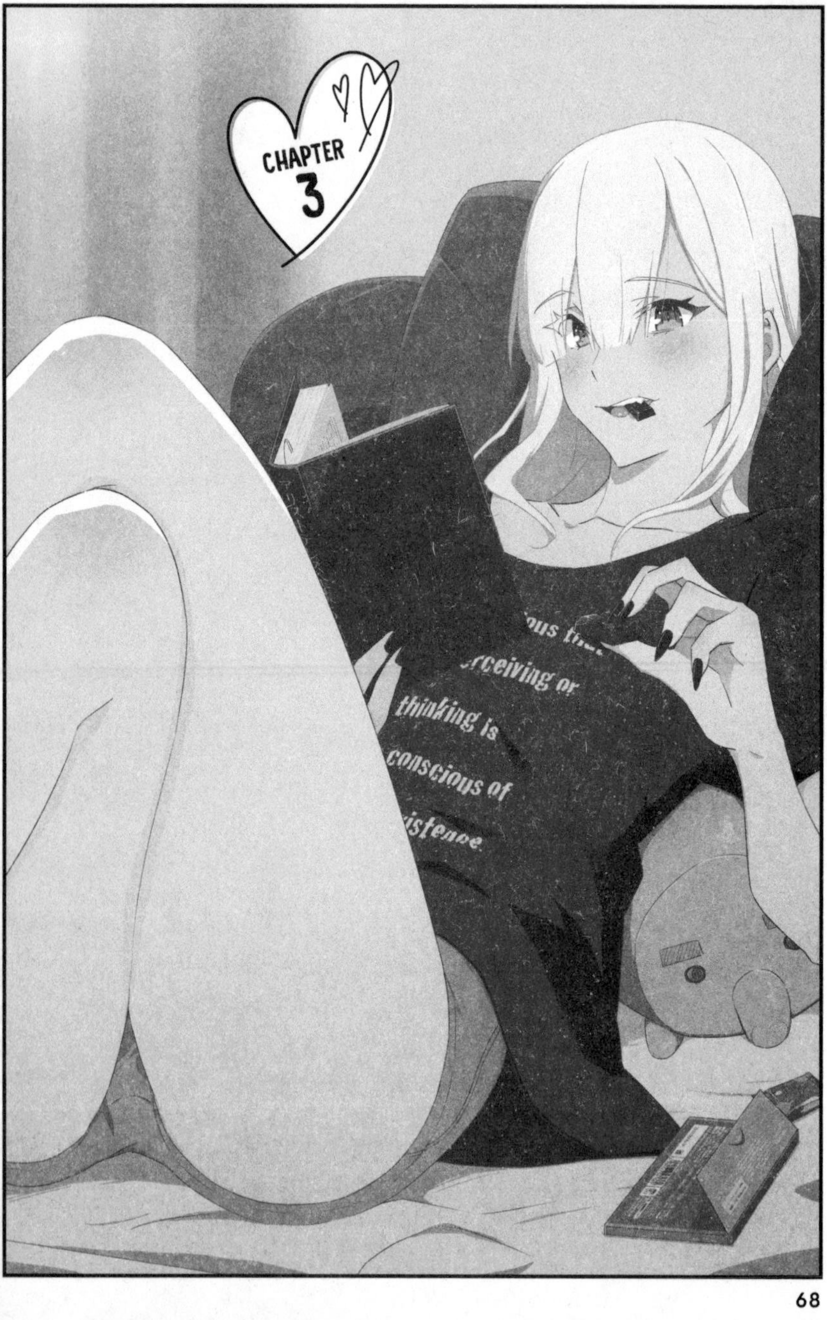
CHAPTER
3
thinking is
conscious of

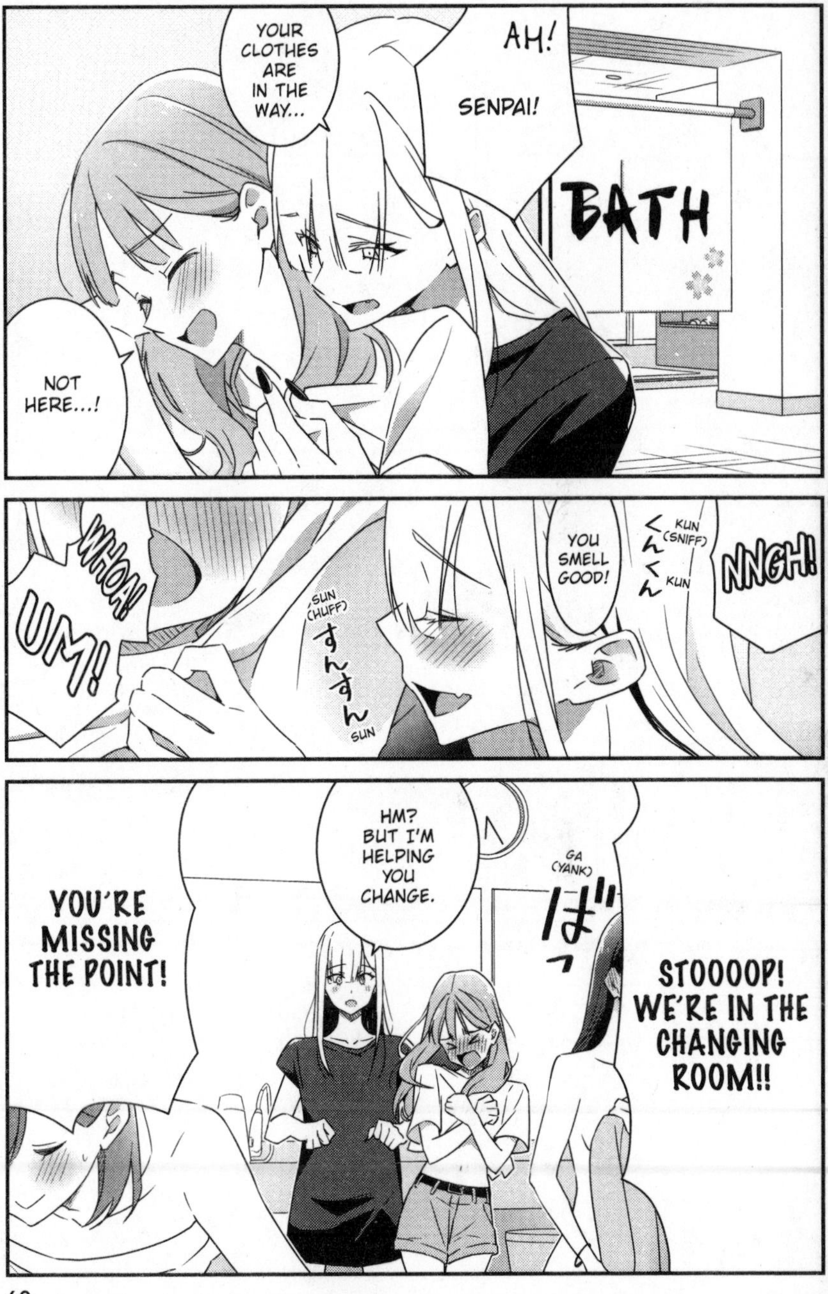

BATH
AH!
SENPAI!
YOUR CLOTHES ARE IN THE WAY...
NOT HERE...!
NNGH!
KUN (SNIFF)
くんくん
KUN
YOU SMELL GOOD!
SUN (HUFF)
すんすん
SUN
WHOA!
UM!
STOOOOP! WE'RE IN THE CHANGING ROOM!!
GA (YANK)
ばっ
HM? BUT I'M HELPING YOU CHANGE.
YOU'RE MISSING THE POINT!

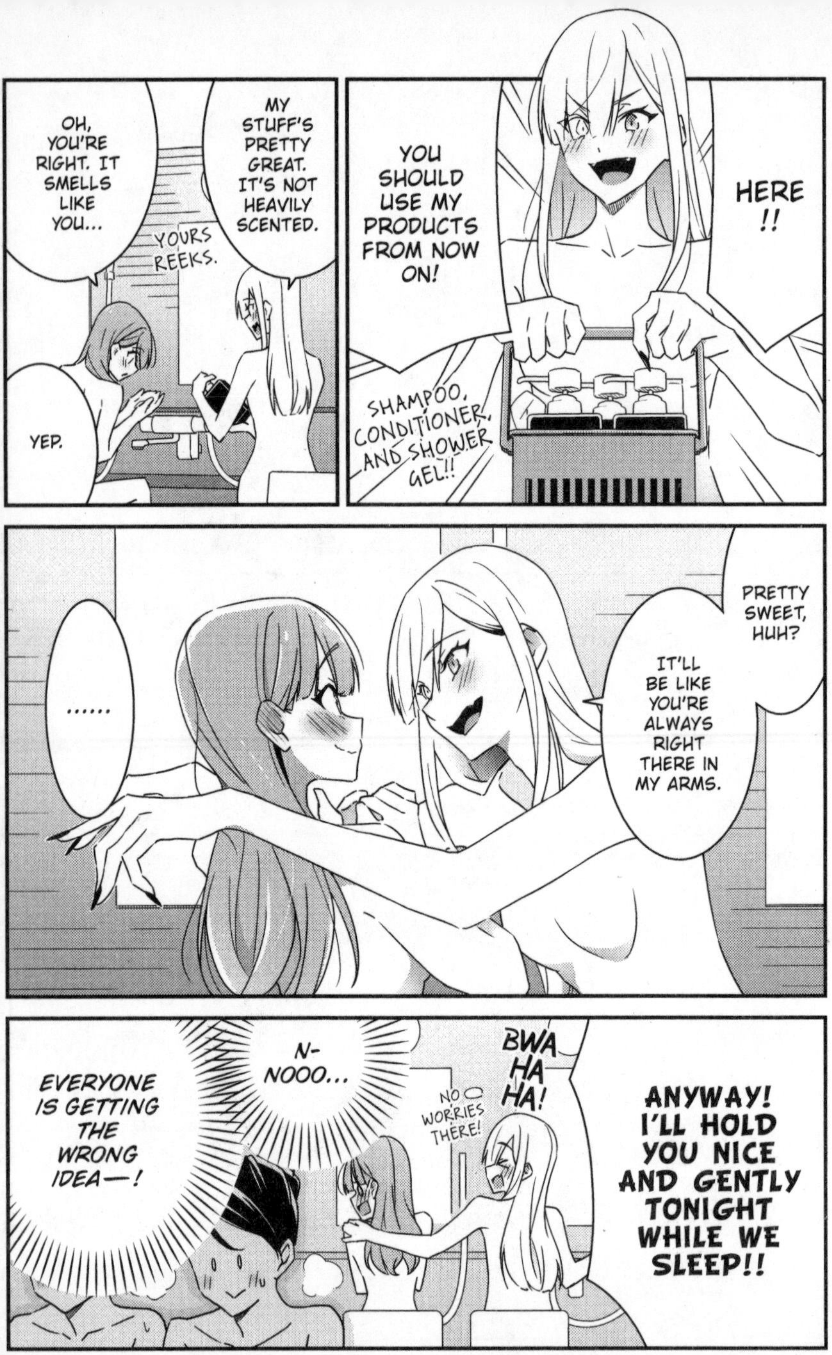
HERE!!
YOU SHOULD USE MY PRODUCTS FROM NOW ON!
SHAMPOO, CONDITIONER, AND SHOWER GEL!!
MY STUFF'S PRETTY GREAT. IT'S NOT HEAVILY SCENTED.
YOURS REEKS.
OH, YOU'RE RIGHT. IT SMELLS LIKE YOU...
YEP.
PRETTY SWEET, HUH?
IT'LL BE LIKE YOU'RE ALWAYS RIGHT THERE IN MY ARMS.
......
ANYWAY! I'LL HOLD YOU NICE AND GENTLY TONIGHT WHILE WE SLEEP!!
BWA HA HA!
NO WORRIES THERE!
N-NOOO...
EVERYONE IS GETTING THE WRONG IDEA—!

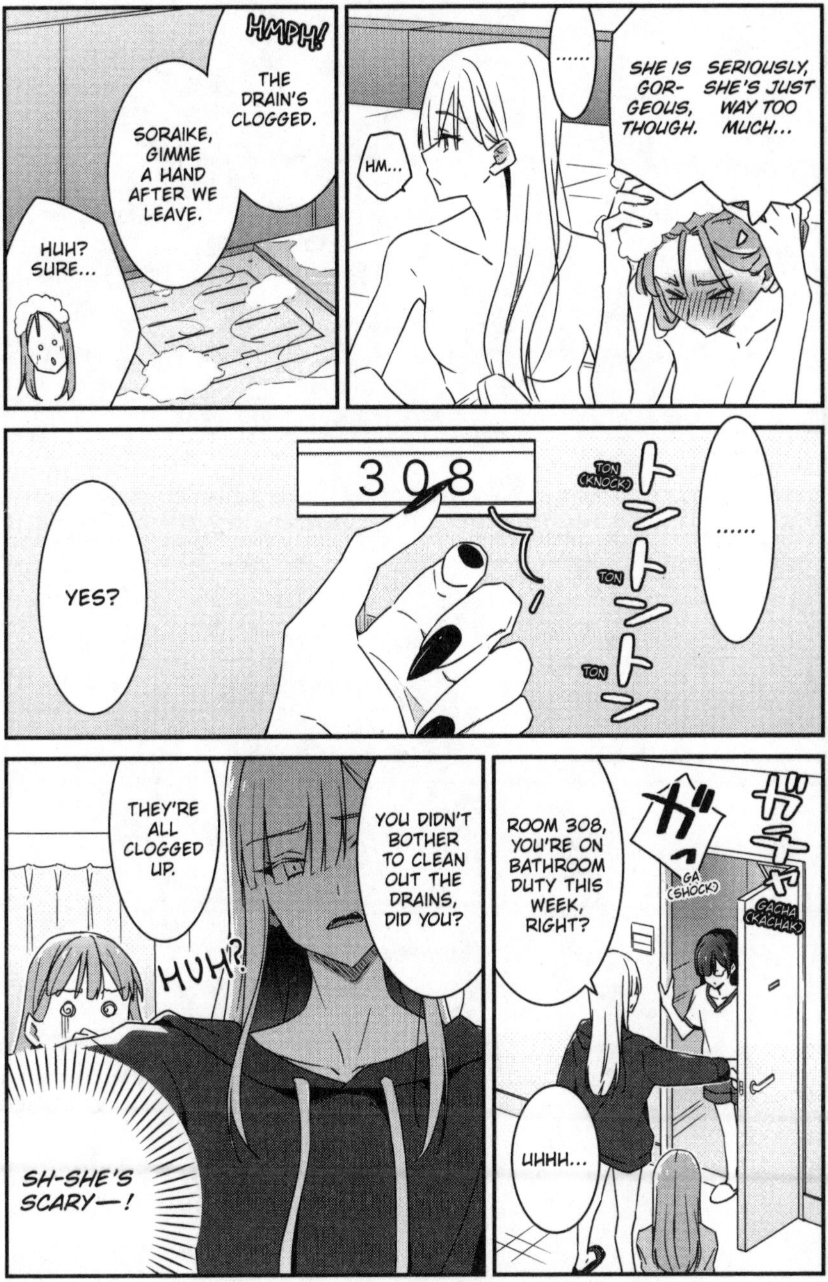
SERIOUSLY, SHE'S JUST WAY TOO MUCH...
SHE IS GORGEOUS, THOUGH.
......
HM...
HMPH!
THE DRAIN'S CLOGGED.
SORAIKE, GIMME A HAND AFTER WE LEAVE.
HUH? SURE...
......
TON (KNOCK)
TON
TON
308
YES?
GACHA (KACHAK)
GA (SHOCK)
ROOM 308, YOU'RE ON BATHROOM DUTY THIS WEEK, RIGHT?
UHHH...
YOU DIDN'T BOTHER TO CLEAN OUT THE DRAINS, DID YOU?
THEY'RE ALL CLOGGED UP.
HUH?
SH-SHE'S SCARY—!

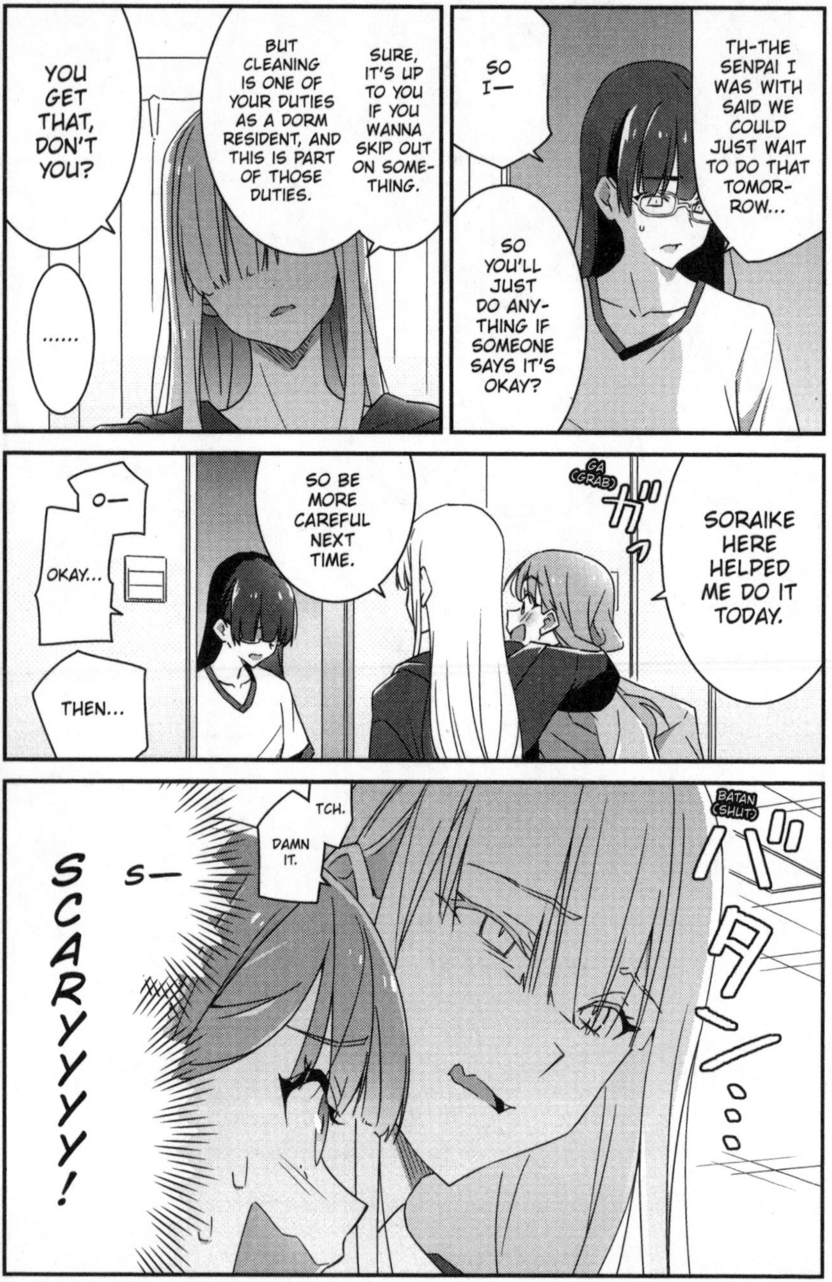
TH-THE SENPAI I WAS WITH SAID WE COULD JUST WAIT TO DO THAT TOMORROW...
SO I—
SO YOU'LL JUST DO ANYTHING IF SOMEONE SAYS IT'S OKAY?
SURE, IT'S UP TO YOU IF YOU WANNA SKIP OUT ON SOMETHING.
BUT CLEANING IS ONE OF YOUR DUTIES AS A DORM RESIDENT, AND THIS IS PART OF THOSE DUTIES.
YOU GET THAT, DON'T YOU?
......
GA (GRAB)
SORAIKE HERE HELPED ME DO IT TODAY.
SO BE MORE CAREFUL NEXT TIME.
O— OKAY...
THEN...
BATAN (SHUT)
TCH.
DAMN IT.
S—
SCARYYYY!

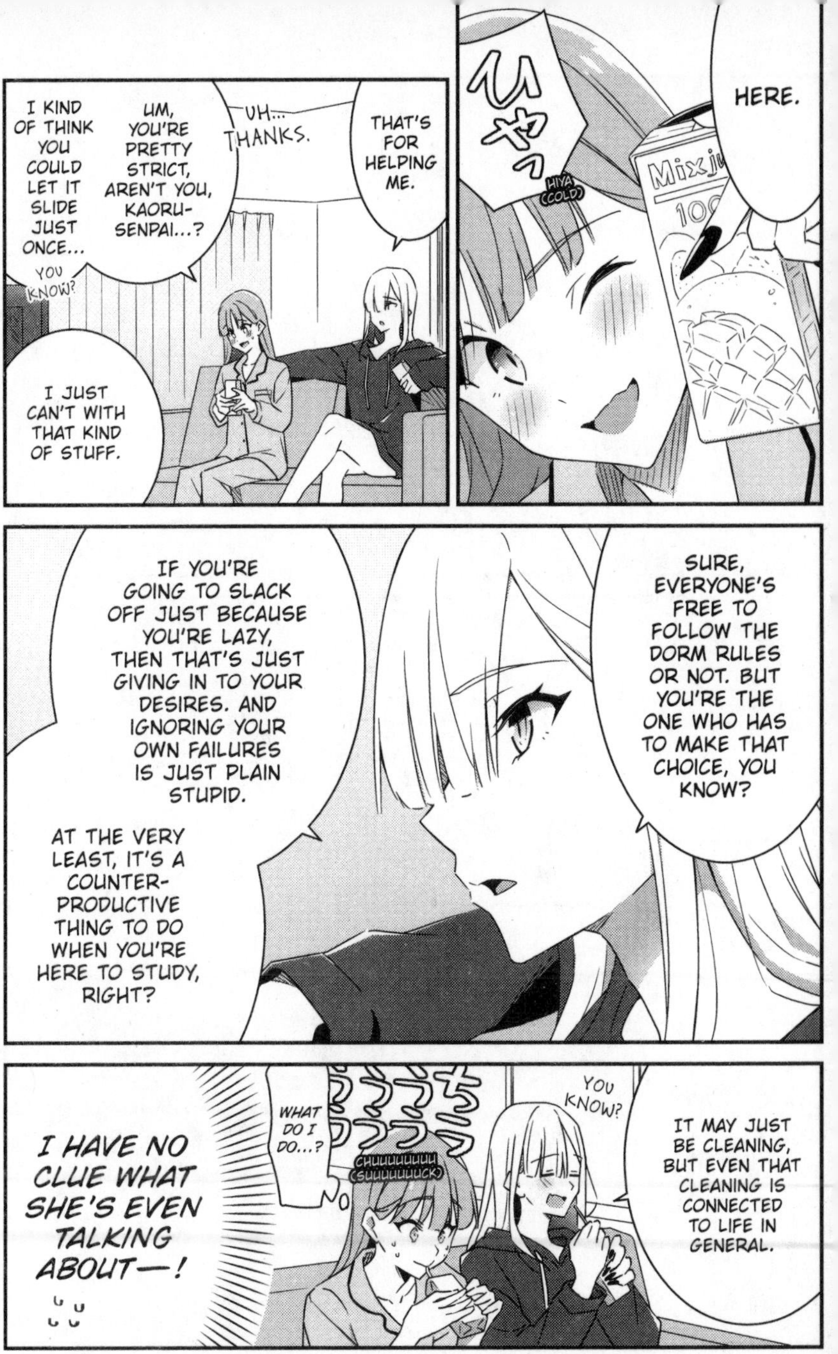

HERE.
ひやっ
HIYA (COLD)
THAT'S FOR HELPING ME.
UH... THANKS.
UM, YOU'RE PRETTY STRICT, AREN'T YOU, KAORU-SENPAI...?
I KIND OF THINK YOU COULD LET IT SLIDE JUST ONCE...
YOU KNOW?
I JUST CAN'T WITH THAT KIND OF STUFF.
SURE, EVERYONE'S FREE TO FOLLOW THE DORM RULES OR NOT. BUT YOU'RE THE ONE WHO HAS TO MAKE THAT CHOICE, YOU KNOW?
IF YOU'RE GOING TO SLACK OFF JUST BECAUSE YOU'RE LAZY, THEN THAT'S JUST GIVING IN TO YOUR DESIRES. AND IGNORING YOUR OWN FAILURES IS JUST PLAIN STUPID.
AT THE VERY LEAST, IT'S A COUNTER-PRODUCTIVE THING TO DO WHEN YOU'RE HERE TO STUDY, RIGHT?
IT MAY JUST BE CLEANING, BUT EVEN THAT CLEANING IS CONNECTED TO LIFE IN GENERAL.
YOU KNOW?
CHUUUUUUUU (SUUUUUUUCK)
WHAT DO I DO...?
I HAVE NO CLUE WHAT SHE'S EVEN TALKING ABOUT—!

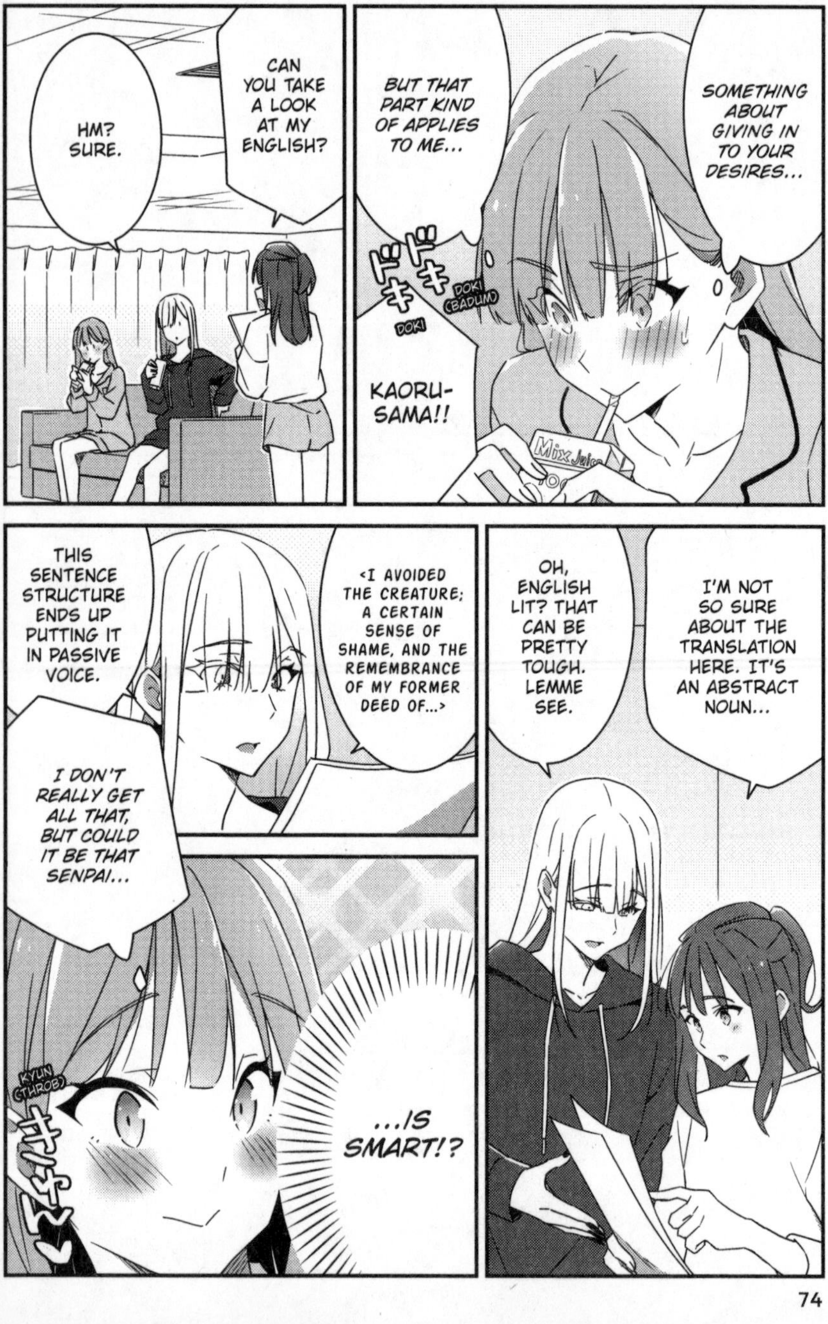
SOMETHING ABOUT GIVING IN TO YOUR DESIRES...
BUT THAT PART KIND OF APPLIES TO ME...
ドキドキ
DOKI (BADUM) DOKI
KAORU-SAMA!!
Mix Juice
CAN YOU TAKE A LOOK AT MY ENGLISH?
HM? SURE.
I'M NOT SO SURE ABOUT THE TRANSLATION HERE. IT'S AN ABSTRACT NOUN...
OH, ENGLISH LIT? THAT CAN BE PRETTY TOUGH. LEMME SEE.
<I AVOIDED THE CREATURE; A CERTAIN SENSE OF SHAME, AND THE REMEMBRANCE OF MY FORMER DEED OF...>
THIS SENTENCE STRUCTURE ENDS UP PUTTING IT IN PASSIVE VOICE.
I DON'T REALLY GET ALL THAT, BUT COULD IT BE THAT SENPAI...
...IS SMART!?
KYUN (THROB)
キュン

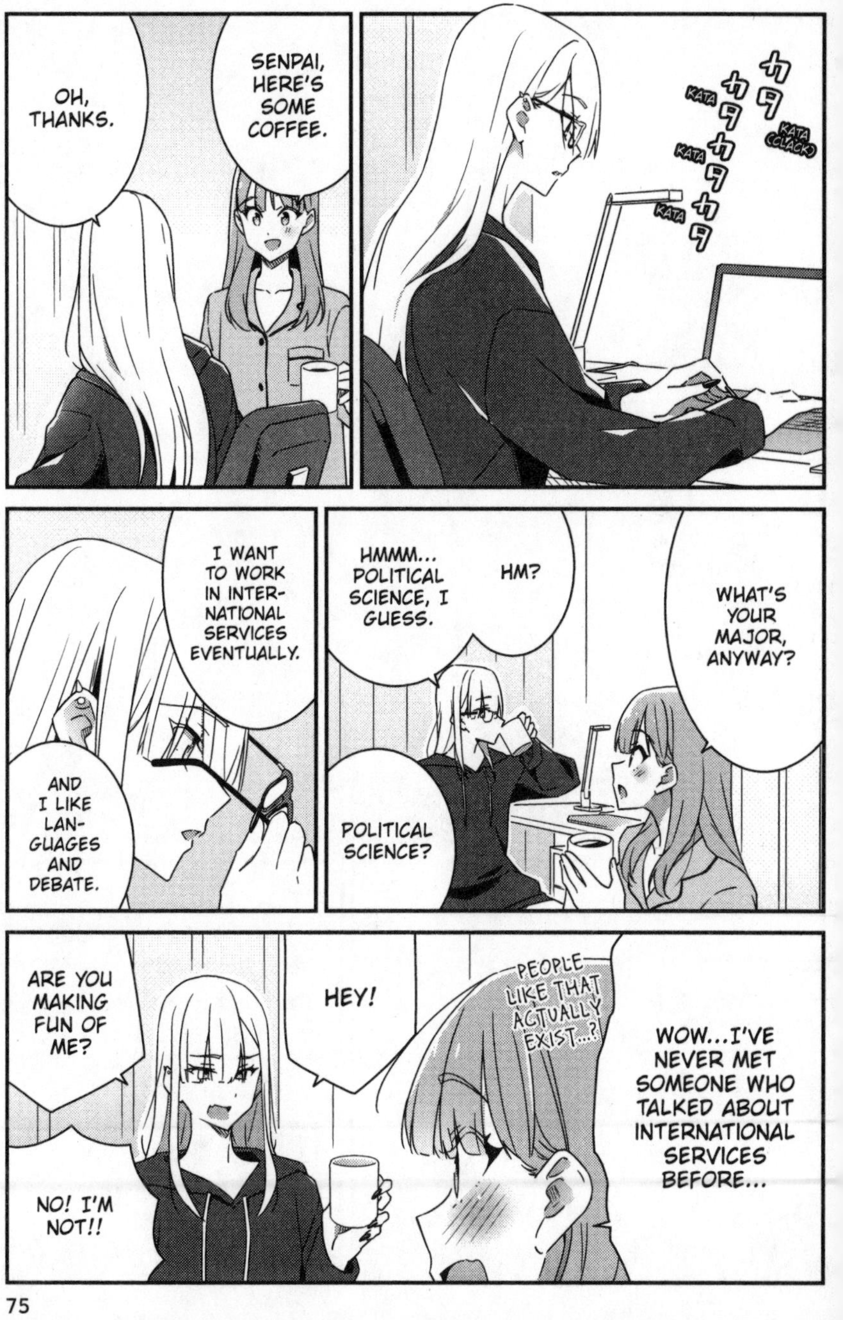
カタ
KATA (CLACK)
カタ
KATA
カタ
KATA
カタ
KATA
SENPAI, HERE'S SOME COFFEE.
OH, THANKS.
WHAT'S YOUR MAJOR, ANYWAY?
HM?
HMMM... POLITICAL SCIENCE, I GUESS.
POLITICAL SCIENCE?
I WANT TO WORK IN INTER-NATIONAL SERVICES EVENTUALLY.
AND I LIKE LAN-GUAGES AND DEBATE.
WOW...I'VE NEVER MET SOMEONE WHO TALKED ABOUT INTERNATIONAL SERVICES BEFORE...
PEOPLE LIKE THAT ACTUALLY EXIST...?
HEY!
ARE YOU MAKING FUN OF ME?
NO! I'M NOT!!

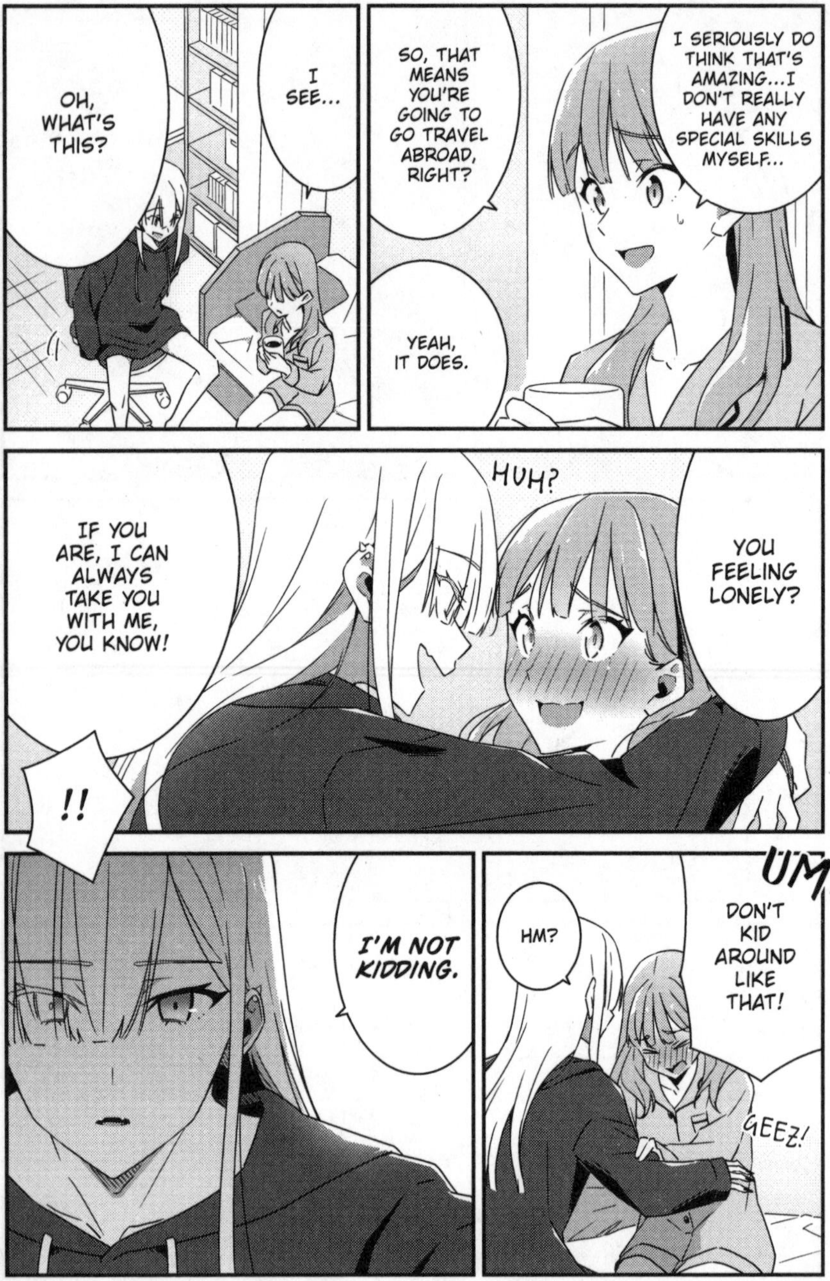
I SERIOUSLY DO THINK THAT'S AMAZING...I DON'T REALLY HAVE ANY SPECIAL SKILLS MYSELF...
SO, THAT MEANS YOU'RE GOING TO GO TRAVEL ABROAD, RIGHT?
YEAH, IT DOES.
I SEE...
OH, WHAT'S THIS?
YOU FEELING LONELY?
HUH?
IF YOU ARE, I CAN ALWAYS TAKE YOU WITH ME, YOU KNOW!
!!
UM!
DON'T KID AROUND LIKE THAT!
HM?
GEEZ!
I'M NOT KIDDING.

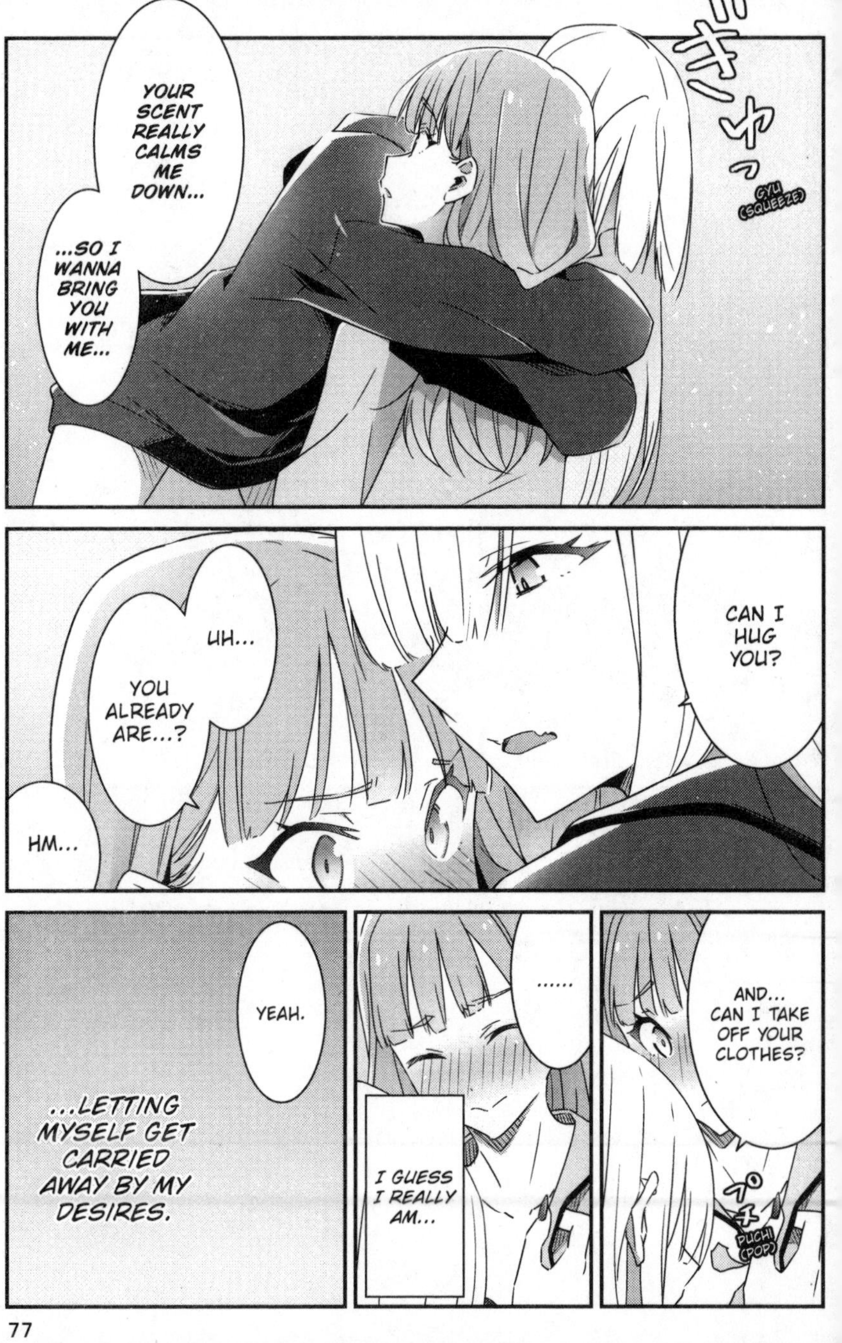

ギュッ
GYU (SQUEEZE)
YOUR SCENT REALLY CALMS ME DOWN...
...SO I WANNA BRING YOU WITH ME...
CAN I HUG YOU?
UH...
YOU ALREADY ARE...?
HM...
AND... CAN I TAKE OFF YOUR CLOTHES?
プチ
PUCHI (POP)
......
I GUESS I REALLY AM...
YEAH.
...LETTING MYSELF GET CARRIED AWAY BY MY DESIRES.

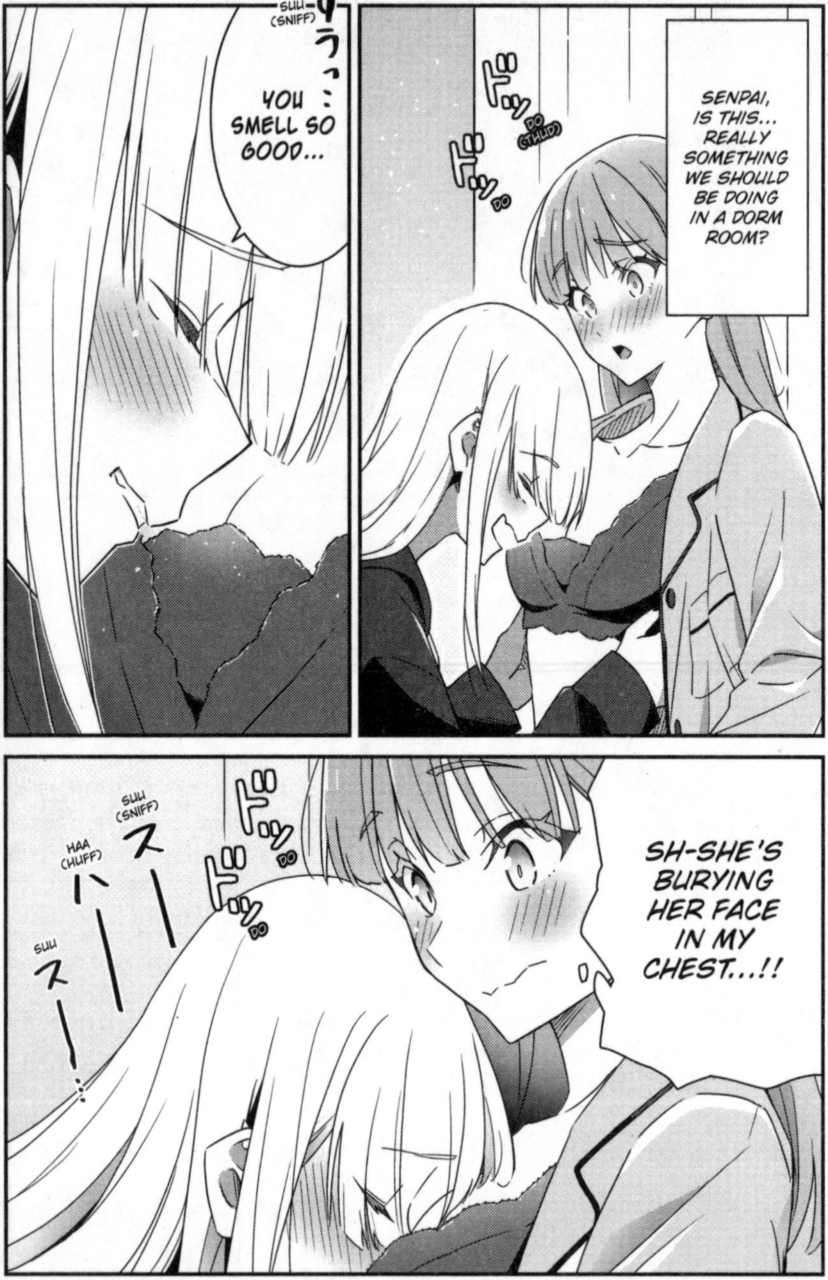
SENPAI, IS THIS... REALLY SOMETHING WE SHOULD BE DOING IN A DORM ROOM?
ドッ DO (THUD)
ドッ DO
すぅっ SUU (SNIFF)
YOU SMELL SO GOOD...
SH-SHE'S BURYING HER FACE IN MY CHEST...!!
ドッ DO
ドッ DO
スー SUU (SNIFF)
ハー HAA (HUFF)
スー... SUU

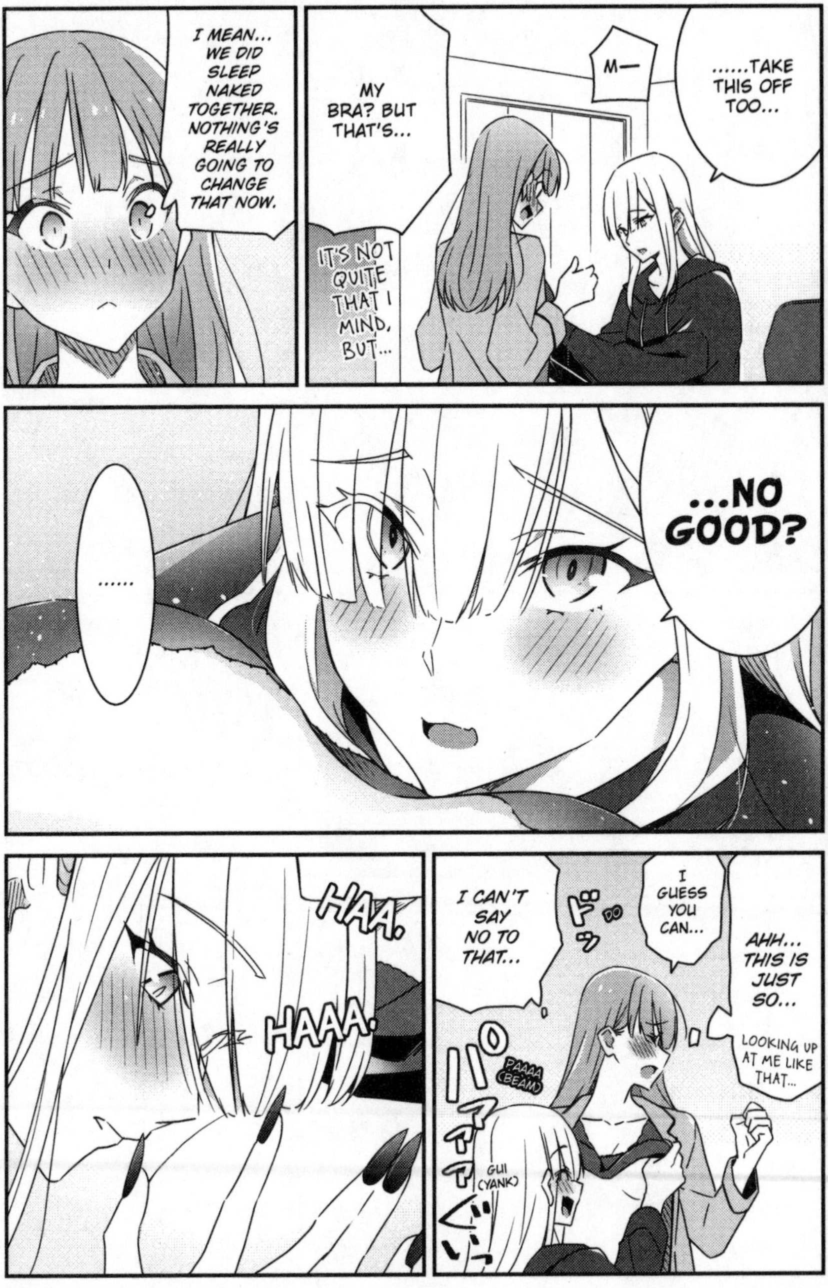

......TAKE THIS OFF TOO...
M—
MY BRA? BUT THAT'S...
IT'S NOT QUITE THAT I MIND, BUT...
I MEAN... WE DID SLEEP NAKED TOGETHER. NOTHING'S REALLY GOING TO CHANGE THAT NOW.
...NO GOOD?
......
I GUESS YOU CAN...
I CAN'T SAY NO TO THAT...
DO
AHH... THIS IS JUST SO...
LOOKING UP AT ME LIKE THAT...
PAAAA (BEAM)
GUI (YANK)
HAA.
HAAA.

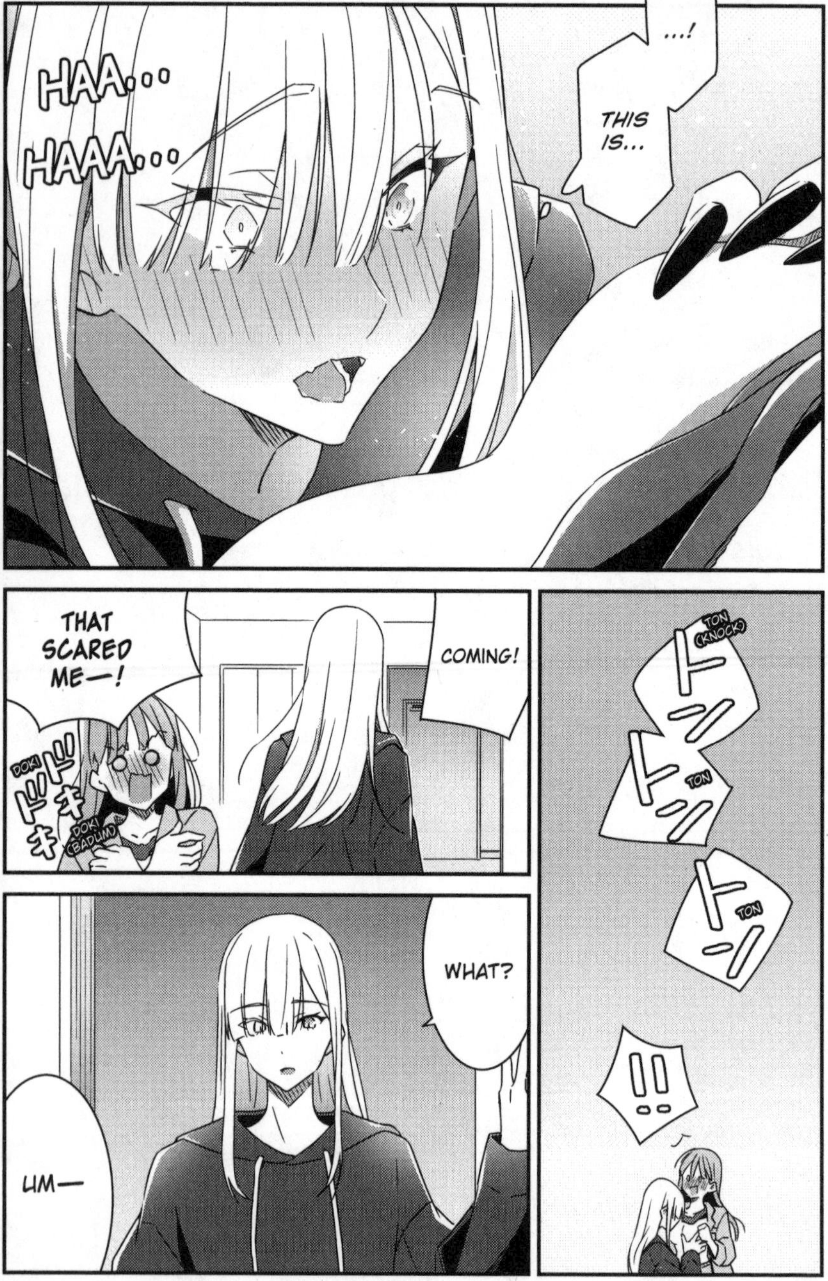

...!
THIS IS...
HAA...
HAAA...
トン
TON (KNOCK)
トン
TON
トン
TON
!!
COMING!
THAT SCARED ME—!
ドキドキ
DOKI DOKI (BADUM)
WHAT?
UM—

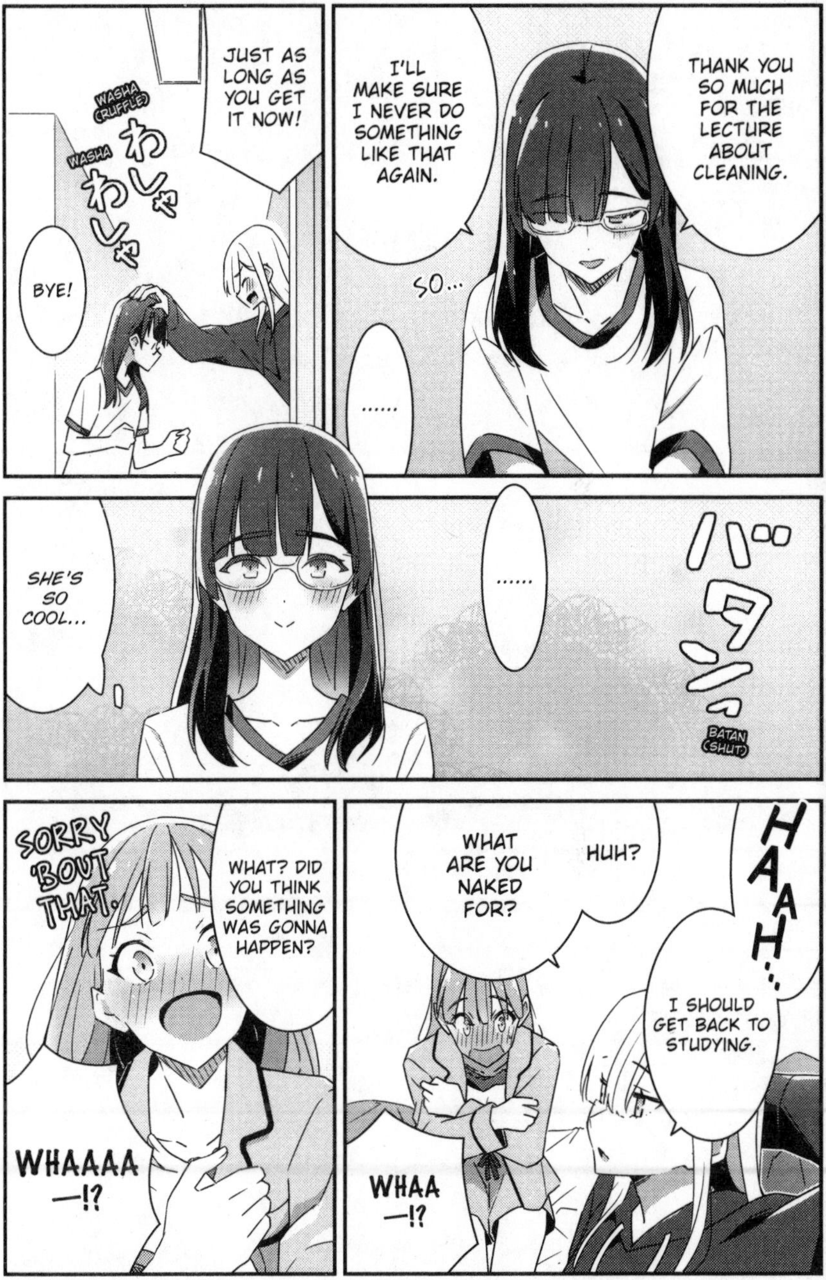
THANK YOU SO MUCH FOR THE LECTURE ABOUT CLEANING.
I'LL MAKE SURE I NEVER DO SOMETHING LIKE THAT AGAIN.
SO...
......
JUST AS LONG AS YOU GET IT NOW!
わしゃ
WASHA (RUFFLE)
わしゃ
WASHA
BYE!
バタン
BATAN (SHUT)
......
SHE'S SO COOL...
HAAH...
I SHOULD GET BACK TO STUDYING.
HUH?
WHAT ARE YOU NAKED FOR?
WHAA—!?
WHAT? DID YOU THINK SOMETHING WAS GONNA HAPPEN?
SORRY 'BOUT THAT.
WHAAAA—!?

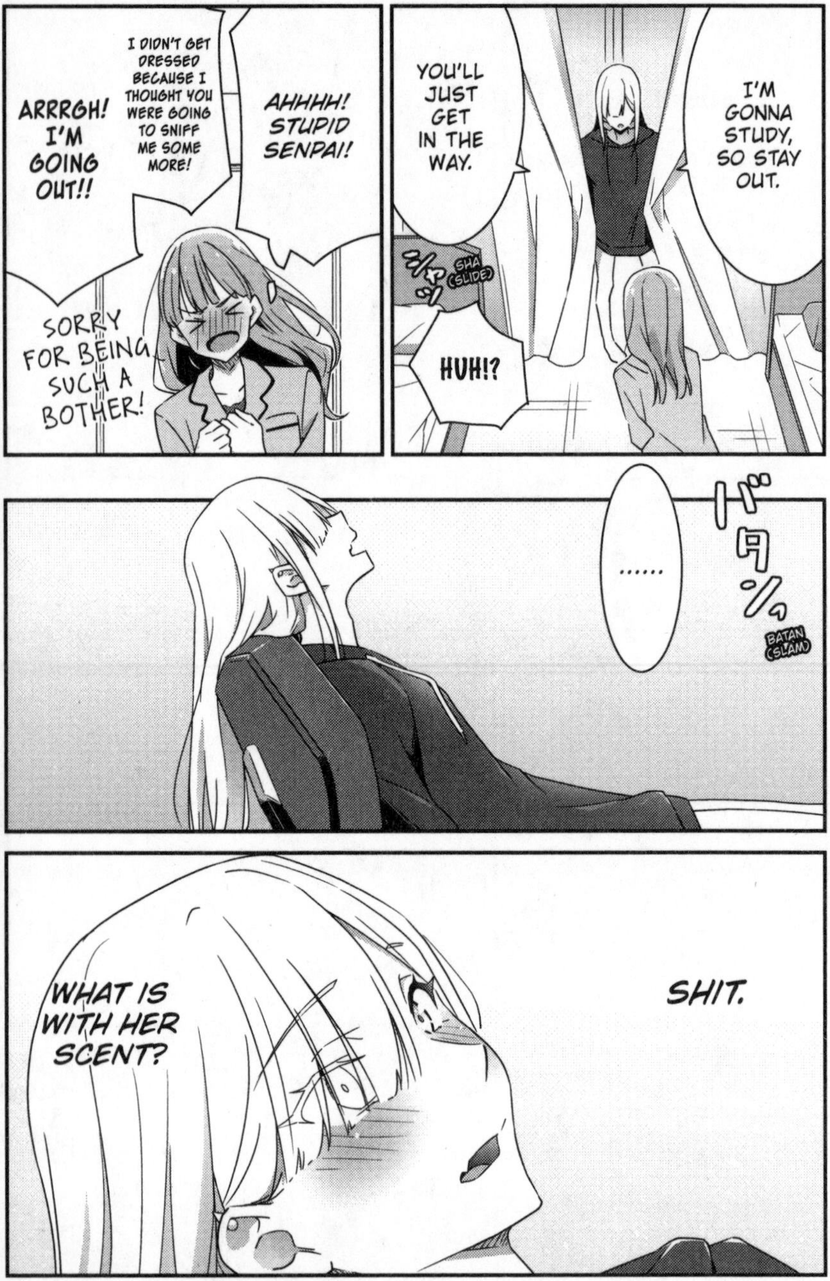
I'M GONNA STUDY, SO STAY OUT.
YOU'LL JUST GET IN THE WAY.
シャッ
SHA (SLIDE)
HUH!?
AHHHH! STUPID SENPAI!
I DIDN'T GET DRESSED BECAUSE I THOUGHT YOU WERE GOING TO SNIFF ME SOME MORE!
ARRRGH! I'M GOING OUT!!
SORRY FOR BEING SUCH A BOTHER!
バタン
BATAN (SLAM)
......
SHIT.
WHAT IS WITH HER SCENT?

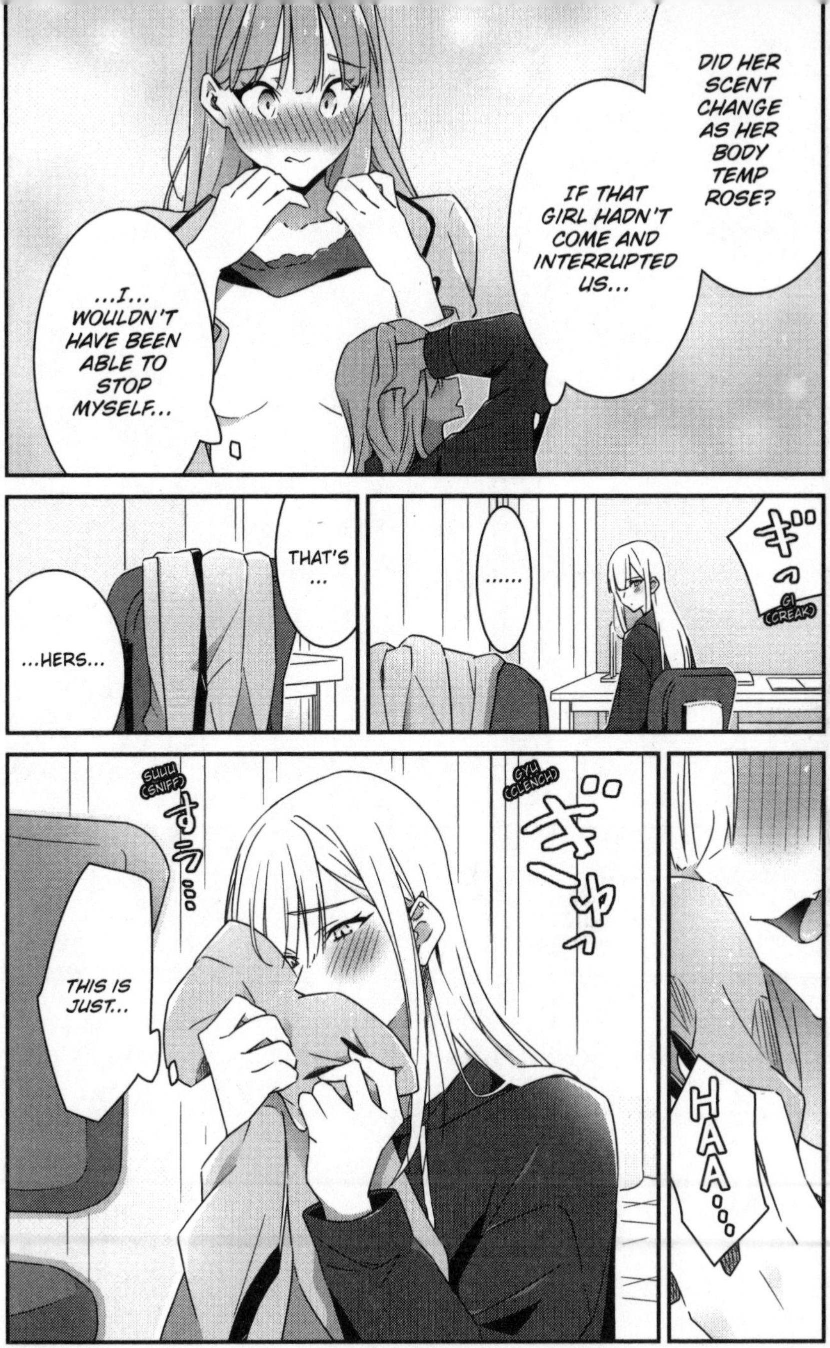
DID HER SCENT CHANGE AS HER BODY TEMP ROSE?
IF THAT GIRL HADN'T COME AND INTERRUPTED US...
...I... WOULDN'T HAVE BEEN ABLE TO STOP MYSELF...
ギッ
GI (CREAK)
......
THAT'S ...
...HERS...
HAA...
ぎゅっ
GYU (CLENCH)
すぅ...
SUUU (SNIFF)
THIS IS JUST...

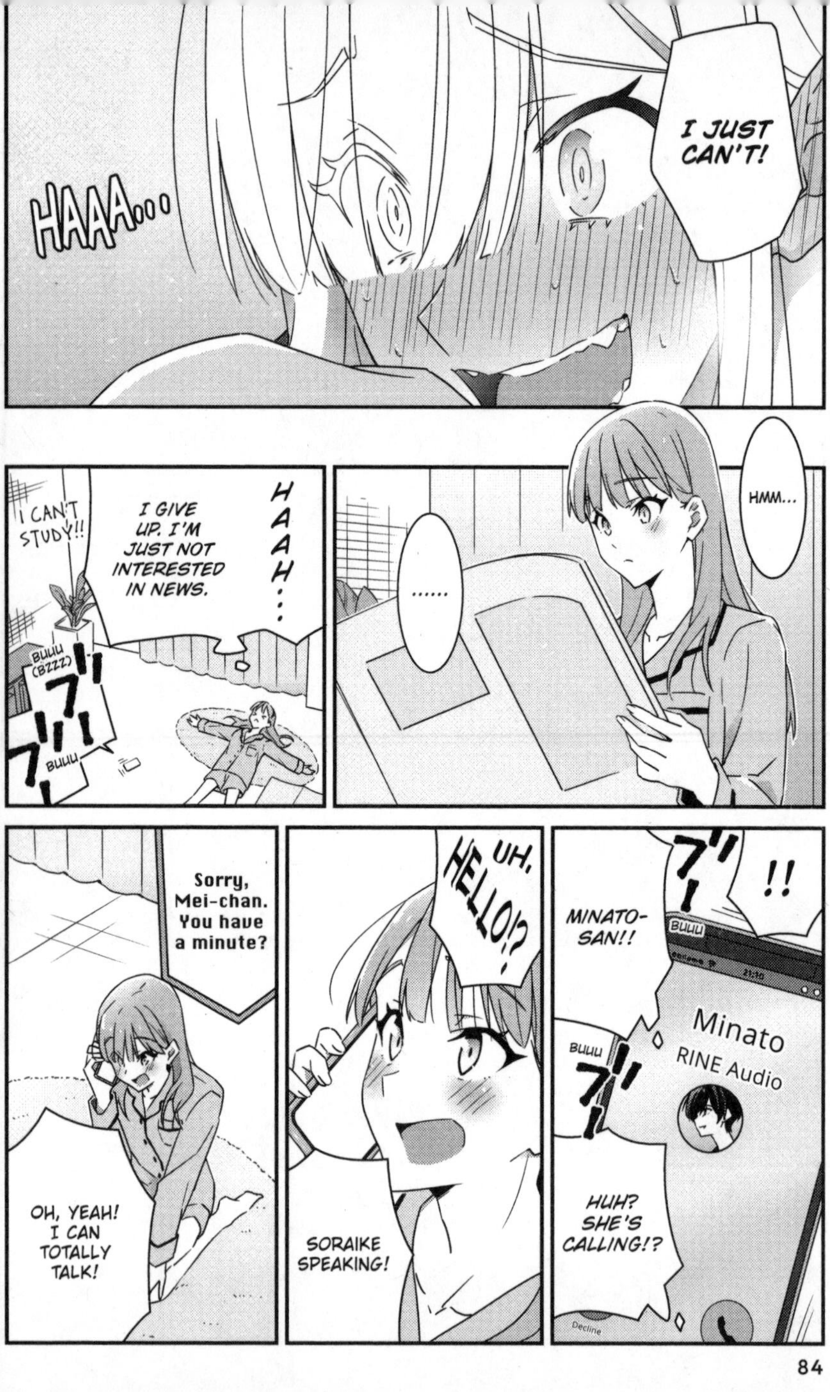
I JUST CAN'T!
HAAA...
HMM...
......
HAAAH...
I GIVE UP. I'M JUST NOT INTERESTED IN NEWS.
I CAN'T STUDY!!
BUUU (BZZZ)
BUUU
!!
BUUU
MINATO-SAN!!
Minato
RINE Audio
BUUU
HUH? SHE'S CALLING!?
Decline
UH, HELLO!?
SORAIKE SPEAKING!
Sorry, Mei-chan. You have a minute?
OH, YEAH! I CAN TOTALLY TALK!

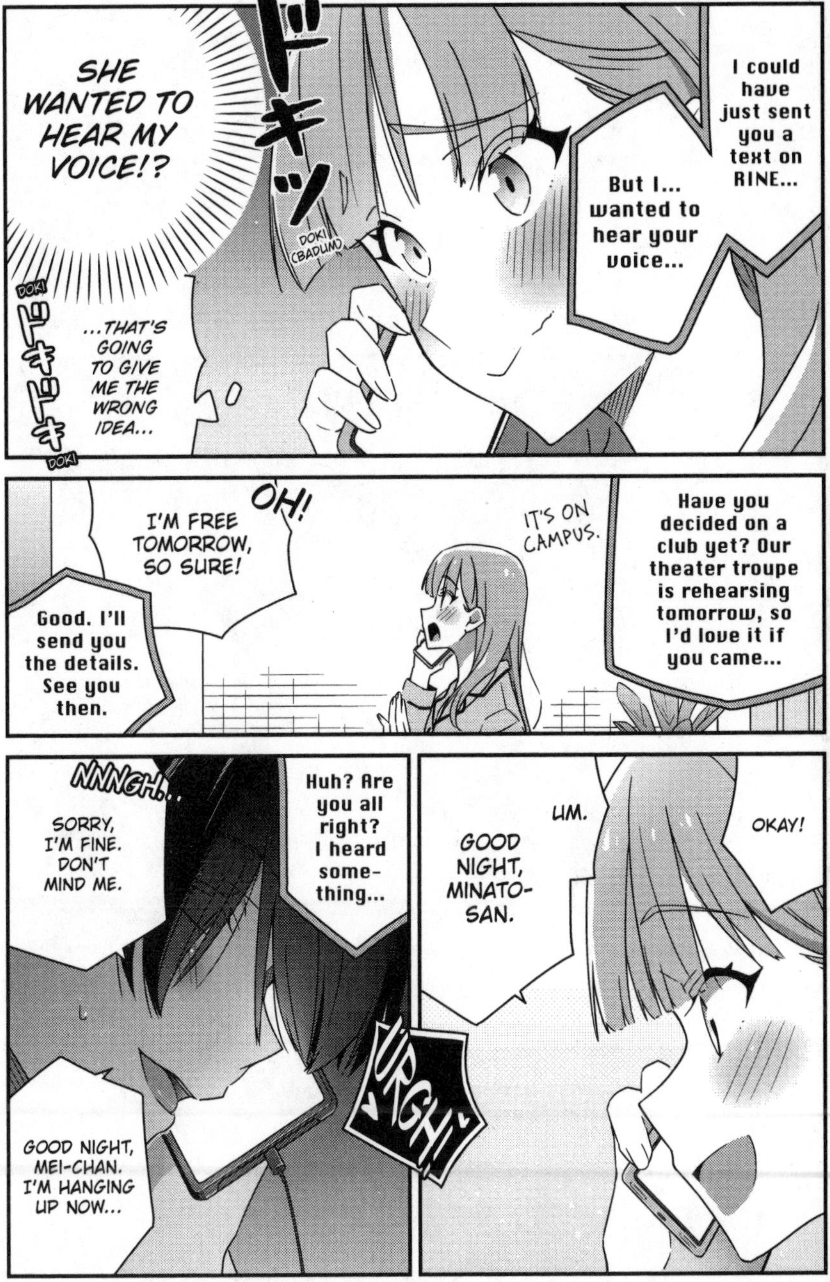
I could have just sent you a text on RINE...
But I... wanted to hear your voice...
ドキッ
DOKI (BADUM)
SHE WANTED TO HEAR MY VOICE!?
...THAT'S GOING TO GIVE ME THE WRONG IDEA...
ドキドキ
DOKI DOKI
Have you decided on a club yet? Our theater troupe is rehearsing tomorrow, so I'd love it if you came...
IT'S ON CAMPUS.
OH!
I'M FREE TOMORROW, SO SURE!
Good. I'll send you the details. See you then.
OKAY!
UM.
GOOD NIGHT, MINATO-SAN.
Huh? Are you all right? I heard something...
NNNGH...
SORRY, I'M FINE. DON'T MIND ME.
URGH!
GOOD NIGHT, MEI-CHAN. I'M HANGING UP NOW...

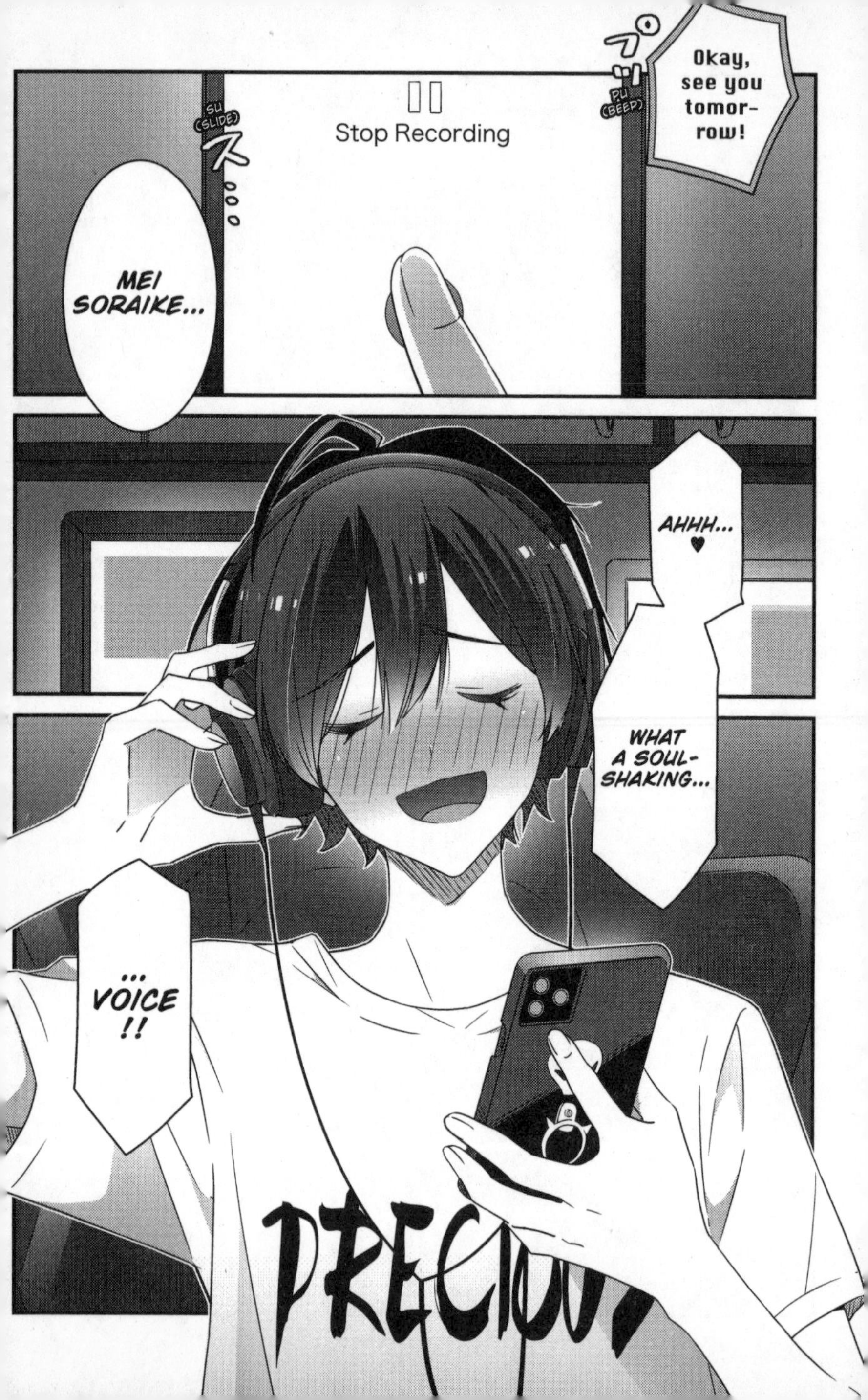
Okay, see you tomorrow!
PU (BEEP)
Stop Recording
SU (SLIDE)
MEI SORAIKE...
AHHH... ♥
WHAT A SOUL-SHAKING...
... VOICE !!
PRECIOU

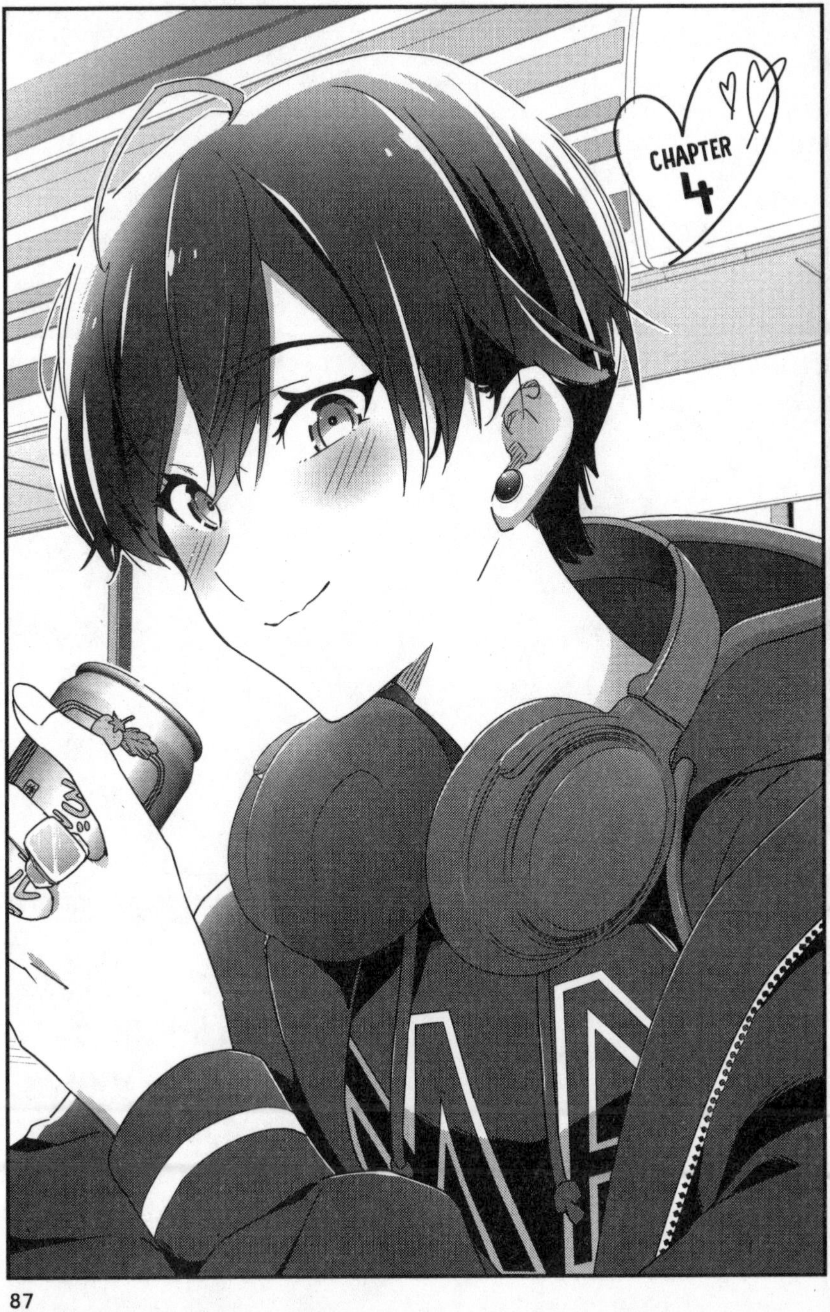
CHAPTER 4

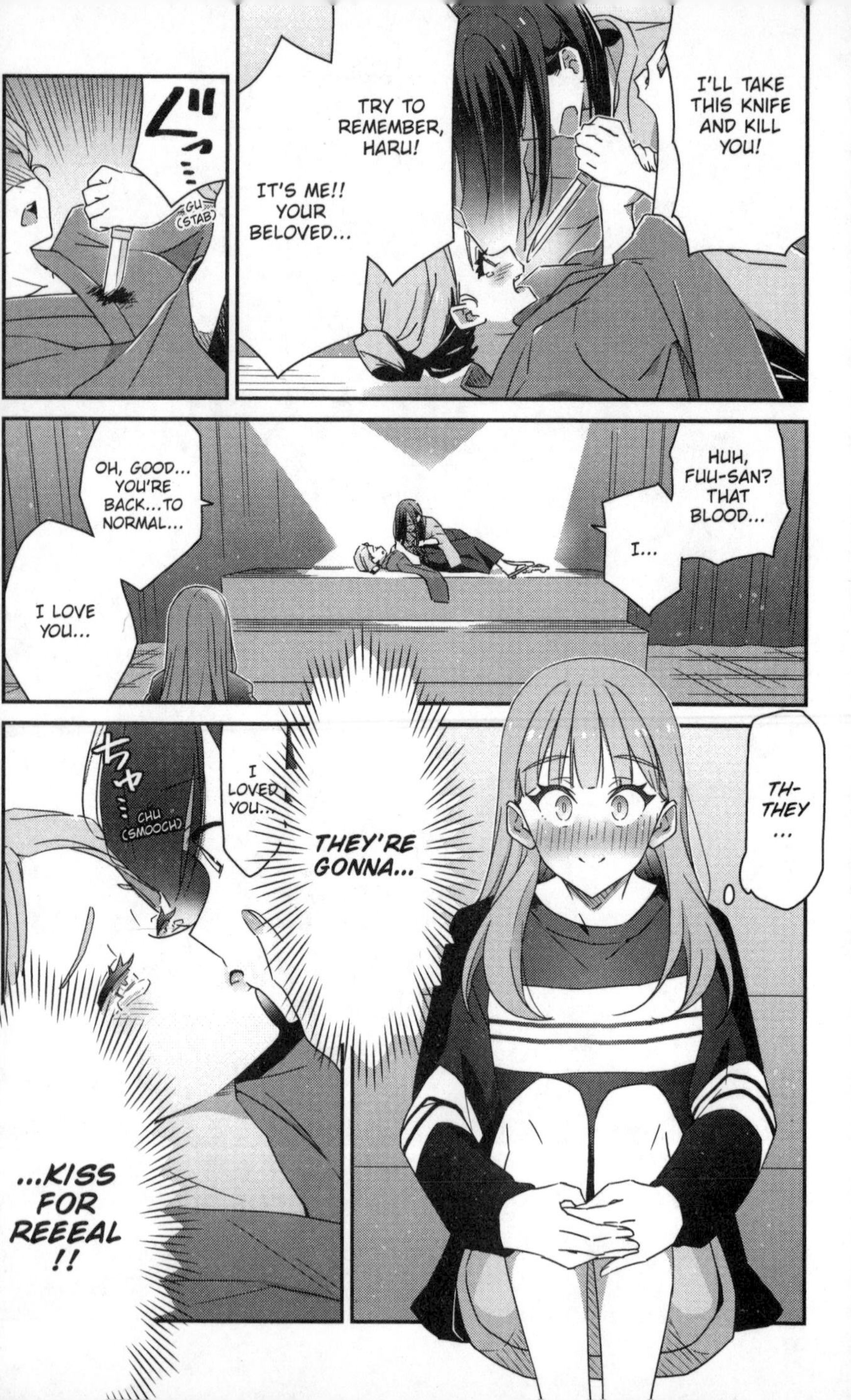
I'LL TAKE THIS KNIFE AND KILL YOU!
TRY TO REMEMBER, HARU!
IT'S ME!! YOUR BELOVED...
GU (STAB)
HUH, FUU-SAN? THAT BLOOD...
I...
OH, GOOD... YOU'RE BACK...TO NORMAL...
I LOVE YOU...
TH-THEY ...
I LOVED YOU...
THEY'RE GONNA...
CHU (SMOOCH)
...KISS FOR REEEAL!!

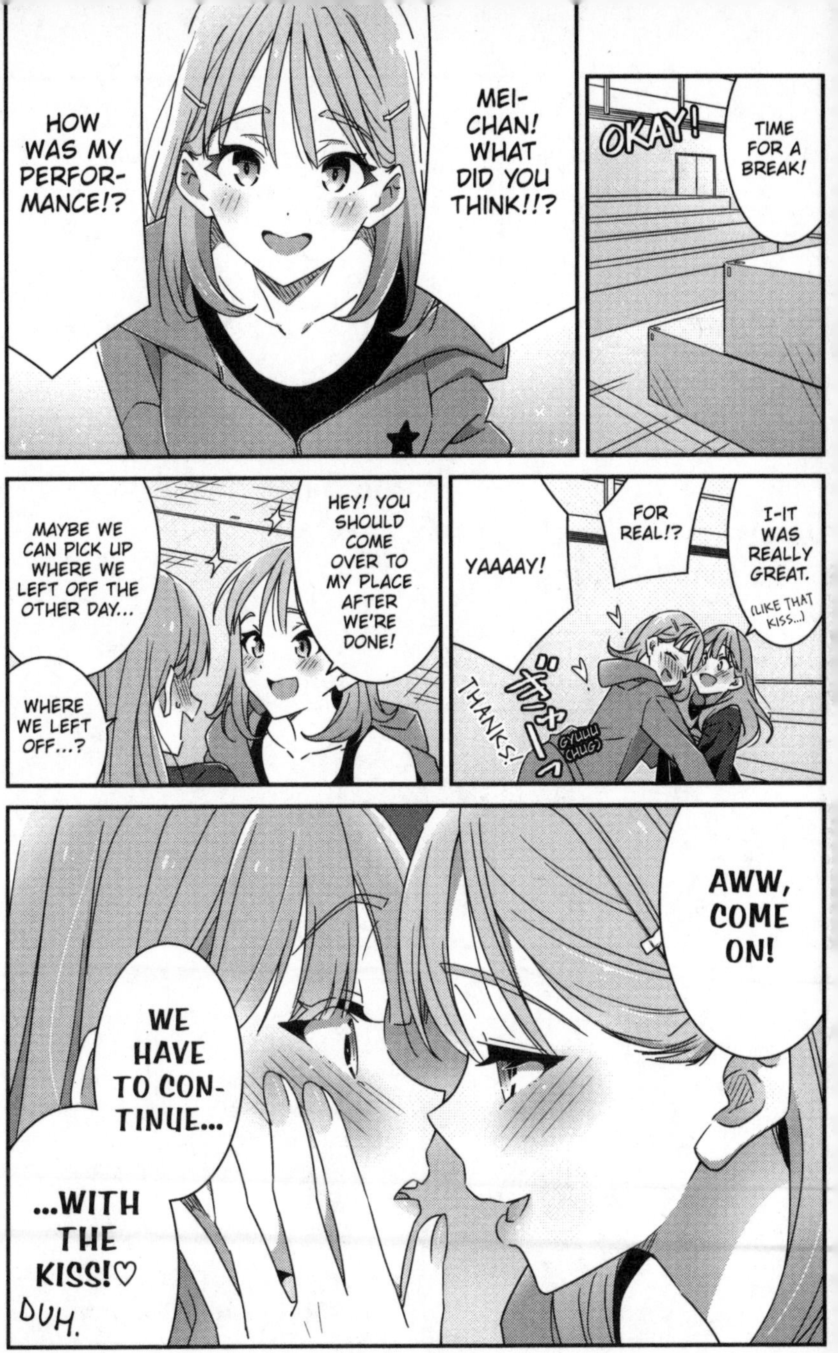
OKAY!
TIME FOR A BREAK!
MEI-CHAN! WHAT DID YOU THINK!!?
HOW WAS MY PERFORMANCE!?
I-IT WAS REALLY GREAT.
(LIKE THAT KISS...)
FOR REAL!?
YAAAAY!
THANKS!
GYUUU (HUG)
HEY! YOU SHOULD COME OVER TO MY PLACE AFTER WE'RE DONE!
MAYBE WE CAN PICK UP WHERE WE LEFT OFF THE OTHER DAY...
WHERE WE LEFT OFF...?
AWW, COME ON!
WE HAVE TO CONTINUE...
...WITH THE KISS!♡
DUH.

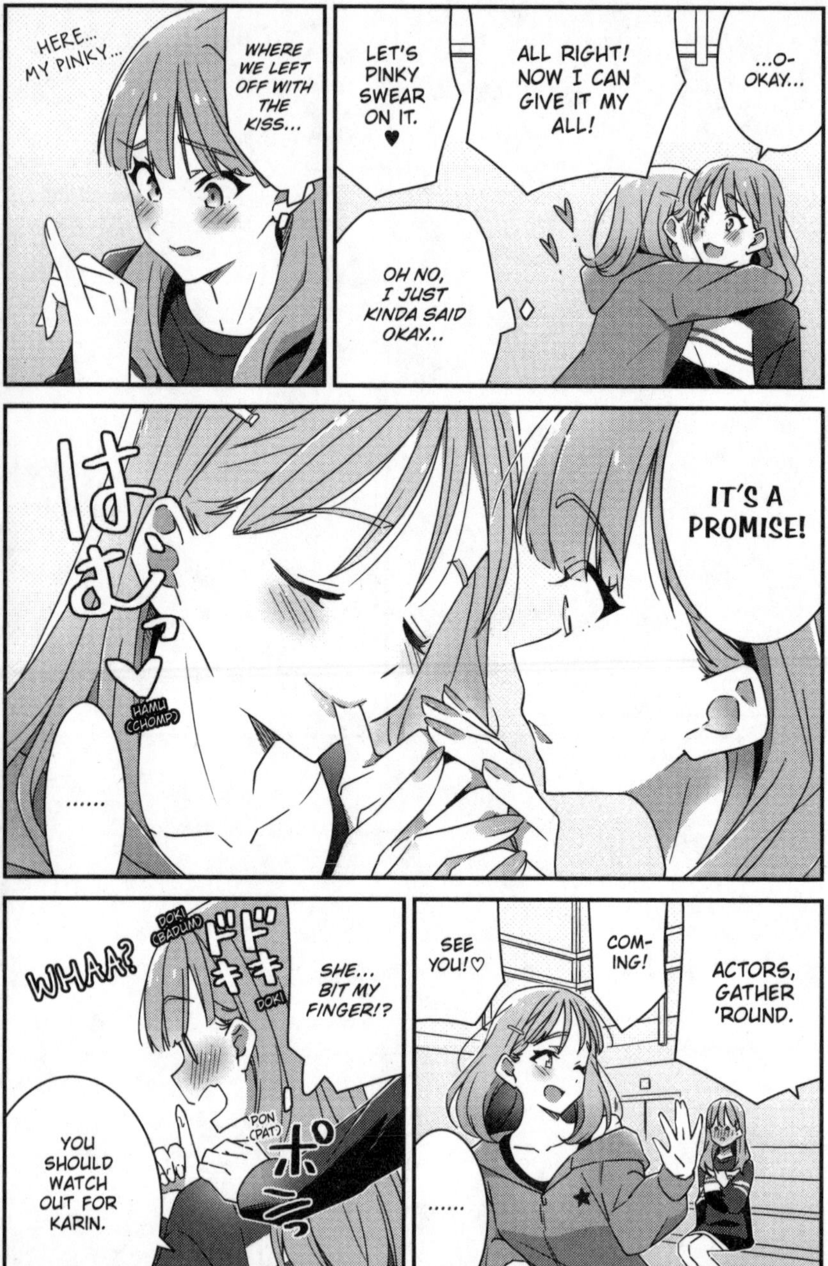
...O-OKAY...
ALL RIGHT! NOW I CAN GIVE IT MY ALL!
LET'S PINKY SWEAR ON IT. ♥
OH NO, I JUST KINDA SAID OKAY...
WHERE WE LEFT OFF WITH THE KISS...
HERE... MY PINKY...
IT'S A PROMISE!
はむっ
HAMU (CHOMP)
......
ACTORS, GATHER 'ROUND.
COM-ING!
SEE YOU!♡
......
SHE... BIT MY FINGER!?
ドキドキ
DOKI (BADUM)
DOKI
WHAA?
ポン
PON (PAT)
YOU SHOULD WATCH OUT FOR KARIN.

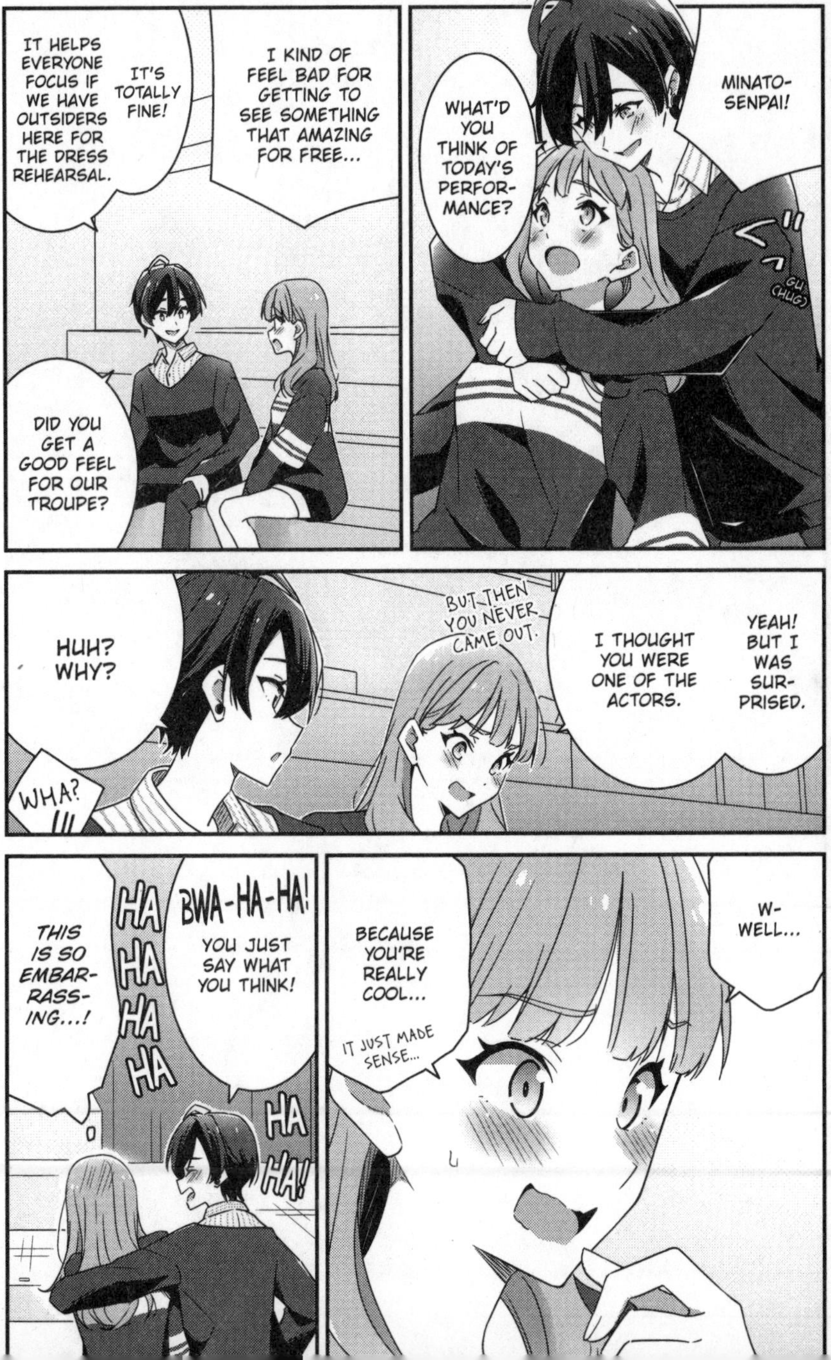
MINATO-SENPAI!
WHAT'D YOU THINK OF TODAY'S PERFORMANCE?
GU (HUG)
I KIND OF FEEL BAD FOR GETTING TO SEE SOMETHING THAT AMAZING FOR FREE...
IT'S TOTALLY FINE!
IT HELPS EVERYONE FOCUS IF WE HAVE OUTSIDERS HERE FOR THE DRESS REHEARSAL.
DID YOU GET A GOOD FEEL FOR OUR TROUPE?
YEAH! BUT I WAS SURPRISED.
I THOUGHT YOU WERE ONE OF THE ACTORS.
BUT THEN YOU NEVER CAME OUT.
HUH? WHY?
WHA?!
W-WELL...
BECAUSE YOU'RE REALLY COOL...
IT JUST MADE SENSE...
BWA-HA-HA!
YOU JUST SAY WHAT YOU THINK!
HA HA HA HA
HA HA!
THIS IS SO EMBARRASSING...!

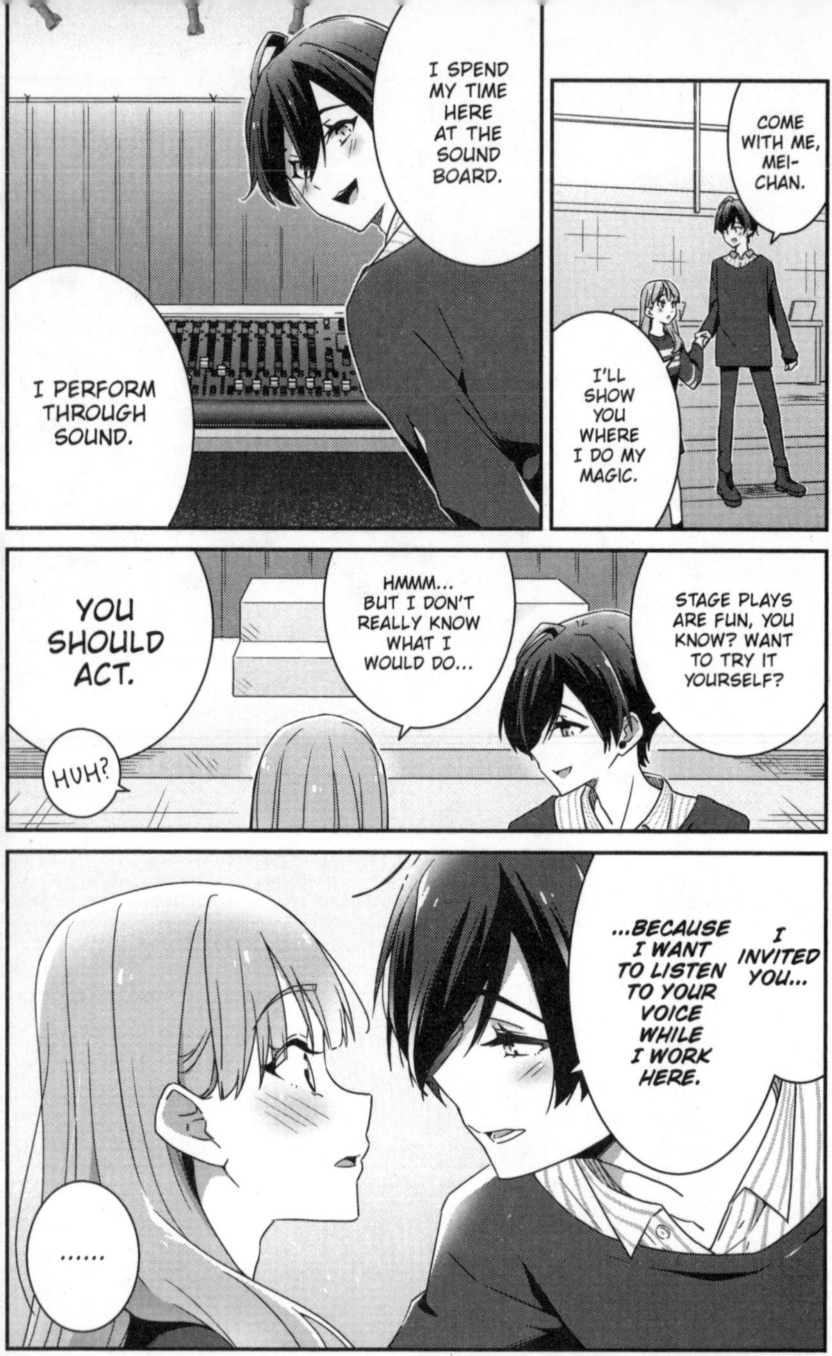
COME WITH ME, MEI-CHAN.
I'LL SHOW YOU WHERE I DO MY MAGIC.
I SPEND MY TIME HERE AT THE SOUND BOARD.
I PERFORM THROUGH SOUND.
STAGE PLAYS ARE FUN, YOU KNOW? WANT TO TRY IT YOURSELF?
HMMM... BUT I DON'T REALLY KNOW WHAT I WOULD DO...
YOU SHOULD ACT.
HUH?
I INVITED YOU...
...BECAUSE I WANT TO LISTEN TO YOUR VOICE WHILE I WORK HERE.
......

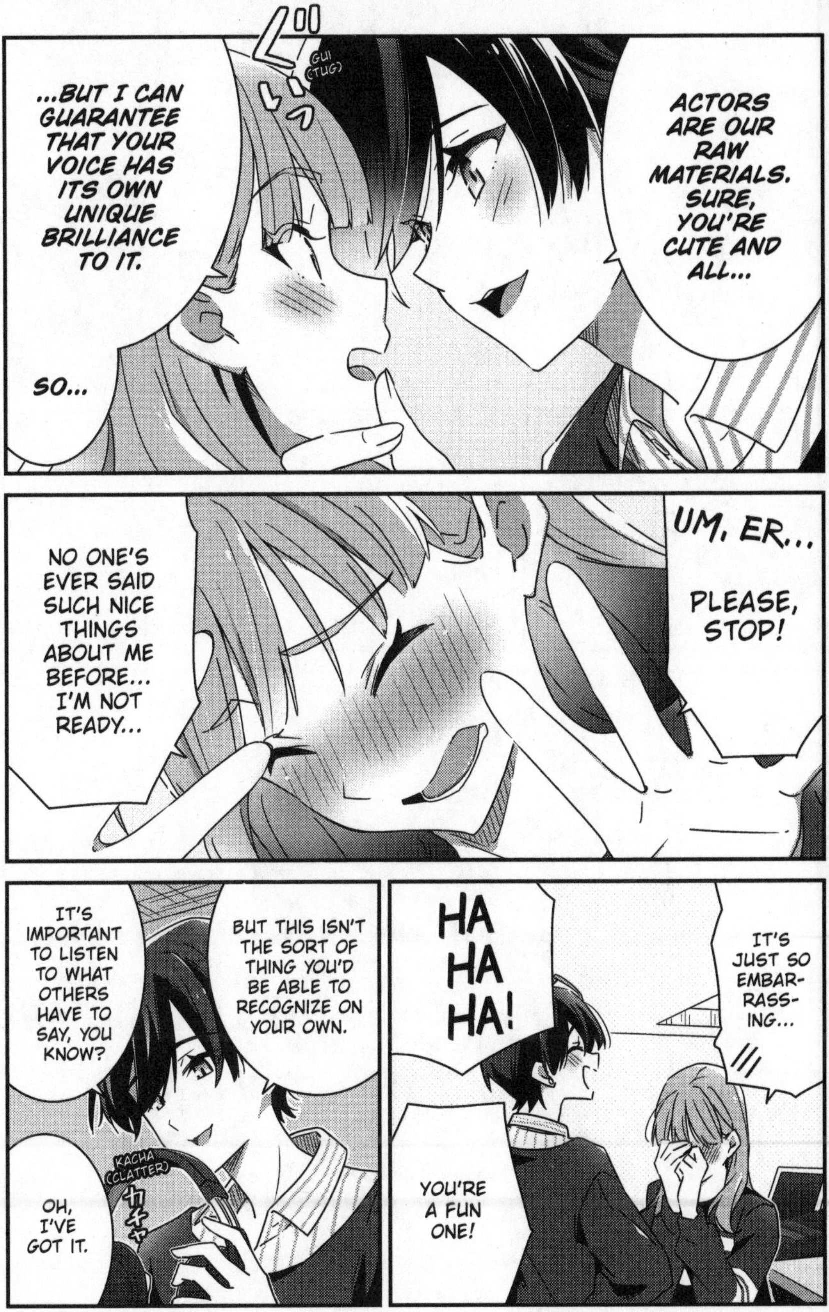
ACTORS ARE OUR RAW MATERIALS. SURE, YOU'RE CUTE AND ALL...
GUI (TUG)
...BUT I CAN GUARANTEE THAT YOUR VOICE HAS ITS OWN UNIQUE BRILLIANCE TO IT.
SO...
UM, ER...
PLEASE, STOP!
NO ONE'S EVER SAID SUCH NICE THINGS ABOUT ME BEFORE... I'M NOT READY...
IT'S JUST SO EMBAR-RASS-ING...
HA HA HA!
YOU'RE A FUN ONE!
BUT THIS ISN'T THE SORT OF THING YOU'D BE ABLE TO RECOGNIZE ON YOUR OWN.
IT'S IMPORTANT TO LISTEN TO WHAT OTHERS HAVE TO SAY, YOU KNOW?
KACHA (CLATTER)
OH, I'VE GOT IT.

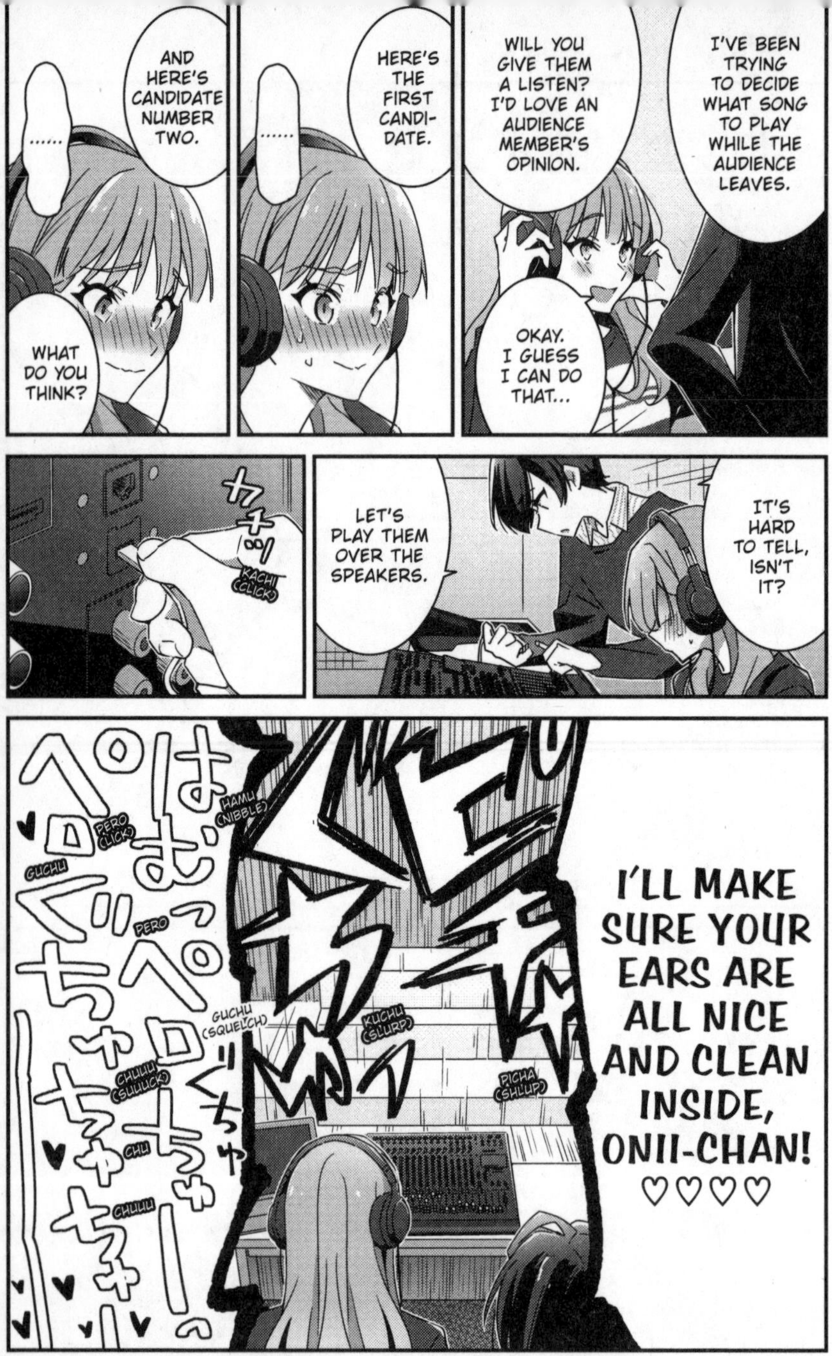
I'VE BEEN TRYING TO DECIDE WHAT SONG TO PLAY WHILE THE AUDIENCE LEAVES.
WILL YOU GIVE THEM A LISTEN? I'D LOVE AN AUDIENCE MEMBER'S OPINION.
OKAY. I GUESS I CAN DO THAT...
HERE'S THE FIRST CANDIDATE.
......
AND HERE'S CANDIDATE NUMBER TWO.
......
WHAT DO YOU THINK?
IT'S HARD TO TELL, ISN'T IT?
LET'S PLAY THEM OVER THE SPEAKERS.
カチッ
KACHI (CLICK)
I'LL MAKE SURE YOUR EARS ARE ALL NICE AND CLEAN INSIDE, ONII-CHAN! ♡♡♡♡
PICHA (SHLUP)
KUCHU (SLURP)
GUCHU (SQUELCH)
HAMU (NIBBLE)
PERO (LICK)
GUCHU
PERO
CHUUU (SUUUCK)
CHU
CHUUU

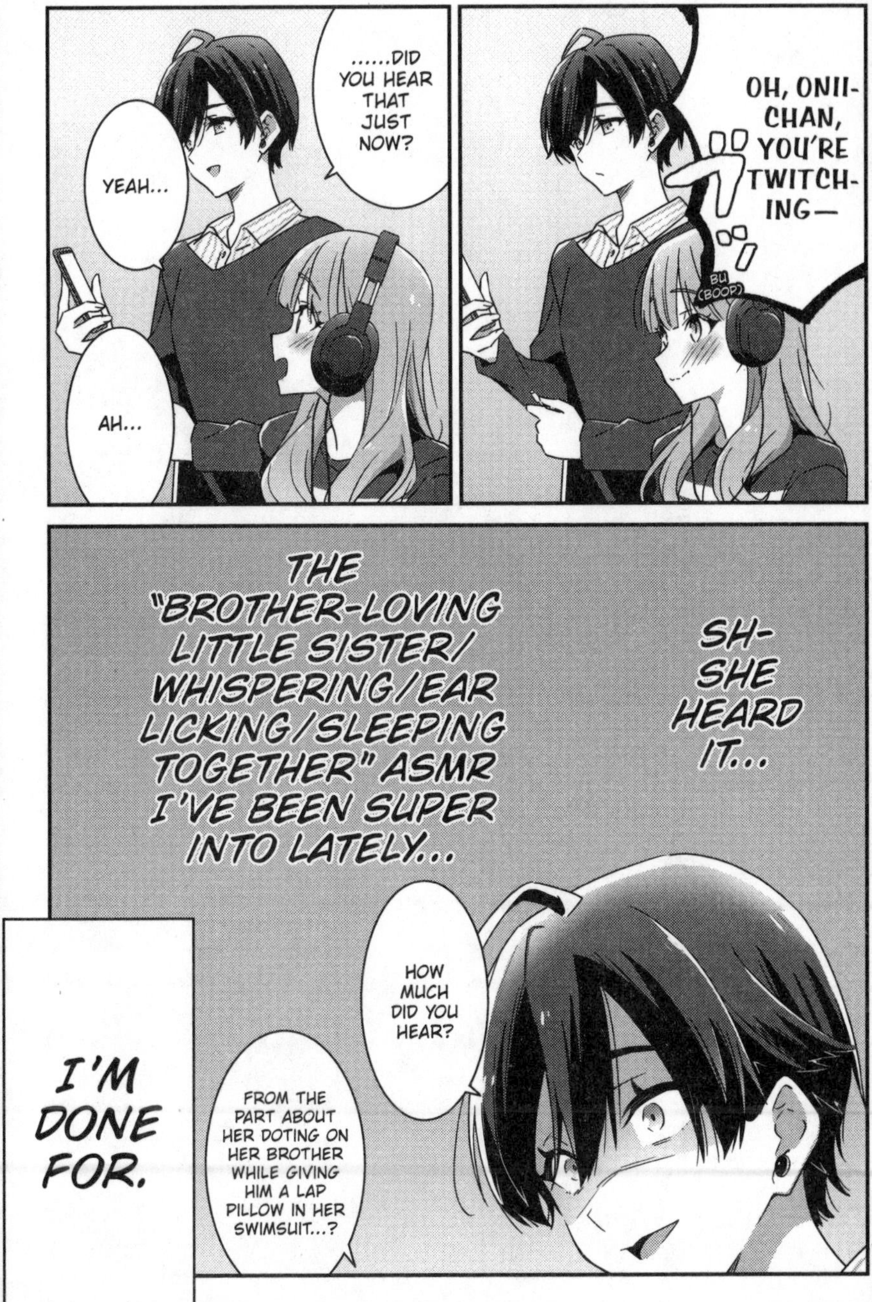
OH, ONII-CHAN, YOU'RE TWITCH-ING—
BU (BOOP)
......DID YOU HEAR THAT JUST NOW?
YEAH...
AH...
SH-SHE HEARD IT...
THE "BROTHER-LOVING LITTLE SISTER/WHISPERING/EAR LICKING/SLEEPING TOGETHER" ASMR I'VE BEEN SUPER INTO LATELY...
HOW MUCH DID YOU HEAR?
FROM THE PART ABOUT HER DOTING ON HER BROTHER WHILE GIVING HIM A LAP PILLOW IN HER SWIMSUIT...?
I'M DONE FOR.

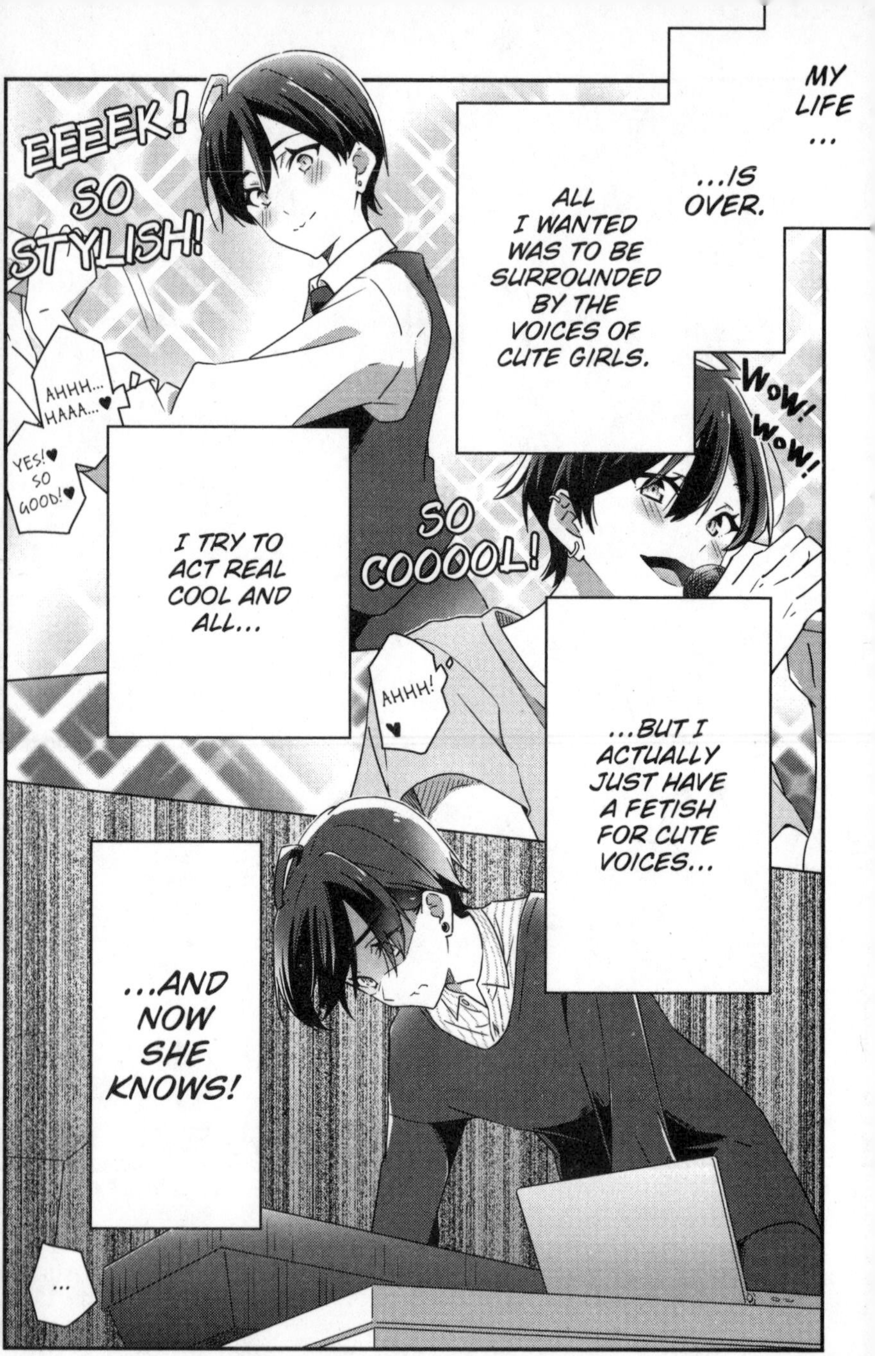
MY LIFE...
...IS OVER.
ALL I WANTED WAS TO BE SURROUNDED BY THE VOICES OF CUTE GIRLS.
WOW! WOW!
SO COOOOL!
AHHH! ♥
EEEEK! SO STYLISH!
AHHH... HAAA...♥
YES!♥ SO GOOD!♥
I TRY TO ACT REAL COOL AND ALL...
...BUT I ACTUALLY JUST HAVE A FETISH FOR CUTE VOICES...
...AND NOW SHE KNOWS!
...

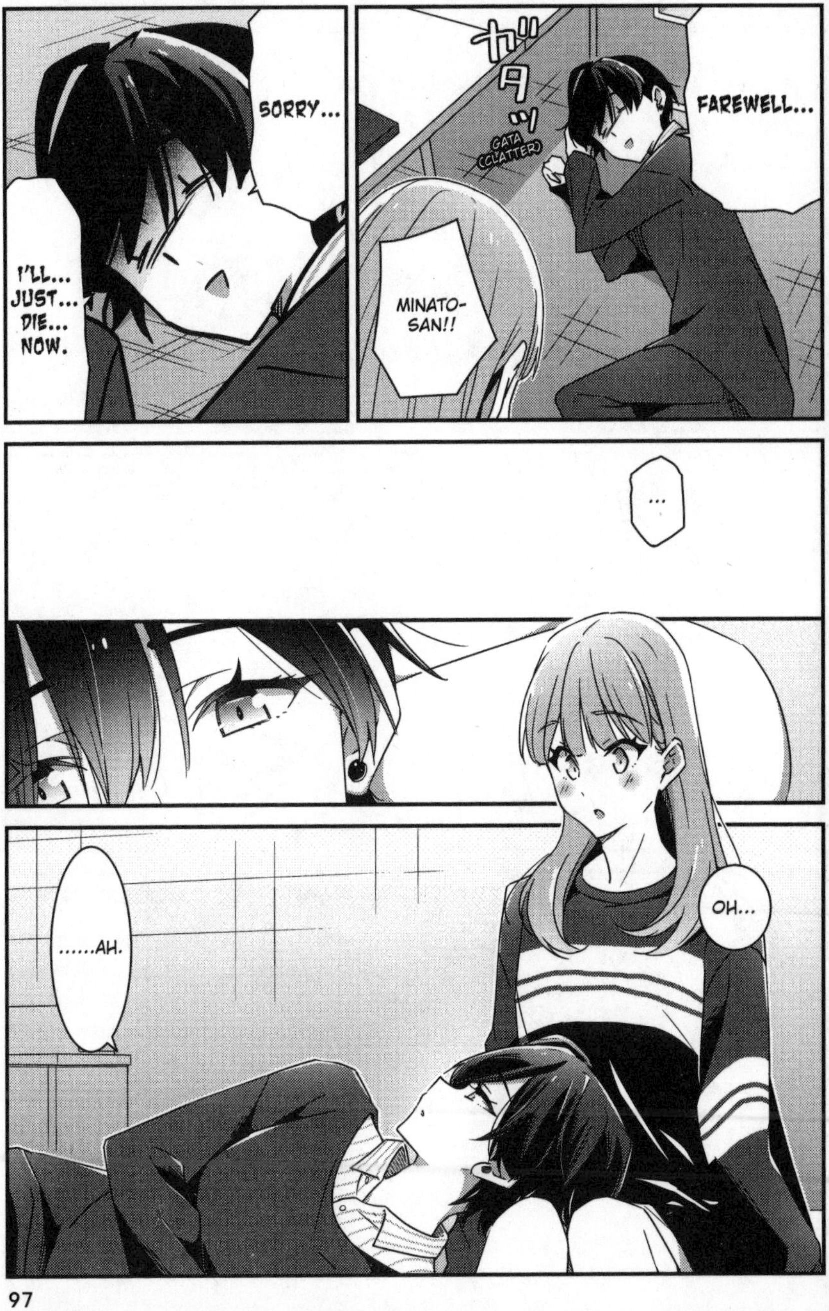

FAREWELL...
カタッ
GATA (CLATTER)
MINATO-SAN!!
SORRY...
I'LL... JUST... DIE... NOW.
...
OH...
......AH.

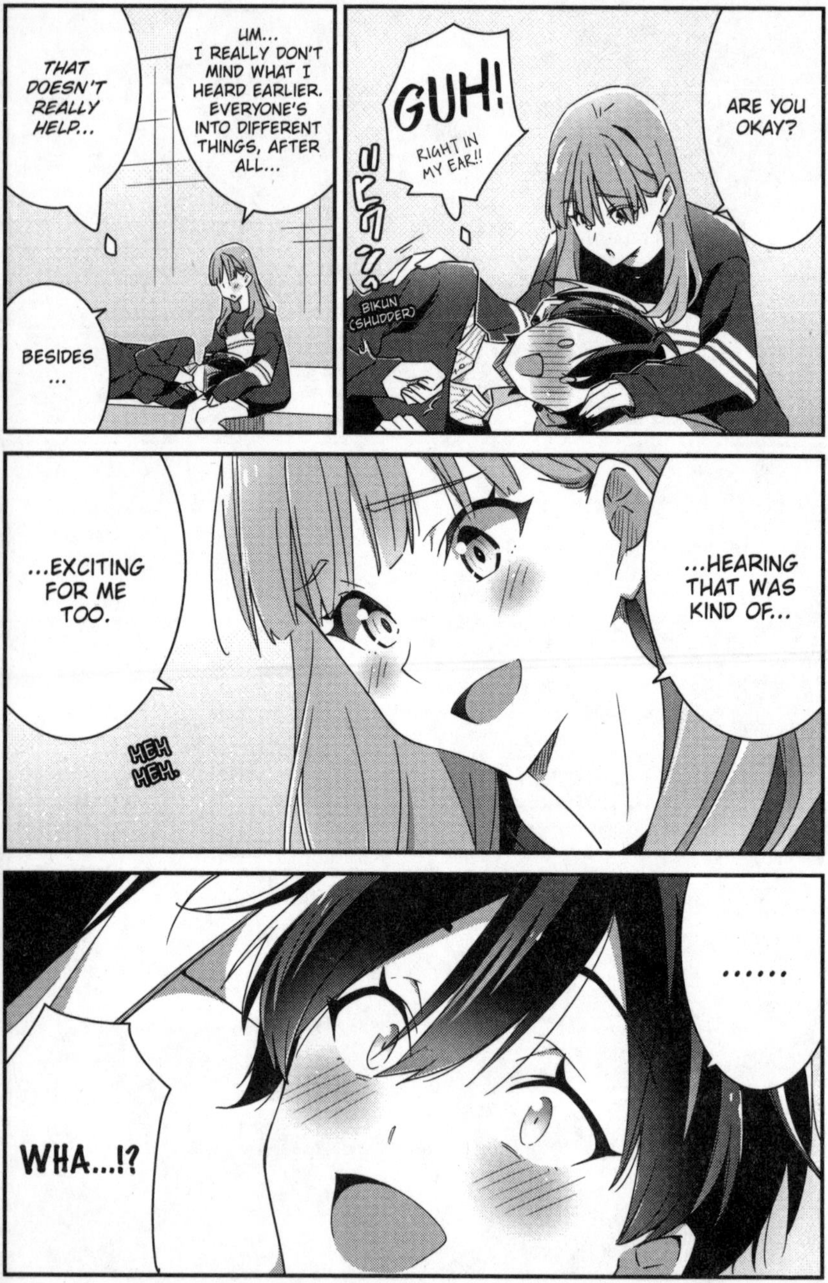
ARE YOU OKAY?
GUH!
RIGHT IN MY EAR!!
BIKUN (SHUDDER)
UM... I REALLY DON'T MIND WHAT I HEARD EARLIER. EVERYONE'S INTO DIFFERENT THINGS, AFTER ALL...
THAT DOESN'T REALLY HELP...
BESIDES ...
...HEARING THAT WAS KIND OF...
...EXCITING FOR ME TOO.
HEH HEH.
......
WHA...!?

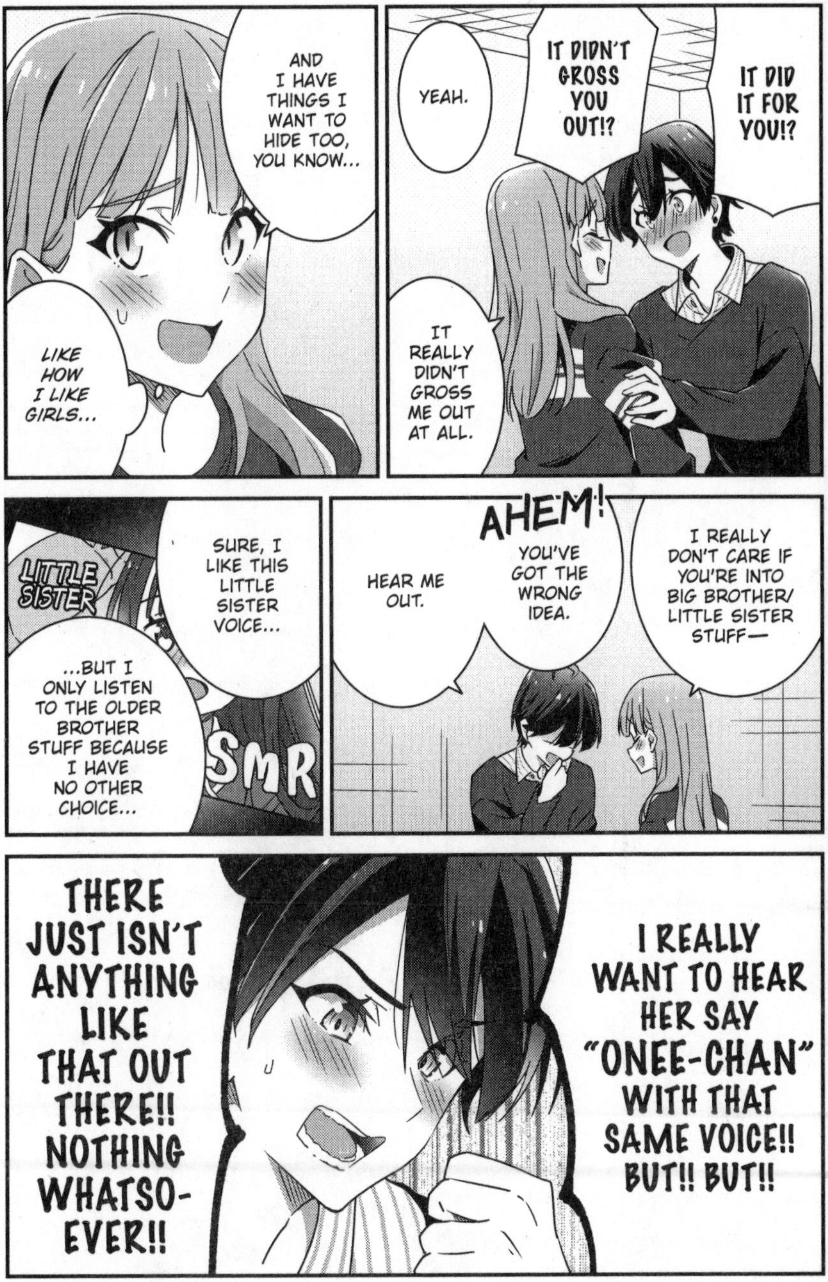
IT DID IT FOR YOU!?
IT DIDN'T GROSS YOU OUT!?
YEAH.
IT REALLY DIDN'T GROSS ME OUT AT ALL.
AND I HAVE THINGS I WANT TO HIDE TOO, YOU KNOW...
LIKE HOW I LIKE GIRLS...
I REALLY DON'T CARE IF YOU'RE INTO BIG BROTHER/ LITTLE SISTER STUFF—
AHEM!
YOU'VE GOT THE WRONG IDEA.
HEAR ME OUT.
SURE, I LIKE THIS LITTLE SISTER VOICE...
LITTLE SISTER
...BUT I ONLY LISTEN TO THE OLDER BROTHER STUFF BECAUSE I HAVE NO OTHER CHOICE...
SMR
I REALLY WANT TO HEAR HER SAY "ONEE-CHAN" WITH THAT SAME VOICE!! BUT!! BUT!!
THERE JUST ISN'T ANYTHING LIKE THAT OUT THERE!! NOTHING WHATSO-EVER!!

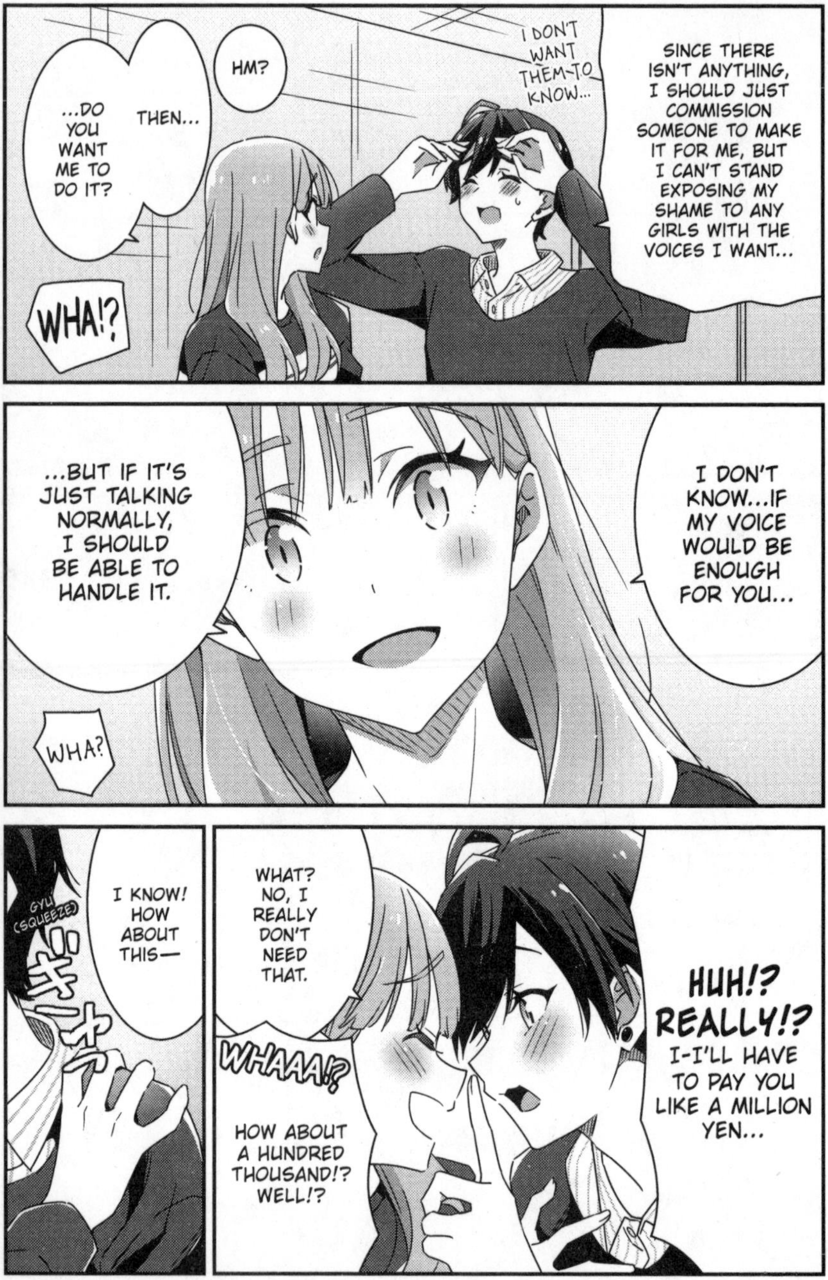
SINCE THERE ISN'T ANYTHING, I SHOULD JUST COMMISSION SOMEONE TO MAKE IT FOR ME, BUT I CAN'T STAND EXPOSING MY SHAME TO ANY GIRLS WITH THE VOICES I WANT...
I DON'T WANT THEM TO KNOW...
HM?
THEN...
...DO YOU WANT ME TO DO IT?
WHA!?
I DON'T KNOW...IF MY VOICE WOULD BE ENOUGH FOR YOU...
...BUT IF IT'S JUST TALKING NORMALLY, I SHOULD BE ABLE TO HANDLE IT.
WHA?
HUH!? REALLY!? I-I'LL HAVE TO PAY YOU LIKE A MILLION YEN...
WHAT? NO, I REALLY DON'T NEED THAT.
WHAAA!?
HOW ABOUT A HUNDRED THOUSAND!? WELL!?
I KNOW! HOW ABOUT THIS—
GYU (SQUEEZE)

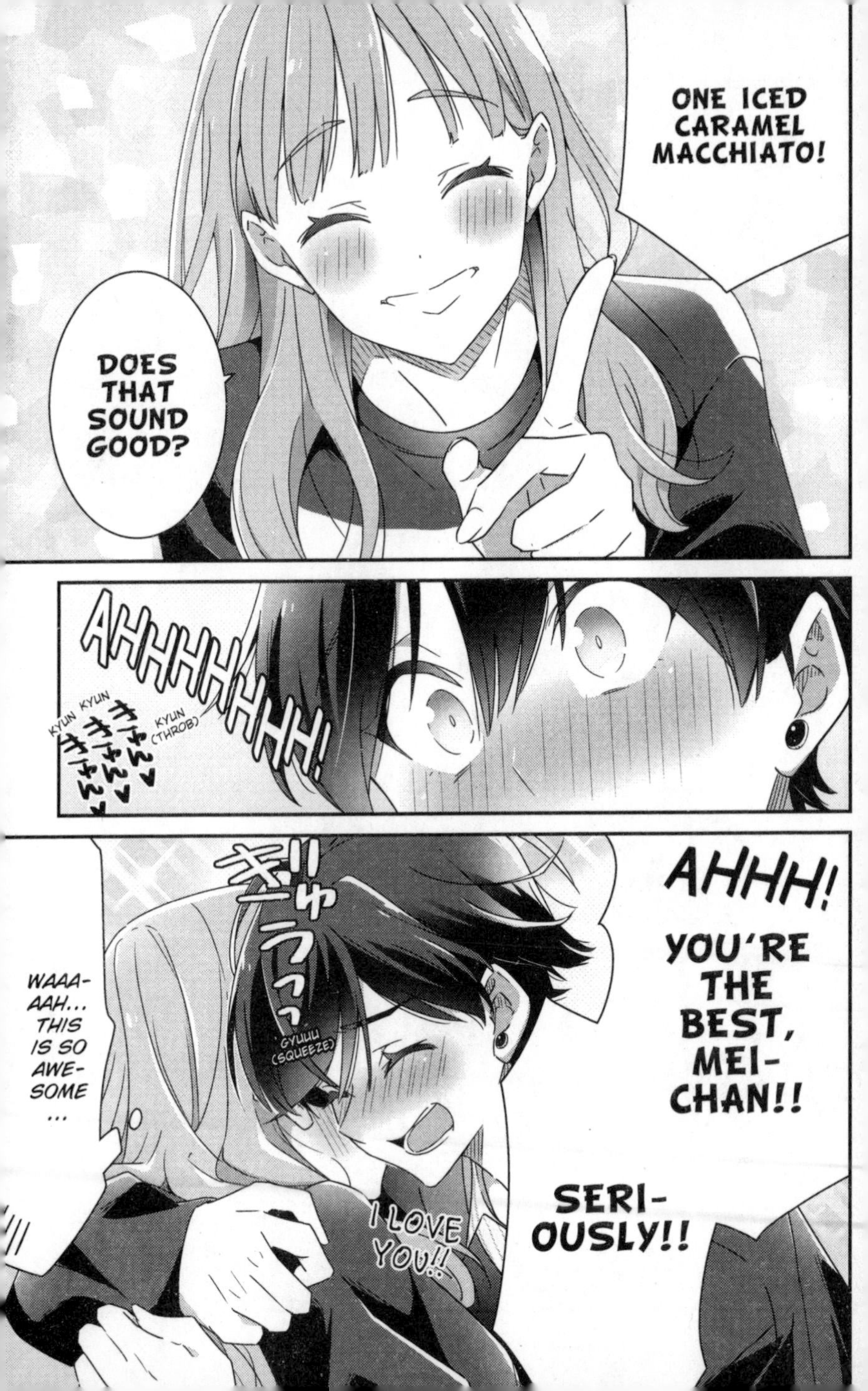
ONE ICED CARAMEL MACCHIATO!
DOES THAT SOUND GOOD?
AHHHHHHHH!
KYUN (THROB)
KYUN KYUN
AHHH!
YOU'RE THE BEST, MEI-CHAN!!
SERI-OUSLY!!
GYUUU (SQUEEZE)
WAAAAAH... THIS IS SO AWESOME...
I LOVE YOU!!

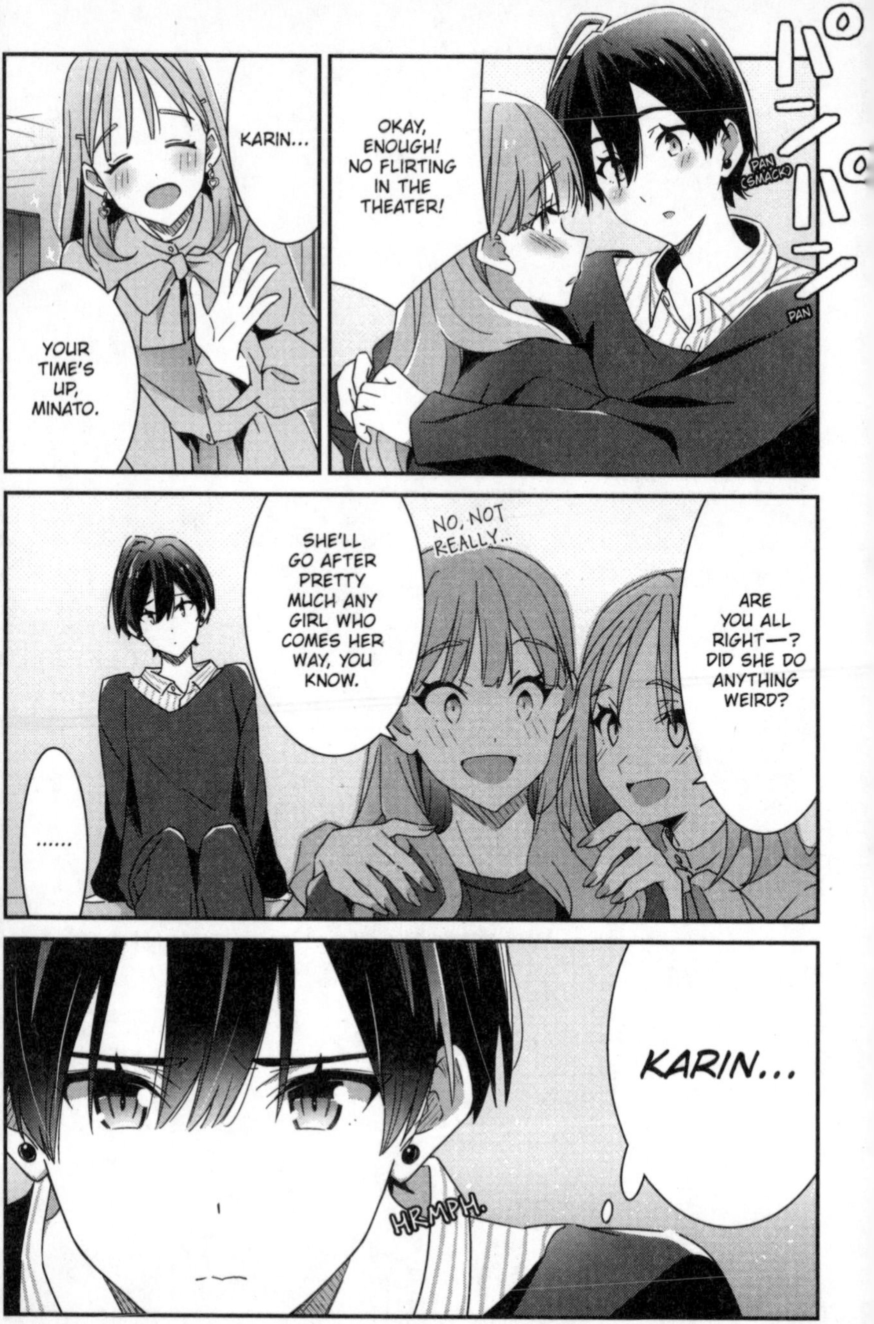
PAN (SMACK)
PAN
OKAY, ENOUGH! NO FLIRTING IN THE THEATER!
KARIN...
YOUR TIME'S UP, MINATO.
ARE YOU ALL RIGHT—? DID SHE DO ANYTHING WEIRD?
NO, NOT REALLY...
SHE'LL GO AFTER PRETTY MUCH ANY GIRL WHO COMES HER WAY, YOU KNOW.
......
KARIN...
HRMPH.

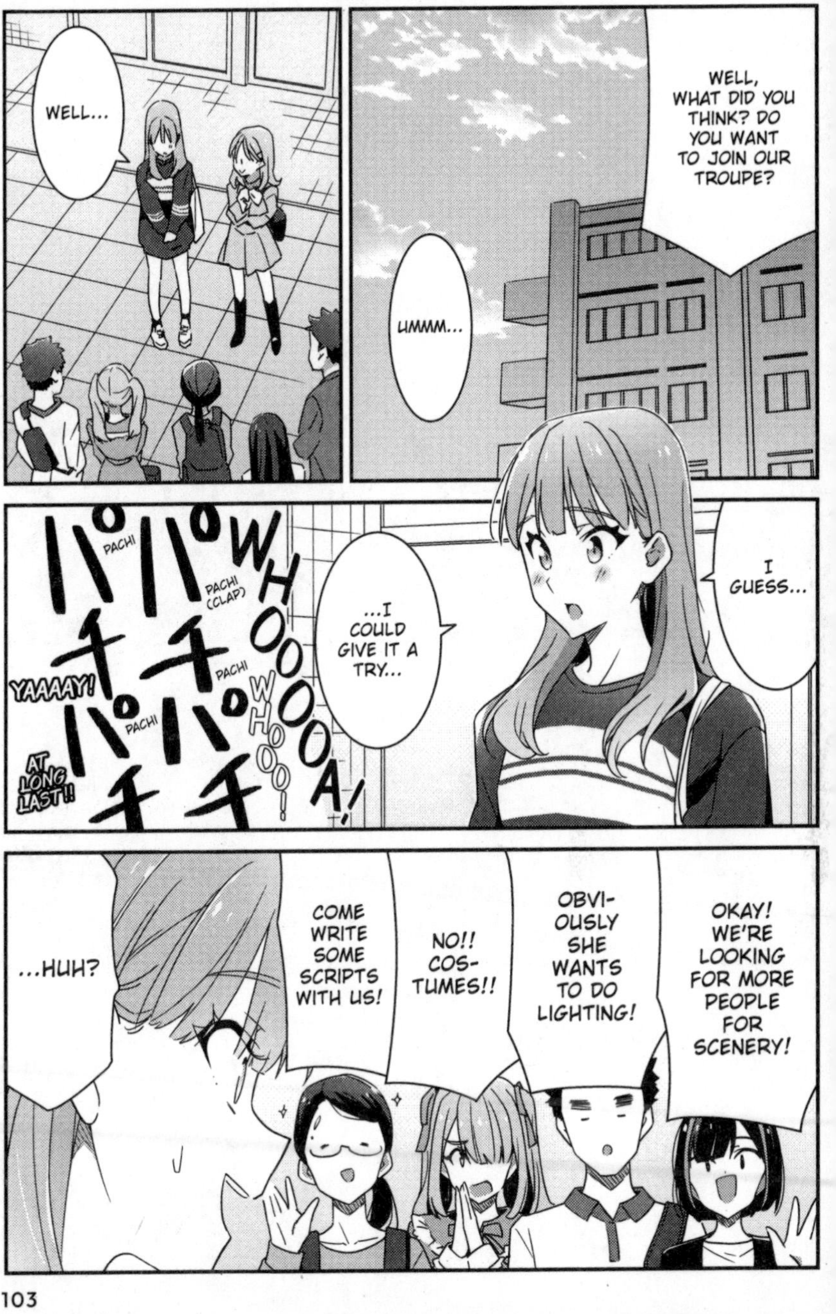
WELL, WHAT DID YOU THINK? DO YOU WANT TO JOIN OUR TROUPE?
UMMM...
WELL...
I GUESS...
...I COULD GIVE IT A TRY...
WHOOOOA!
WHOOOO!
パチパチ
PACHI PACHI (CLAP)
パチパチ
PACHI PACHI
YAAAAY!
AT LONG LAST!!
OKAY! WE'RE LOOKING FOR MORE PEOPLE FOR SCENERY!
OBVI-OUSLY SHE WANTS TO DO LIGHTING!
NO!! COS-TUMES!!
COME WRITE SOME SCRIPTS WITH US!
...HUH?

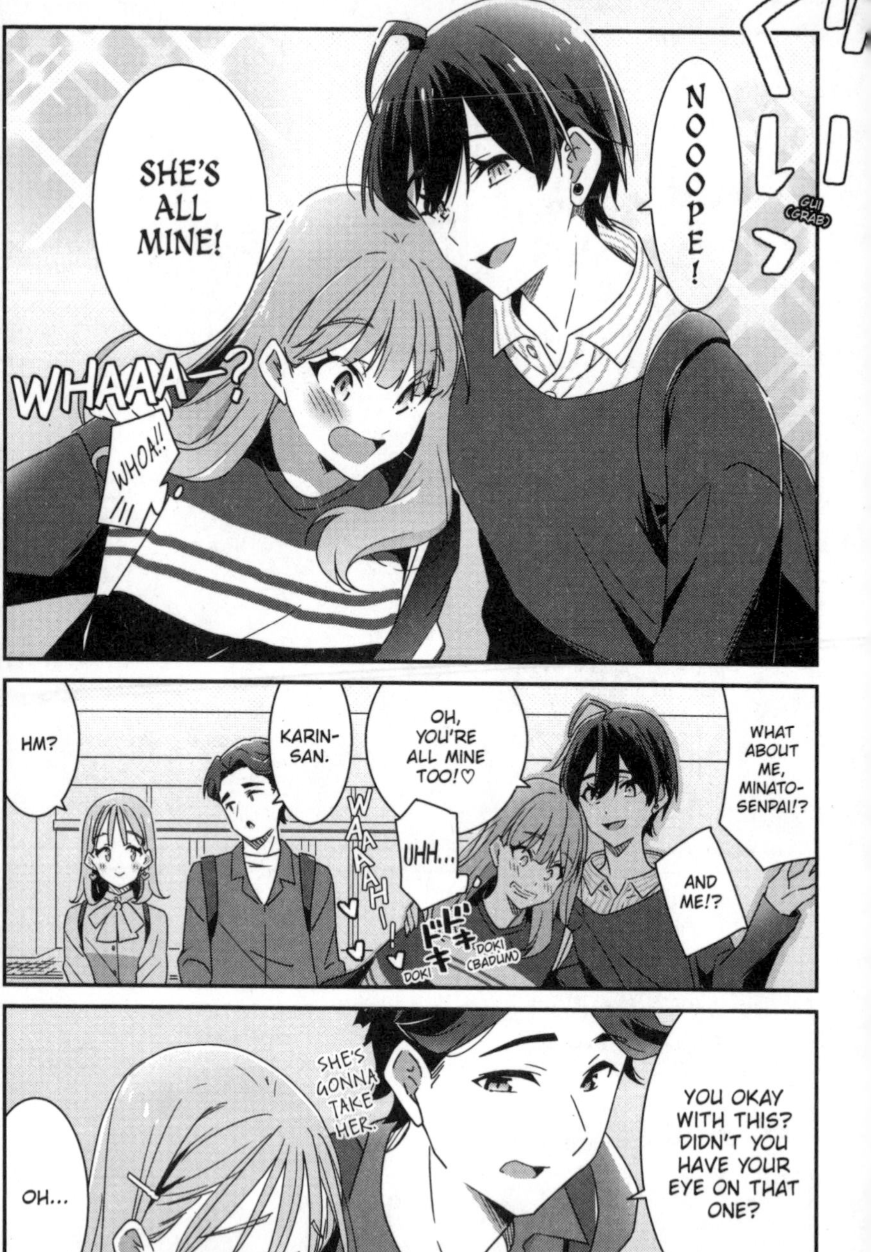
GUI (GRAB)
NOOOPE!
SHE'S ALL MINE!
WHAAA—?
WHOA!!
WHAT ABOUT ME, MINATO-SENPAI!?
AND ME!?
OH, YOU'RE ALL MINE TOO!♡
UHH...
WAAAAH—!
DOKI DOKI (BADUM)
KARIN-SAN.
HM?
YOU OKAY WITH THIS? DIDN'T YOU HAVE YOUR EYE ON THAT ONE?
SHE'S GONNA TAKE HER.
OH...

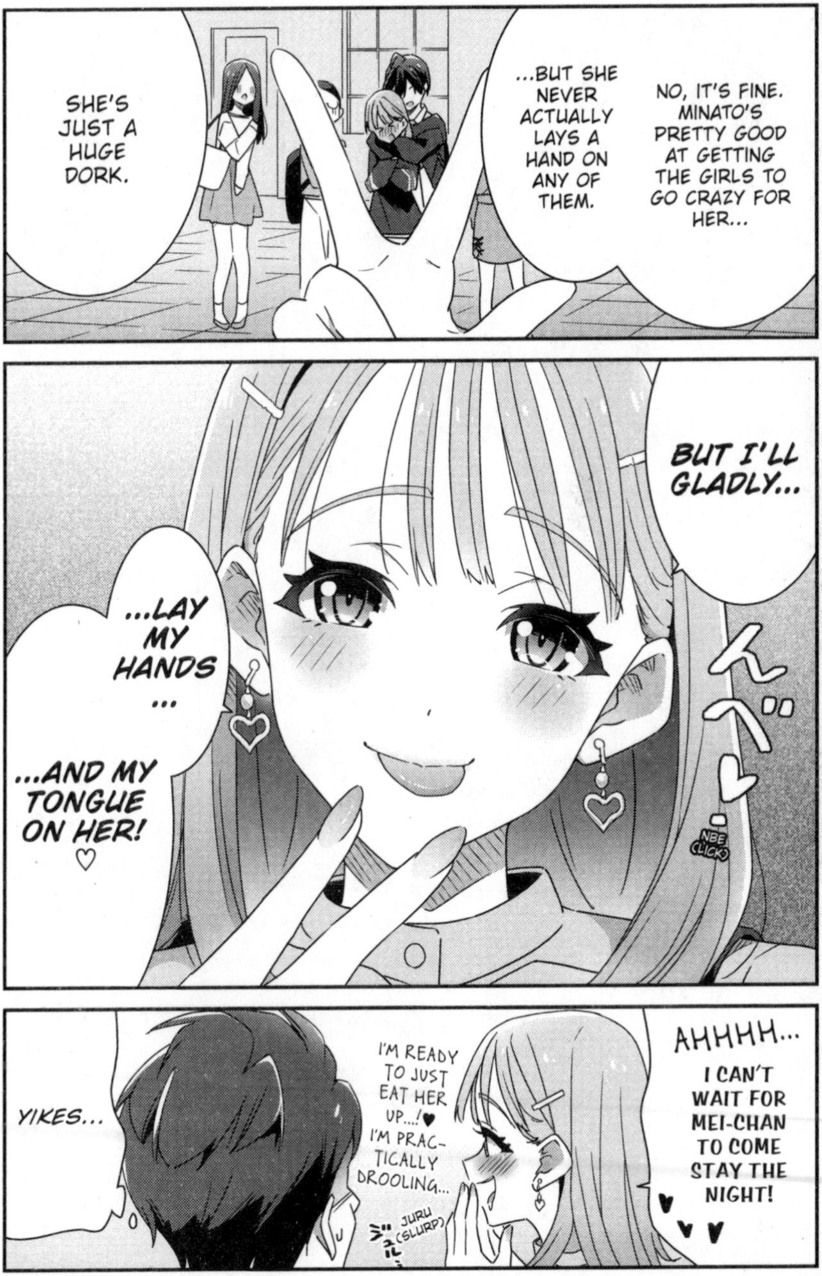
NO, IT'S FINE. MINATO'S PRETTY GOOD AT GETTING THE GIRLS TO GO CRAZY FOR HER...
...BUT SHE NEVER ACTUALLY LAYS A HAND ON ANY OF THEM.
SHE'S JUST A HUGE DORK.
BUT I'LL GLADLY...
NBE (LICK)
...LAY MY HANDS...
...AND MY TONGUE ON HER! ♡
AHHHH... I CAN'T WAIT FOR MEI-CHAN TO COME STAY THE NIGHT! ♥ ♥ ♥
I'M READY TO JUST EAT HER UP...!♥ I'M PRACTICALLY DROOLING...
JURU (SLURP)
YIKES...

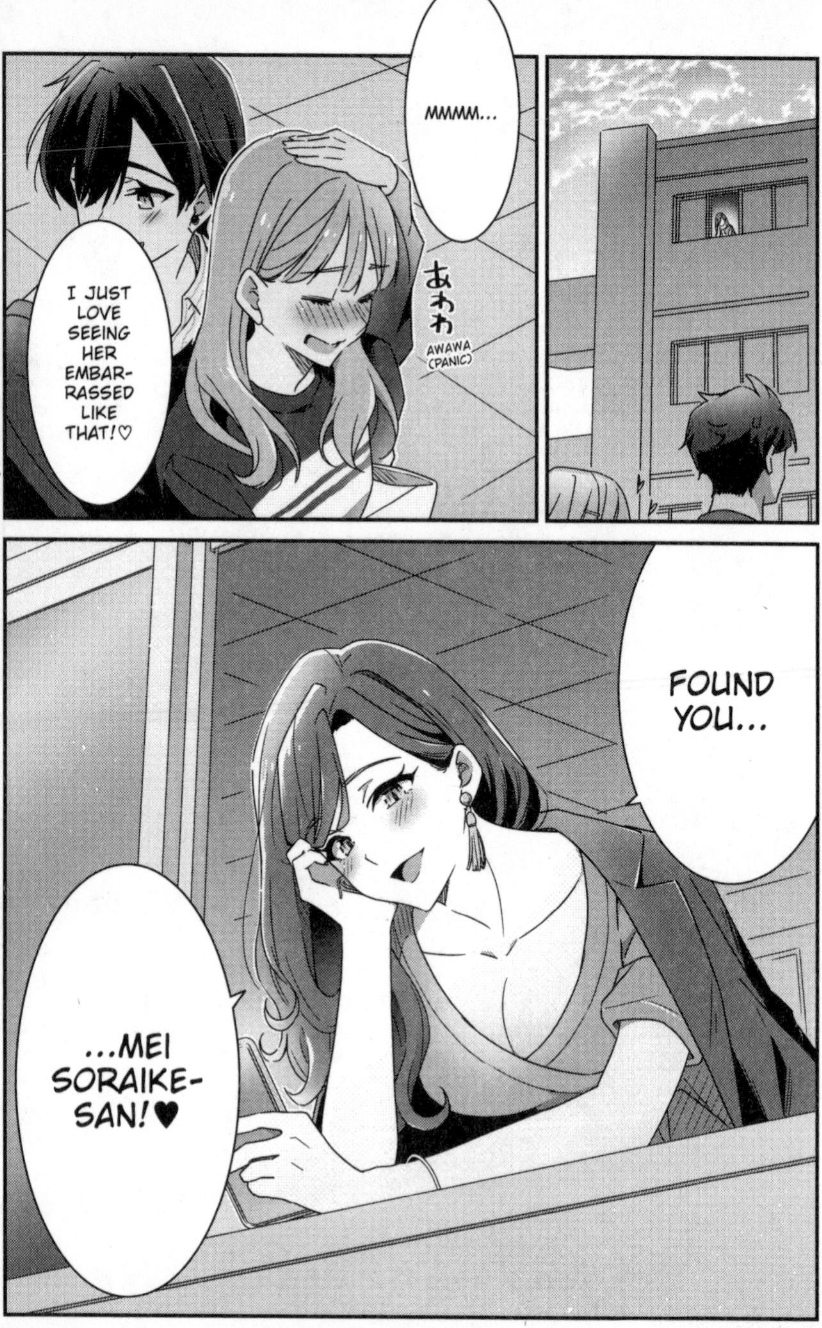

MMMM...
あわわ
AWAWA (PANIC)
I JUST LOVE SEEING HER EMBARRASSED LIKE THAT!♡
FOUND YOU...
...MEI SORAIKE-SAN!♥

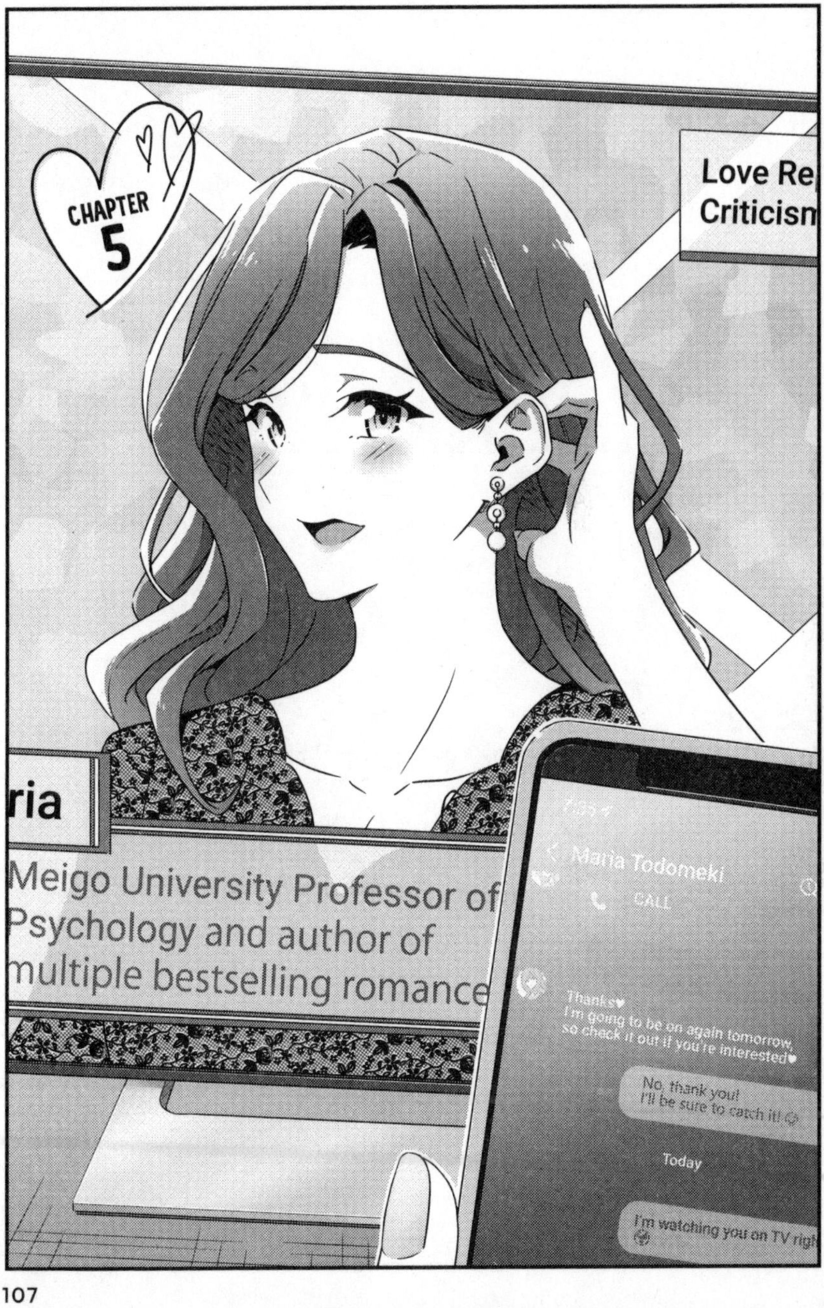
CHAPTER 5
Love
Meigo University Professor of Psychology and author of multiple bestselling romance
Maria Todomeki
CALL
Thanks♥
I'm going to be on again tomorrow, so check it out if you're interested♥
No, thank you!
I'll be sure to catch it!
Today
I'm watching you on TV

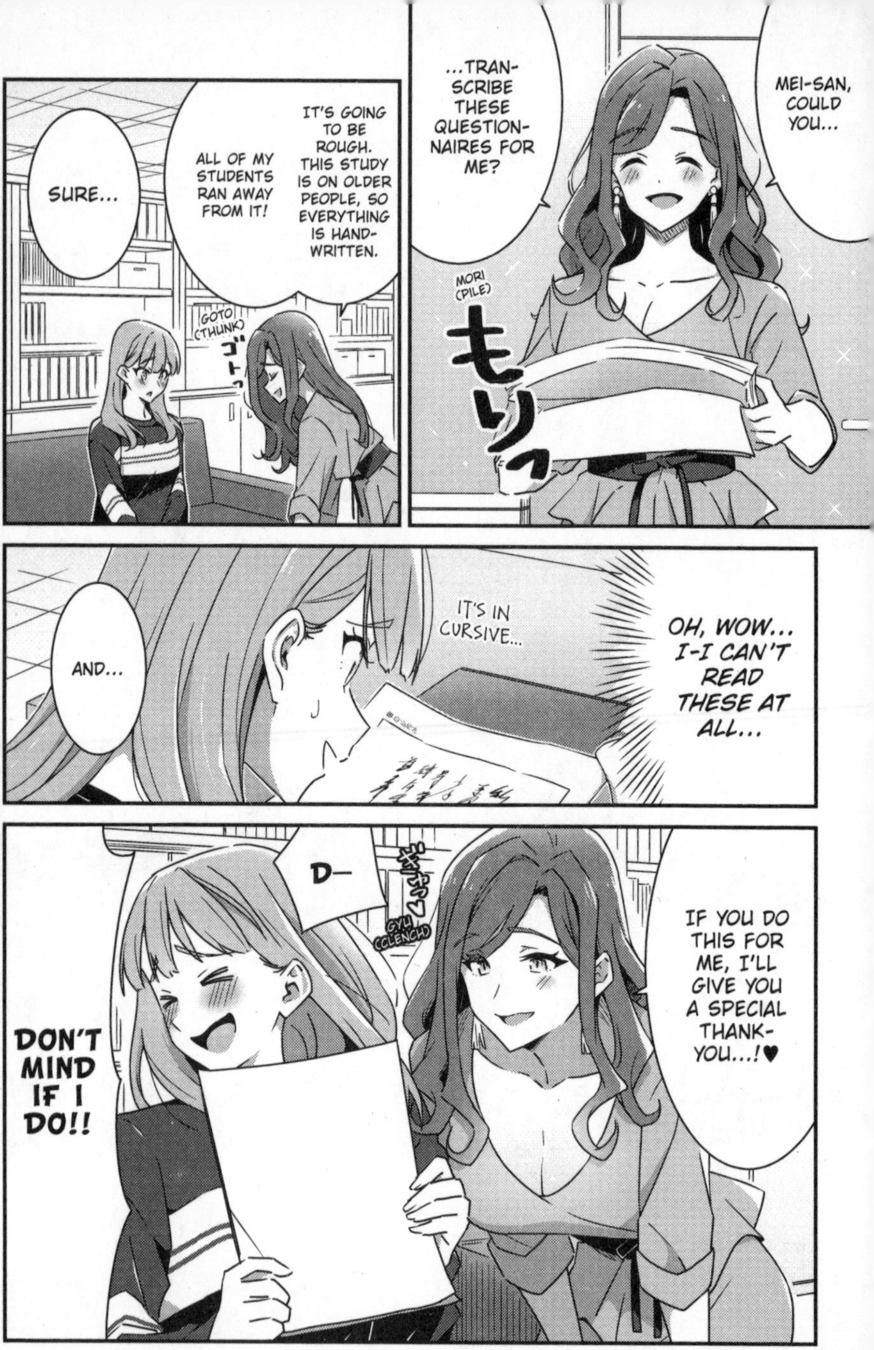
MEI-SAN, COULD YOU...
...TRAN-SCRIBE THESE QUESTION-NAIRES FOR ME?
MORI (PILE)
もりっ
IT'S GOING TO BE ROUGH. THIS STUDY IS ON OLDER PEOPLE, SO EVERYTHING IS HAND-WRITTEN.
ALL OF MY STUDENTS RAN AWAY FROM IT!
GOTO (THUNK)
ゴトッ
SURE...
OH, WOW... I-I CAN'T READ THESE AT ALL...
IT'S IN CURSIVE...
AND...
IF YOU DO THIS FOR ME, I'LL GIVE YOU A SPECIAL THANK-YOU...!♥
GYU (CLENCH)
ぎゅっ♥
D—
DON'T MIND IF I DO!!

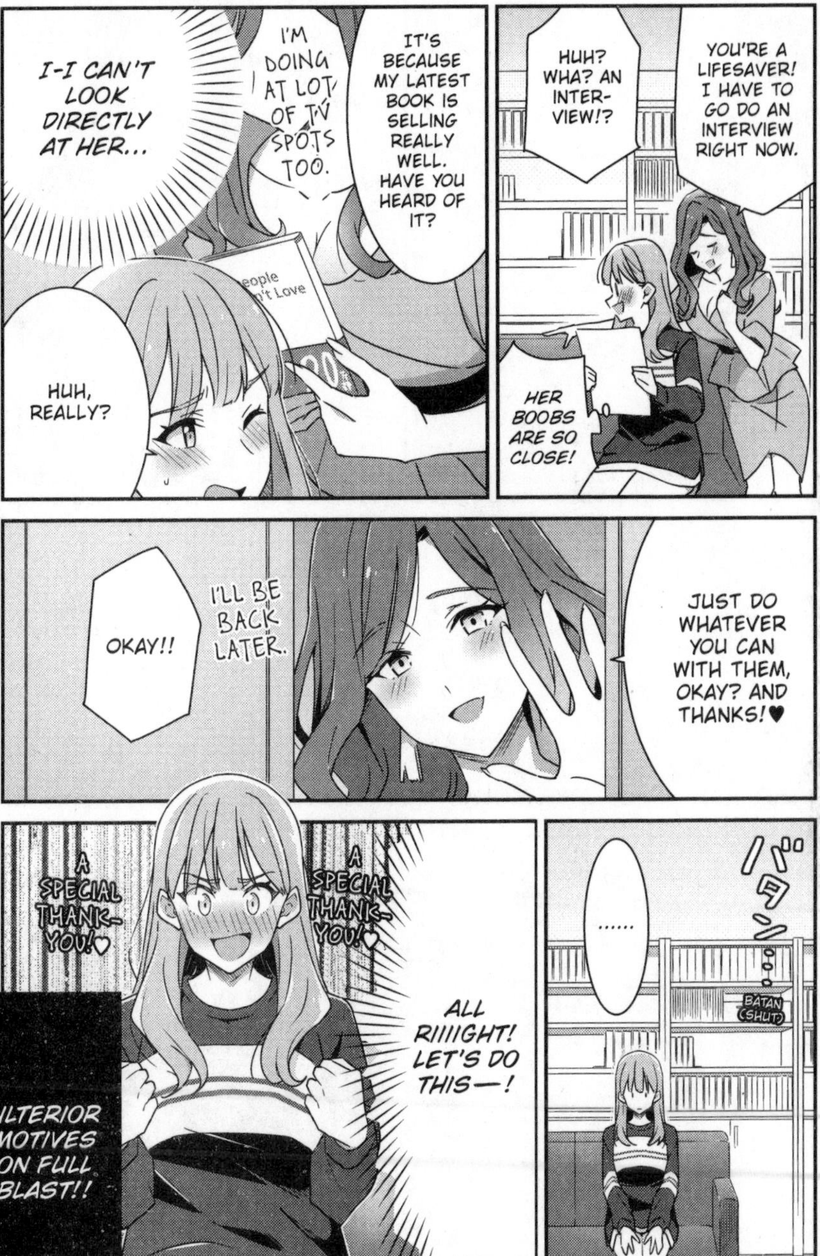
YOU'RE A LIFESAVER! I HAVE TO GO DO AN INTERVIEW RIGHT NOW.
HUH? WHA? AN INTER-VIEW!?
HER BOOBS ARE SO CLOSE!
IT'S BECAUSE MY LATEST BOOK IS SELLING REALLY WELL. HAVE YOU HEARD OF IT?
I'M DOING AT LOT OF TV SPOTS TOO.
I-I CAN'T LOOK DIRECTLY AT HER...
HUH, REALLY?
JUST DO WHATEVER YOU CAN WITH THEM, OKAY? AND THANKS!♥
I'LL BE BACK LATER.
OKAY!!
BATAN (SHUT)
......
A SPECIAL THANK-YOU!♥
ALL RIIIIGHT! LET'S DO THIS—!
A SPECIAL THANK-YOU!♥
ULTERIOR MOTIVES ON FULL BLAST!!

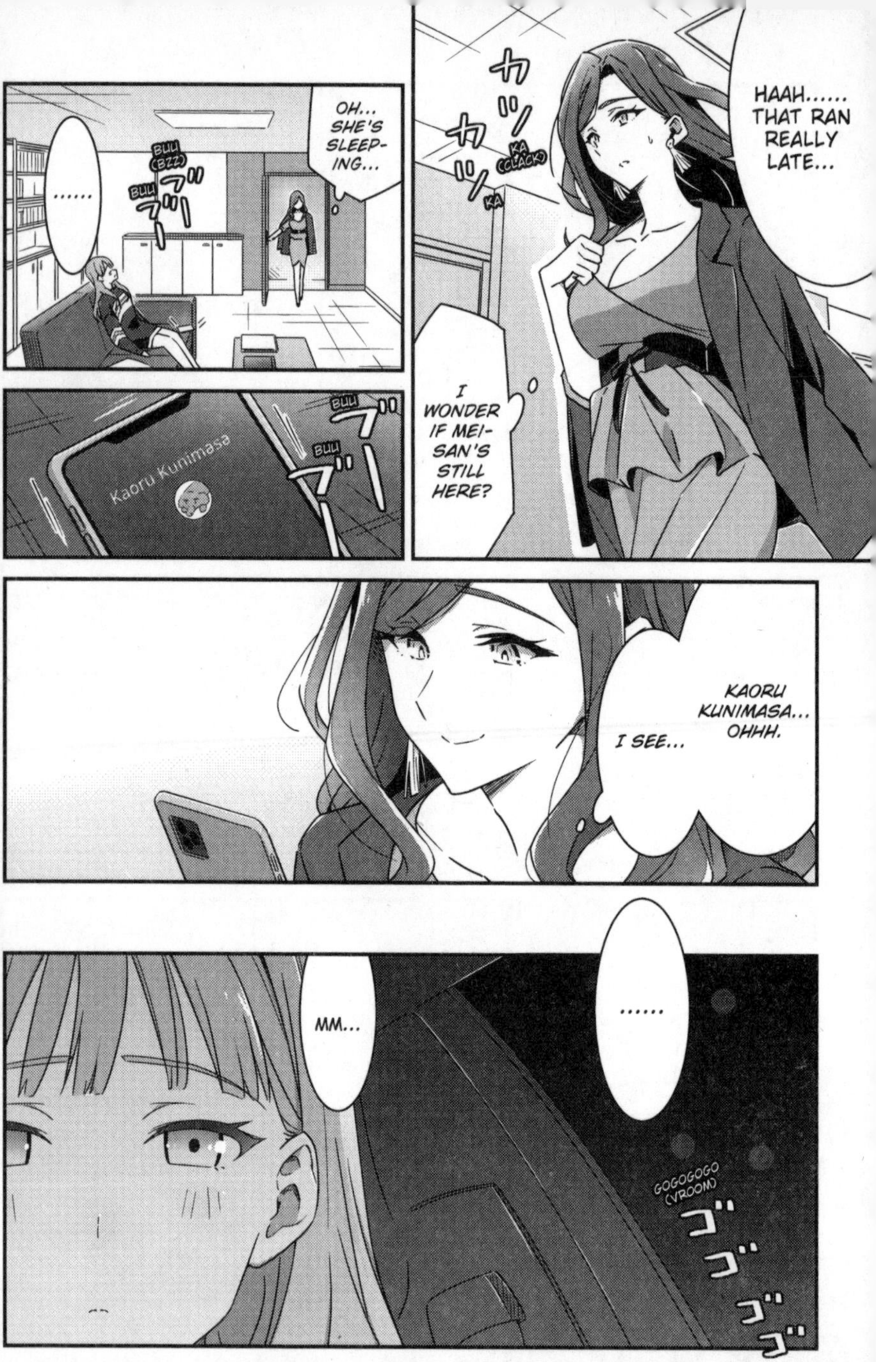
KA (CLACK)
KA
HAAH...... THAT RAN REALLY LATE...
I WONDER IF MEI-SAN'S STILL HERE?
OH... SHE'S SLEEPING...
BUU (BZZ)
BUU
......
BUU
BUU
Kaoru Kunimasa
KAORU KUNIMASA... OHHH.
I SEE...
......
MM...
GOGOGOGO (VROOM)

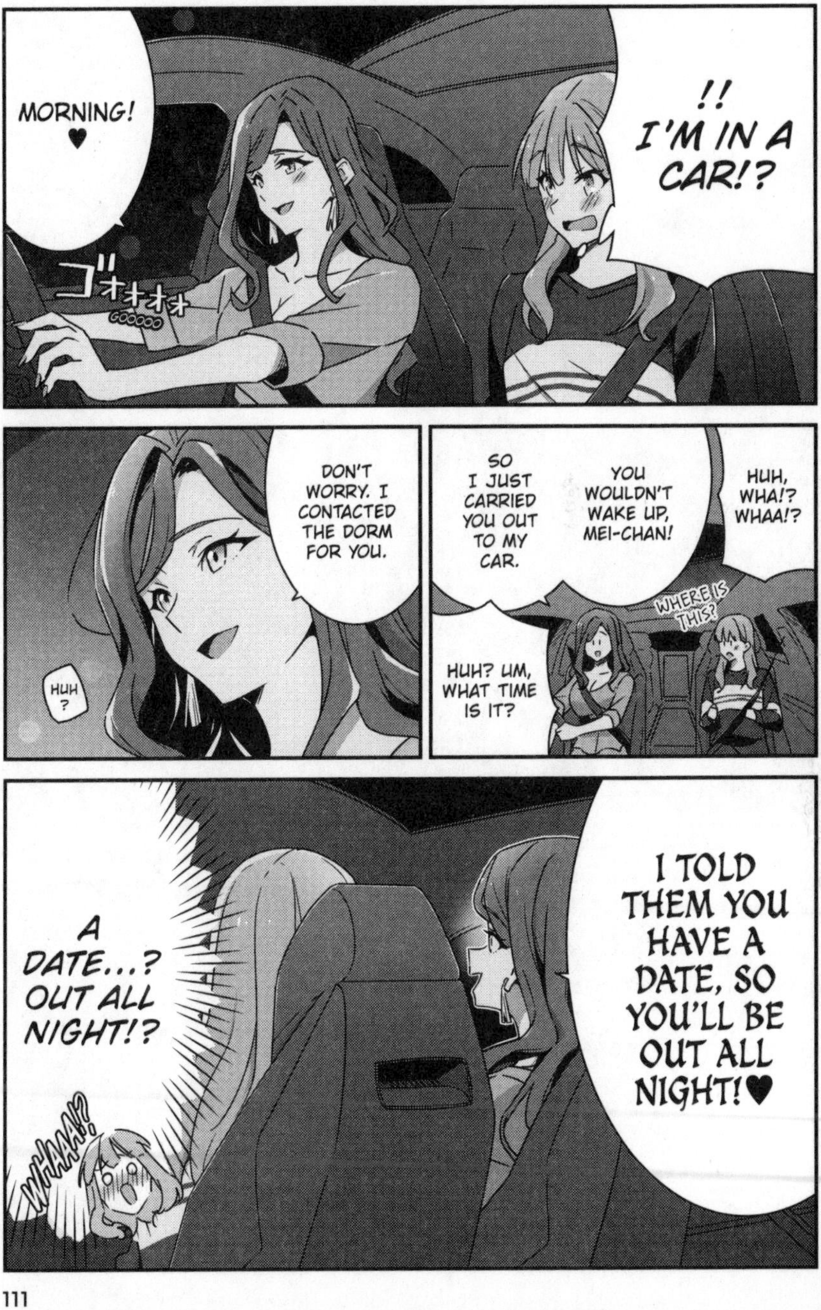
!! I'M IN A CAR!?
MORNING! ♥
ゴオオオオ
GOOOOO
HUH, WHA!? WHAA!?
YOU WOULDN'T WAKE UP, MEI-CHAN!
SO I JUST CARRIED YOU OUT TO MY CAR.
WHERE IS THIS?
HUH? UM, WHAT TIME IS IT?
DON'T WORRY. I CONTACTED THE DORM FOR YOU.
HUH ?
I TOLD THEM YOU HAVE A DATE, SO YOU'LL BE OUT ALL NIGHT! ♥
A DATE...? OUT ALL NIGHT!?
WHAAA!?

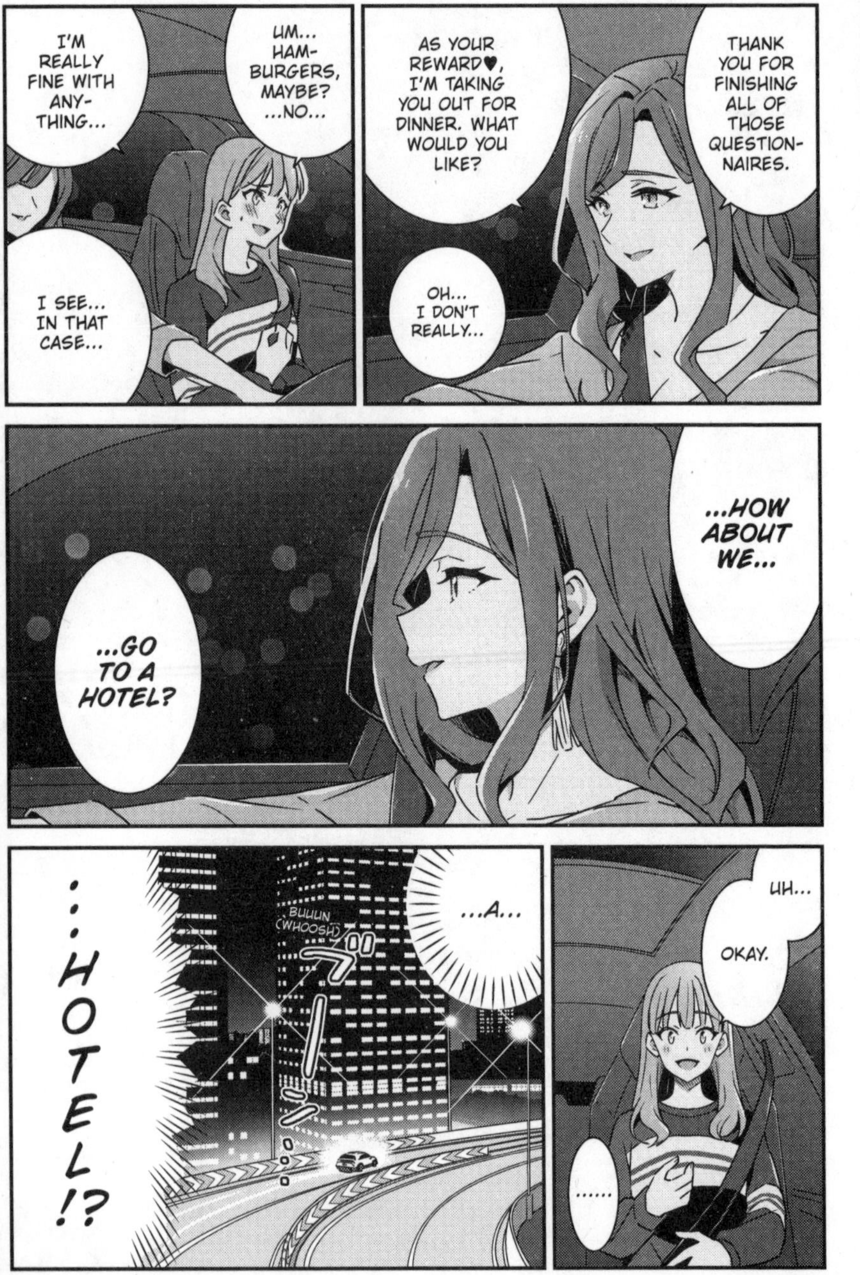
THANK YOU FOR FINISHING ALL OF THOSE QUESTIONNAIRES.
AS YOUR REWARD♥, I'M TAKING YOU OUT FOR DINNER. WHAT WOULD YOU LIKE?
OH... I DON'T REALLY...
UM... HAMBURGERS, MAYBE? ...NO...
I'M REALLY FINE WITH ANYTHING...
I SEE... IN THAT CASE...
...HOW ABOUT WE...
...GO TO A HOTEL?
UH...
OKAY.
......
...A...
BUUUN (WHOOSH)
...HOTEL!?

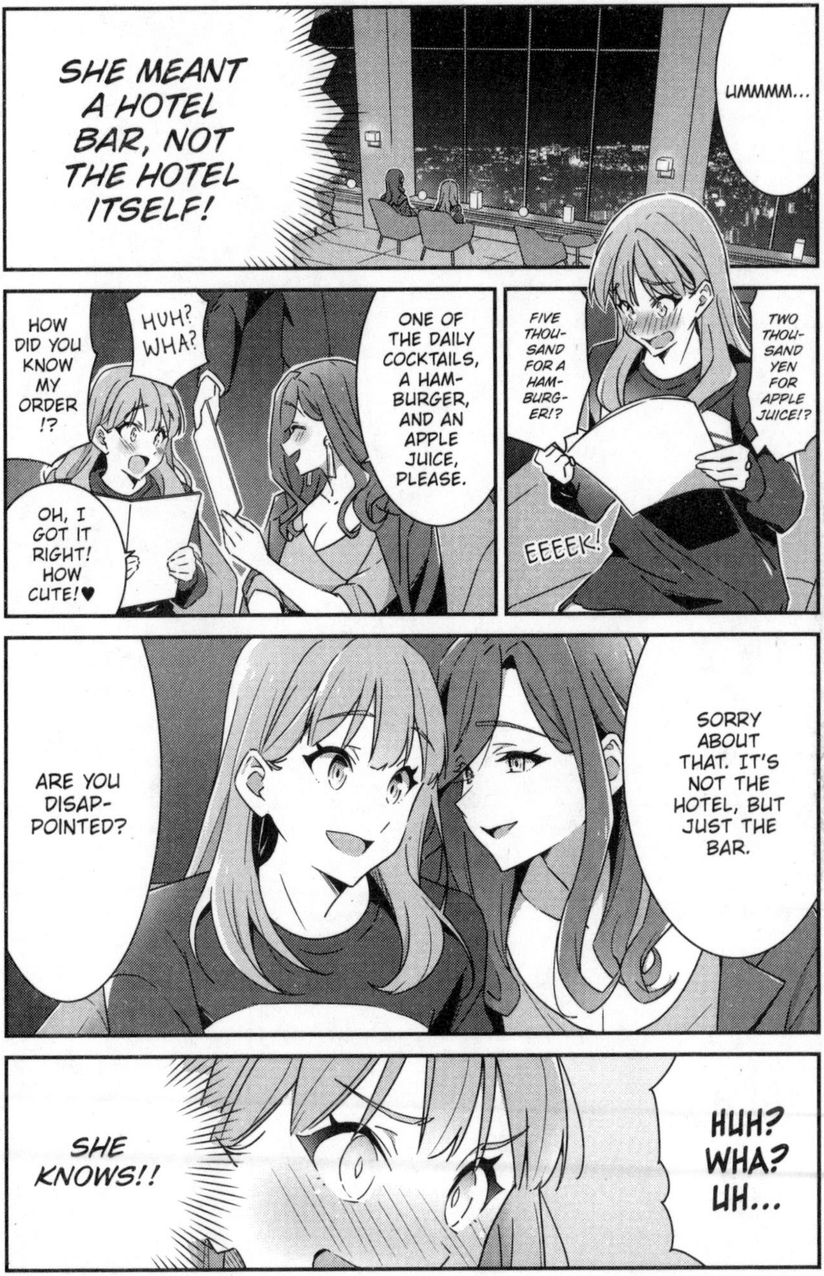
UMMMM...
SHE MEANT A HOTEL BAR, NOT THE HOTEL ITSELF!
TWO THOUSAND YEN FOR APPLE JUICE!?
FIVE THOUSAND FOR A HAMBURGER!?
EEEEK!
ONE OF THE DAILY COCKTAILS, A HAMBURGER, AND AN APPLE JUICE, PLEASE.
HUH? WHA?
HOW DID YOU KNOW MY ORDER!?
OH, I GOT IT RIGHT! HOW CUTE!♥
SORRY ABOUT THAT. IT'S NOT THE HOTEL, BUT JUST THE BAR.
ARE YOU DISAPPOINTED?
HUH? WHA? UH...
SHE KNOWS!!

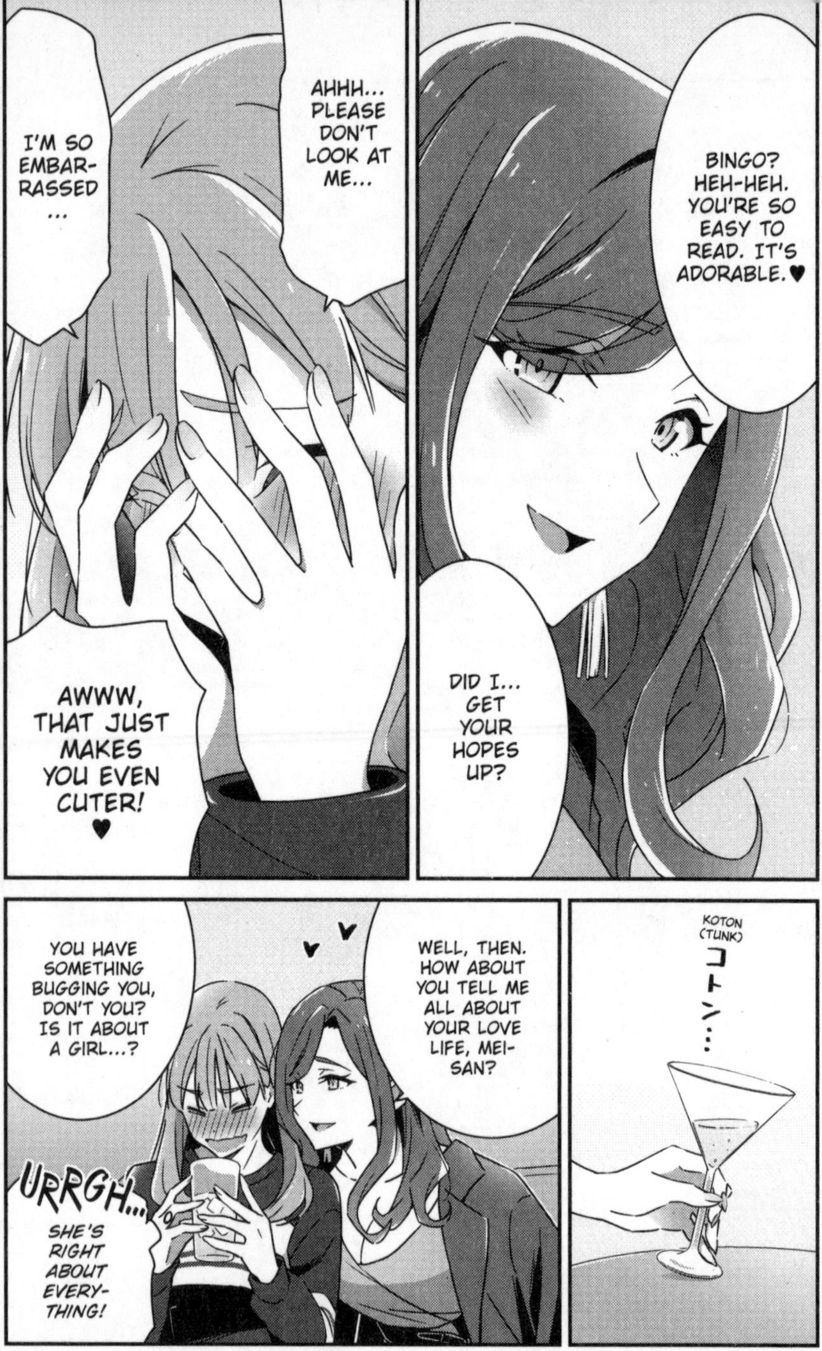
BINGO? HEH-HEH. YOU'RE SO EASY TO READ. IT'S ADORABLE.♥
DID I... GET YOUR HOPES UP?
AHHH... PLEASE DON'T LOOK AT ME...
I'M SO EMBAR-RASSED...
AWWW, THAT JUST MAKES YOU EVEN CUTER! ♥
KOTON (TUNK)
コトン…
WELL, THEN. HOW ABOUT YOU TELL ME ALL ABOUT YOUR LOVE LIFE, MEI-SAN?
YOU HAVE SOMETHING BUGGING YOU, DON'T YOU? IS IT ABOUT A GIRL...?
URRGH...
SHE'S RIGHT ABOUT EVERY-THING!

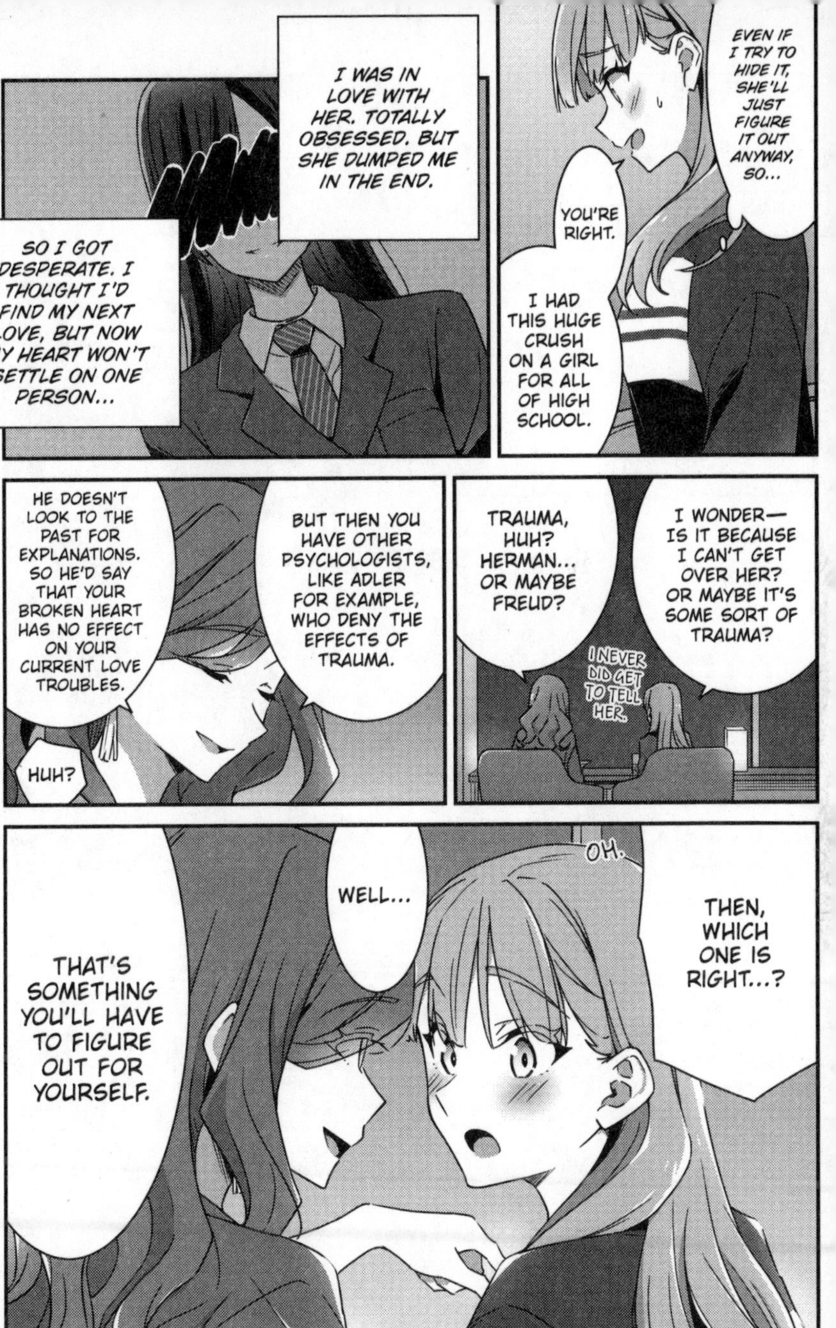
EVEN IF I TRY TO HIDE IT, SHE'LL JUST FIGURE IT OUT ANYWAY, SO...
YOU'RE RIGHT.
I HAD THIS HUGE CRUSH ON A GIRL FOR ALL OF HIGH SCHOOL.
I WAS IN LOVE WITH HER. TOTALLY OBSESSED. BUT SHE DUMPED ME IN THE END.
SO I GOT DESPERATE. I THOUGHT I'D FIND MY NEXT LOVE, BUT NOW MY HEART WON'T SETTLE ON ONE PERSON...
I WONDER— IS IT BECAUSE I CAN'T GET OVER HER? OR MAYBE IT'S SOME SORT OF TRAUMA?
TRAUMA, HUH? HERMAN... OR MAYBE FREUD?
I NEVER DID GET TO TELL HER.
BUT THEN YOU HAVE OTHER PSYCHOLOGISTS, LIKE ADLER FOR EXAMPLE, WHO DENY THE EFFECTS OF TRAUMA.
HE DOESN'T LOOK TO THE PAST FOR EXPLANATIONS. SO HE'D SAY THAT YOUR BROKEN HEART HAS NO EFFECT ON YOUR CURRENT LOVE TROUBLES.
HUH?
OH.
THEN, WHICH ONE IS RIGHT...?
WELL...
THAT'S SOMETHING YOU'LL HAVE TO FIGURE OUT FOR YOURSELF.

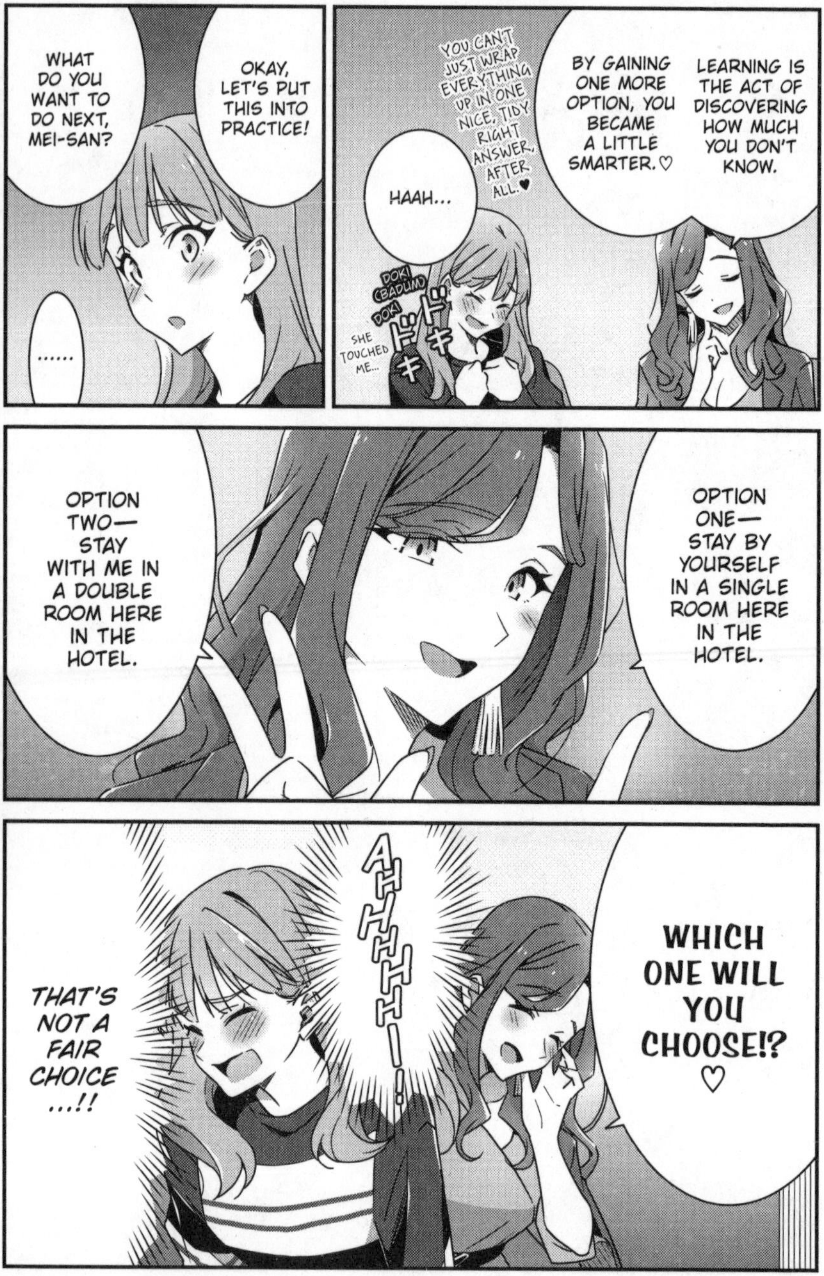
LEARNING IS THE ACT OF DISCOVERING HOW MUCH YOU DON'T KNOW.
BY GAINING ONE MORE OPTION, YOU BECAME A LITTLE SMARTER.♡
YOU CAN'T JUST WRAP EVERYTHING UP IN ONE NICE, TIDY RIGHT ANSWER, AFTER ALL.♥
HAAH...
DOKI (BADUM) DOKI
SHE TOUCHED ME...
OKAY, LET'S PUT THIS INTO PRACTICE!
WHAT DO YOU WANT TO DO NEXT, MEI-SAN?
......
OPTION ONE—STAY BY YOURSELF IN A SINGLE ROOM HERE IN THE HOTEL.
OPTION TWO—STAY WITH ME IN A DOUBLE ROOM HERE IN THE HOTEL.
WHICH ONE WILL YOU CHOOSE!? ♡
AHHHHHH—!!
THAT'S NOT A FAIR CHOICE...!!

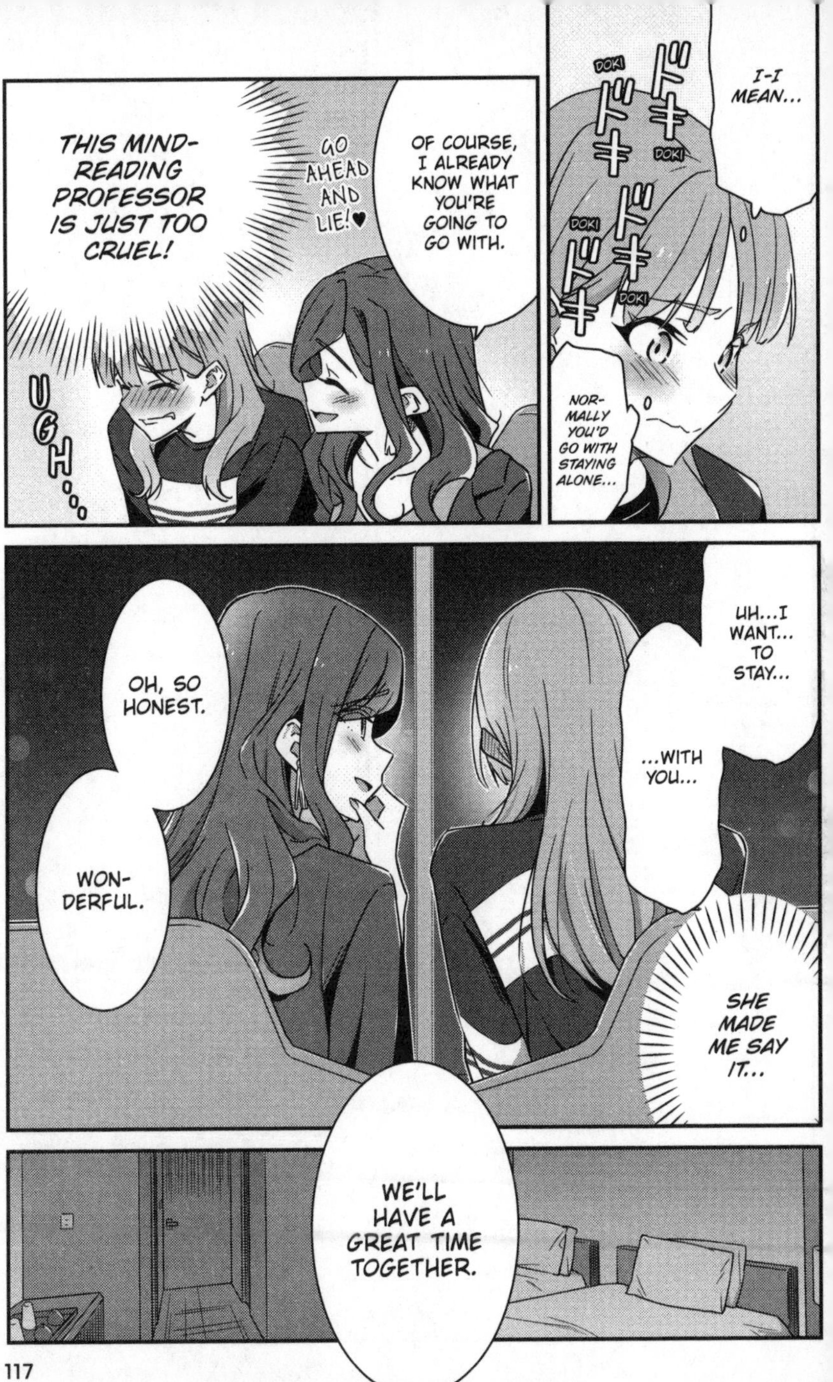
I-I MEAN...
ドキドキ
DOKI DOKI
ドキドキ
DOKI DOKI
NOR-MALLY YOU'D GO WITH STAYING ALONE...
OF COURSE, I ALREADY KNOW WHAT YOU'RE GOING TO GO WITH.
GO AHEAD AND LIE!♥
THIS MIND-READING PROFESSOR IS JUST TOO CRUEL!
UGH...
UH...I WANT... TO STAY...
...WITH YOU...
SHE MADE ME SAY IT...
OH, SO HONEST.
WON-DERFUL.
WE'LL HAVE A GREAT TIME TOGETHER.

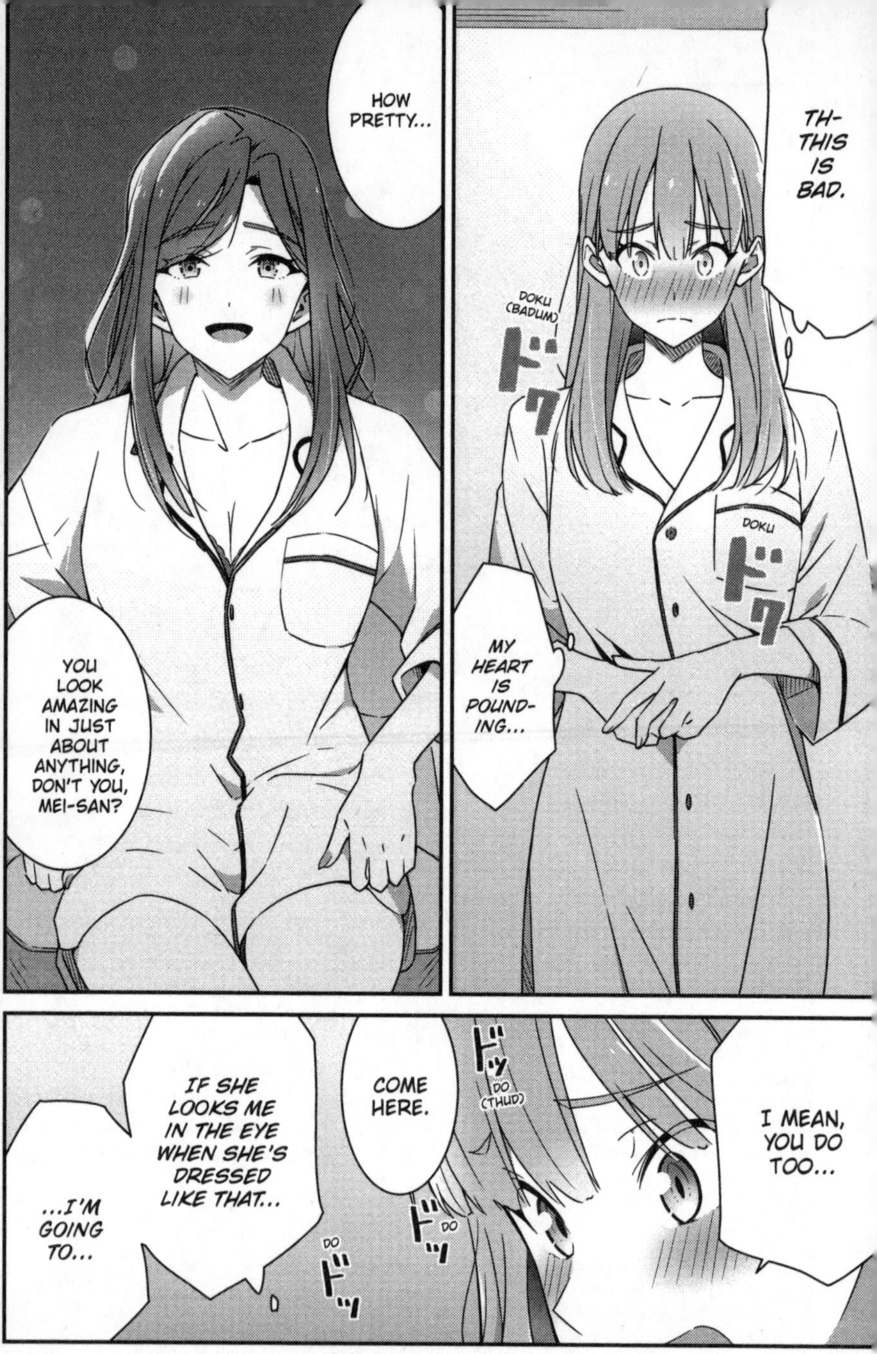
TH- THIS IS BAD.
DOKU (BADUM)
ドク
DOKU
ドク
MY HEART IS POUNDING...
HOW PRETTY...
YOU LOOK AMAZING IN JUST ABOUT ANYTHING, DON'T YOU, MEI-SAN?
I MEAN, YOU DO TOO...
ドッ
DO (THUD)
COME HERE.
ドッ
DO
ドッ
DO
IF SHE LOOKS ME IN THE EYE WHEN SHE'S DRESSED LIKE THAT...
...I'M GOING TO...

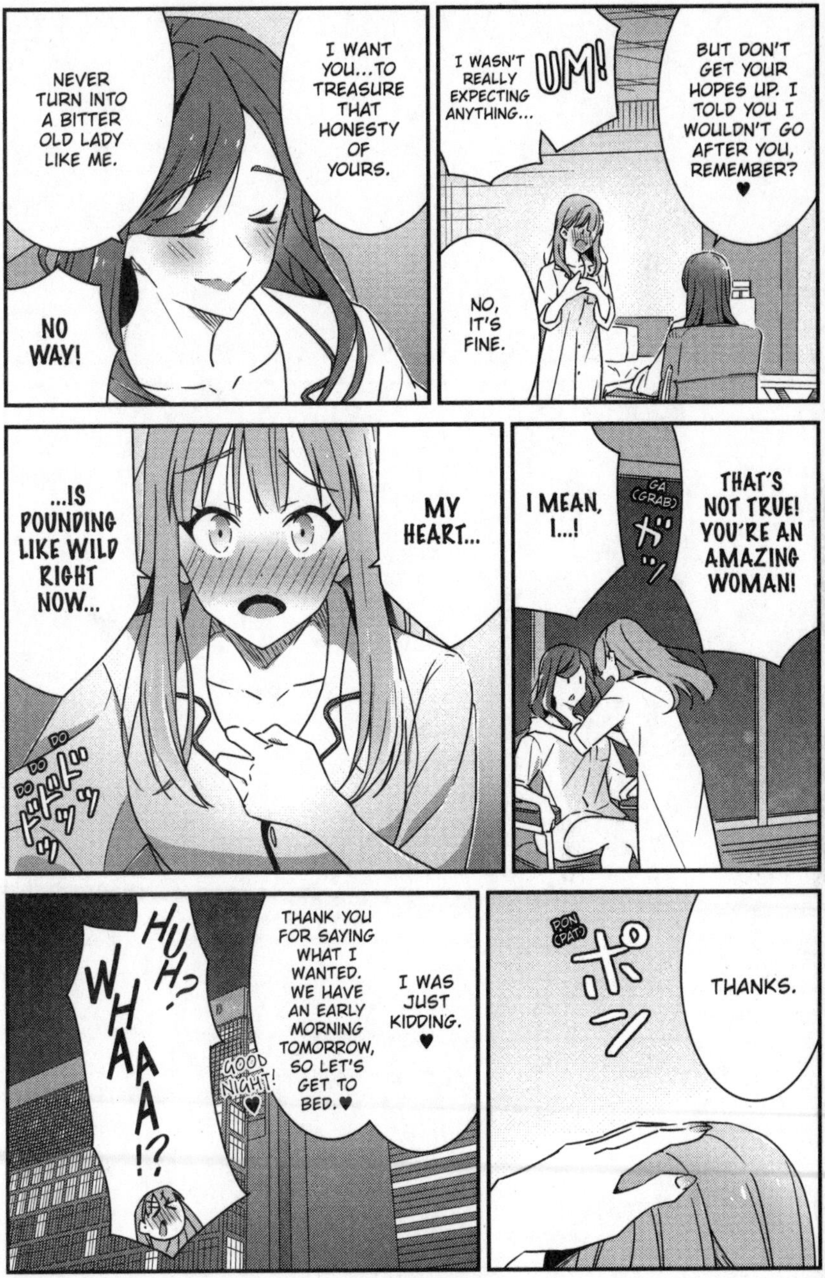
BUT DON'T GET YOUR HOPES UP. I TOLD YOU I WOULDN'T GO AFTER YOU, REMEMBER? ♥
UM!
I WASN'T REALLY EXPECTING ANYTHING...
NO, IT'S FINE.
I WANT YOU...TO TREASURE THAT HONESTY OF YOURS.
NEVER TURN INTO A BITTER OLD LADY LIKE ME.
NO WAY!
THAT'S NOT TRUE! YOU'RE AN AMAZING WOMAN!
GA (GRAB)
I MEAN, I...!
MY HEART...
...IS POUNDING LIKE WILD RIGHT NOW...
DO DO DO
PON (PAT)
THANKS.
I WAS JUST KIDDING. ♥
THANK YOU FOR SAYING WHAT I WANTED. WE HAVE AN EARLY MORNING TOMORROW, SO LET'S GET TO BED. ♥
HUH? WHAAAA!?
GOOD NIGHT! ♥

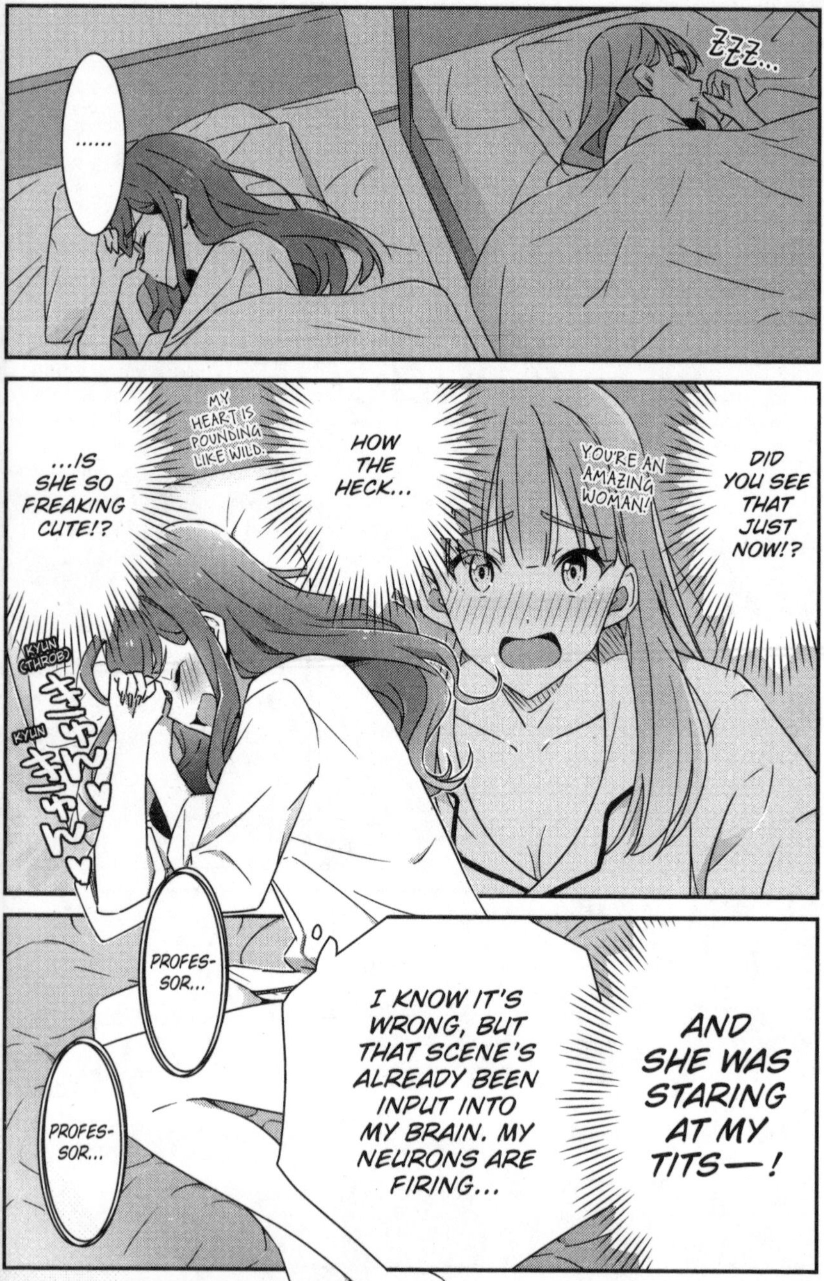

ZZZ...
......
DID YOU SEE THAT JUST NOW!?
YOU'RE AN AMAZING WOMAN!
HOW THE HECK...
MY HEART IS POUNDING LIKE WILD.
...IS SHE SO FREAKING CUTE!?
KYUN (THROB)
KYUN
AND SHE WAS STARING AT MY TITS—!
I KNOW IT'S WRONG, BUT THAT SCENE'S ALREADY BEEN INPUT INTO MY BRAIN. MY NEURONS ARE FIRING...
PROFES-SOR...
PROFES-SOR...

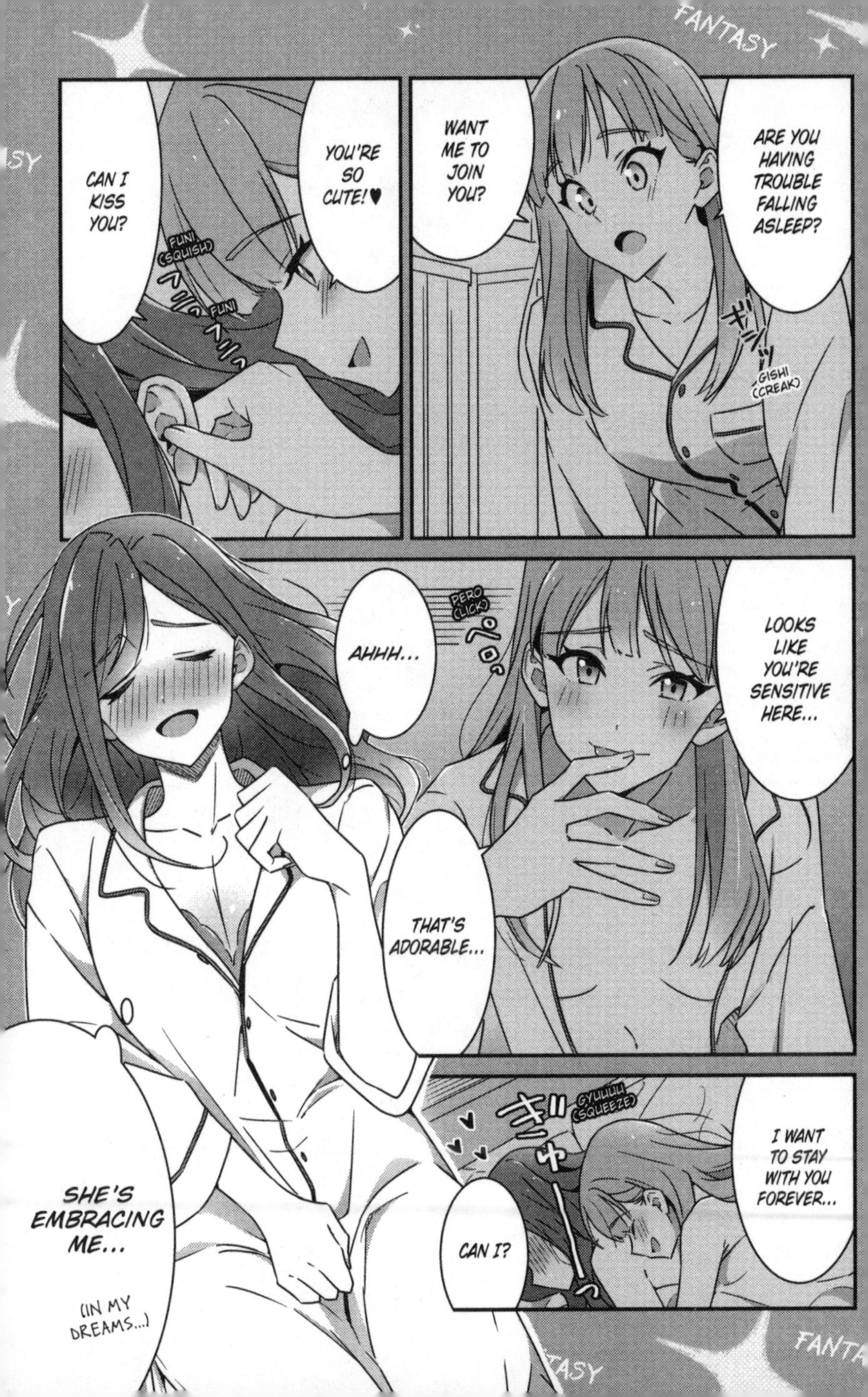
FANTASY
ARE YOU HAVING TROUBLE FALLING ASLEEP?
GISHI (CREAK)
WANT ME TO JOIN YOU?
YOU'RE SO CUTE!♥
FUNI (SQUISH)
FUNI
CAN I KISS YOU?
LOOKS LIKE YOU'RE SENSITIVE HERE...
PERO (LICK)
AHHH...
THAT'S ADORABLE...
I WANT TO STAY WITH YOU FOREVER...
GYUUUU (SQUEEZE)
CAN I?
SHE'S EMBRACING ME...
(IN MY DREAMS...)
FANTASY

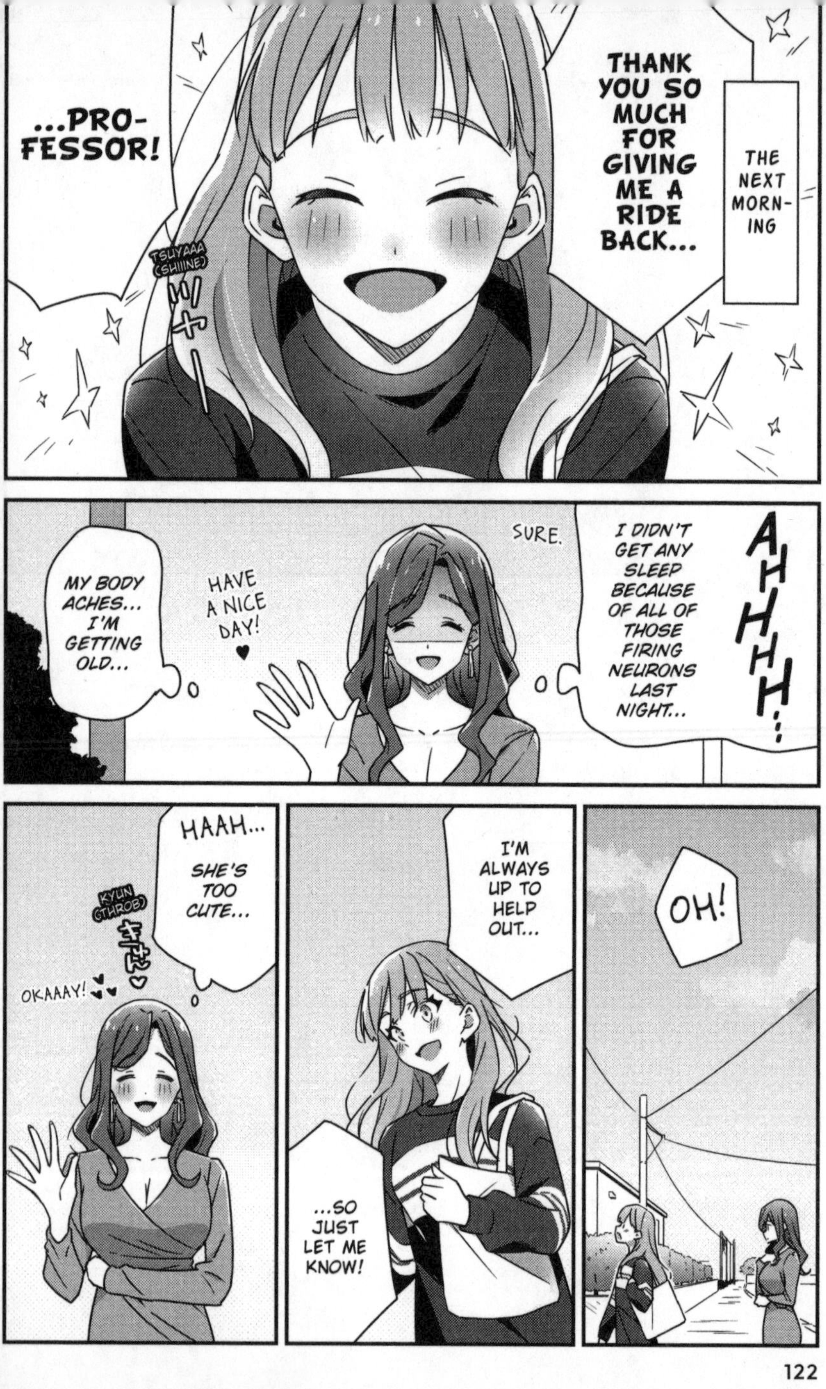
THE NEXT MORNING
THANK YOU SO MUCH FOR GIVING ME A RIDE BACK...
...PRO-FESSOR!
TSUYAAA (SHIIINE)
AHHHH..
I DIDN'T GET ANY SLEEP BECAUSE OF ALL OF THOSE FIRING NEURONS LAST NIGHT...
SURE.
HAVE A NICE DAY! ♥
MY BODY ACHES... I'M GETTING OLD...
OH!
I'M ALWAYS UP TO HELP OUT...
...SO JUST LET ME KNOW!
HAAH... SHE'S TOO CUTE...
KYUN (THROB)
OKAAAY!

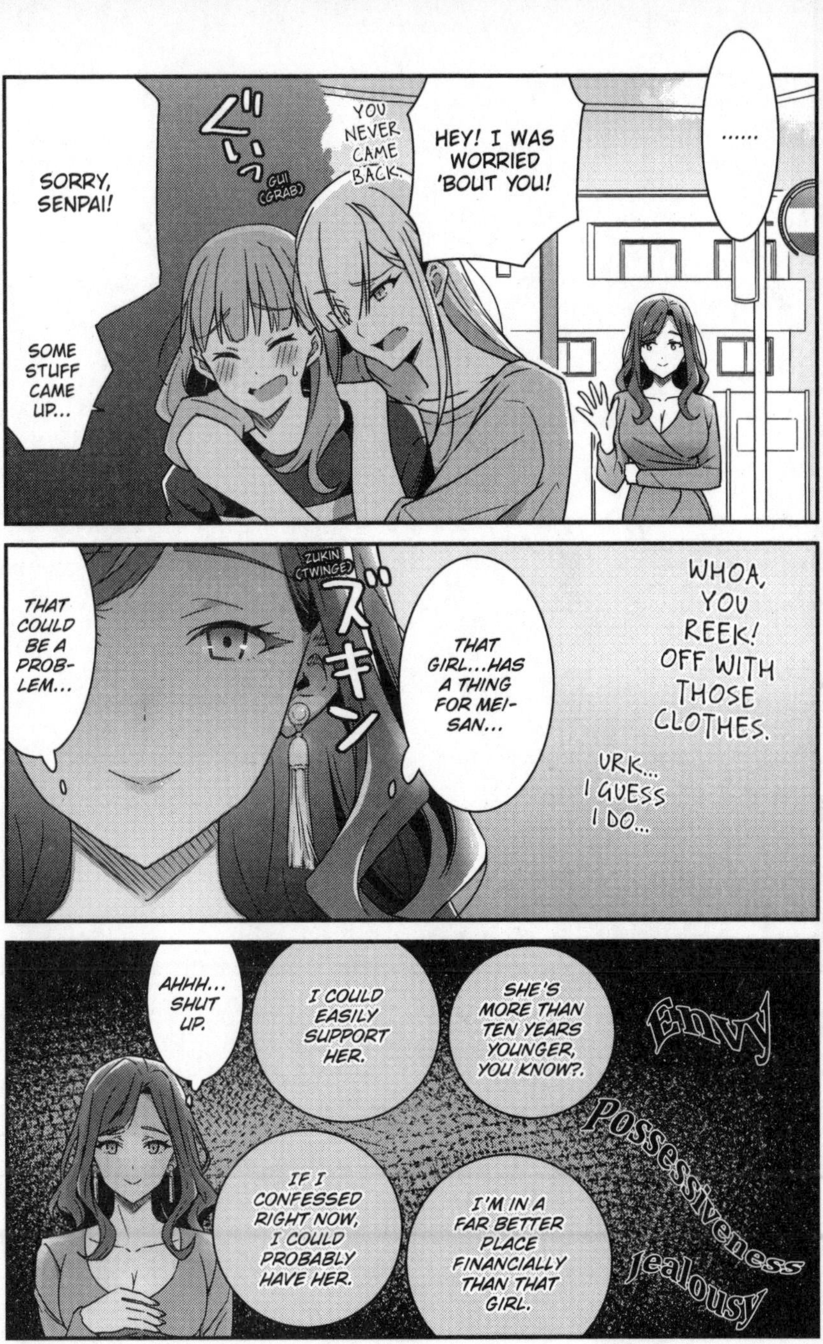
......
HEY! I WAS WORRIED 'BOUT YOU!
YOU NEVER CAME BACK.
ぐいっ
GUI (GRAB)
SORRY, SENPAI!
SOME STUFF CAME UP...
WHOA, YOU REEK! OFF WITH THOSE CLOTHES.
URK... I GUESS I DO...
THAT GIRL...HAS A THING FOR MEI-SAN...
ズキン
ZUKIN (TWINGE)
THAT COULD BE A PROBLEM...
Envy
Possessiveness
Jealousy
SHE'S MORE THAN TEN YEARS YOUNGER, YOU KNOW?.
I COULD EASILY SUPPORT HER.
AHHH... SHUT UP.
I'M IN A FAR BETTER PLACE FINANCIALLY THAN THAT GIRL.
IF I CONFESSED RIGHT NOW, I COULD PROBABLY HAVE HER.

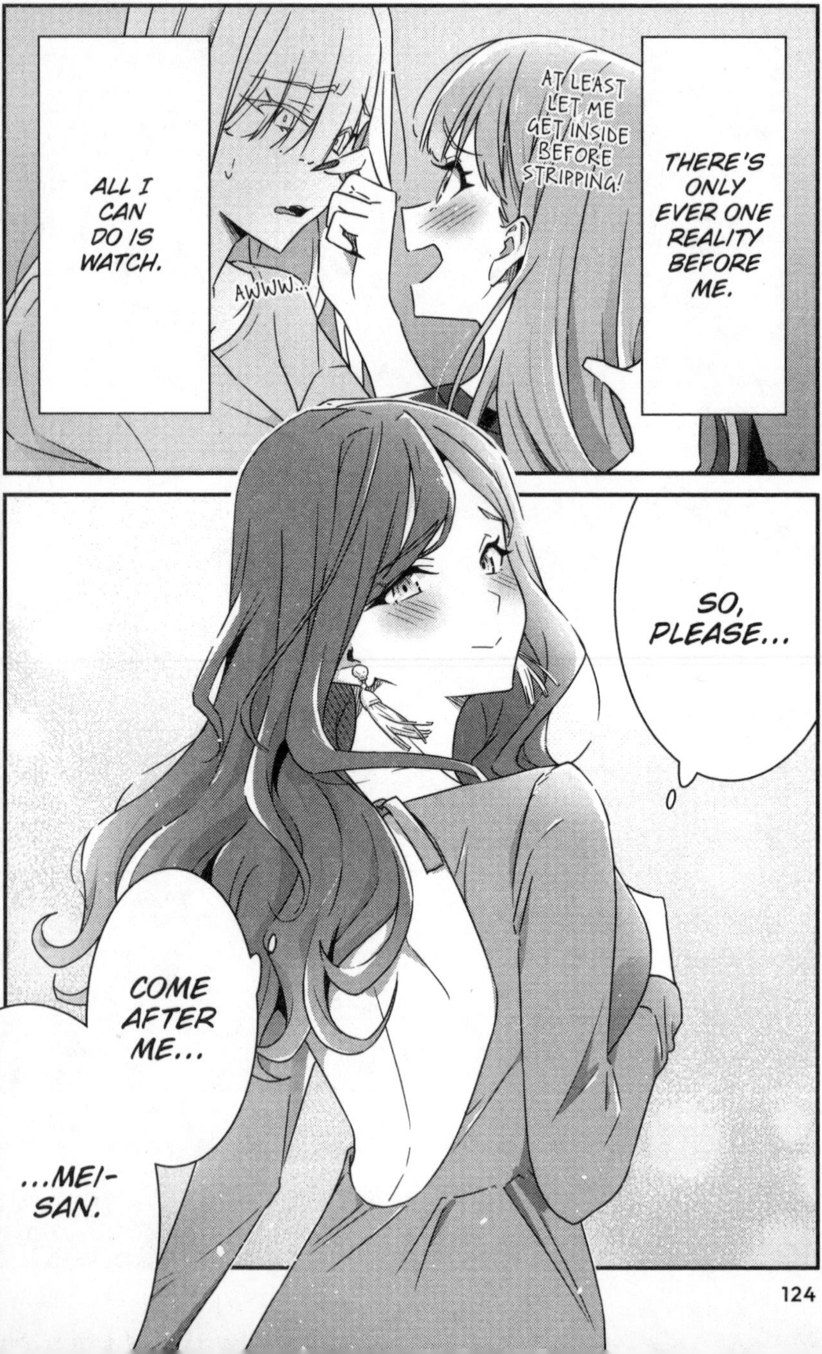
THERE'S ONLY EVER ONE REALITY BEFORE ME.
AT LEAST LET ME GET INSIDE BEFORE STRIPPING!
AWWW...
ALL I CAN DO IS WATCH.
SO, PLEASE...
COME AFTER ME...
...MEI-SAN.

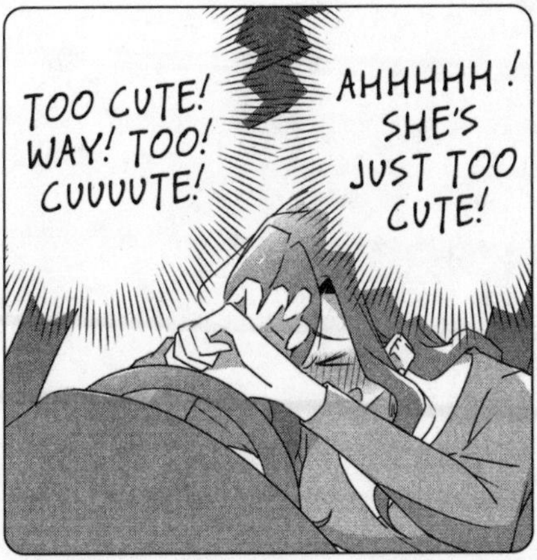
AHHHHH! SHE'S JUST TOO CUTE!
TOO CUTE! WAY! TOO! CUUUUTE!

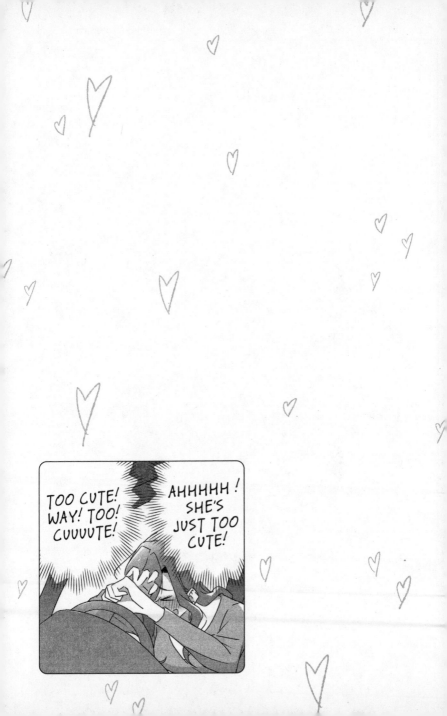

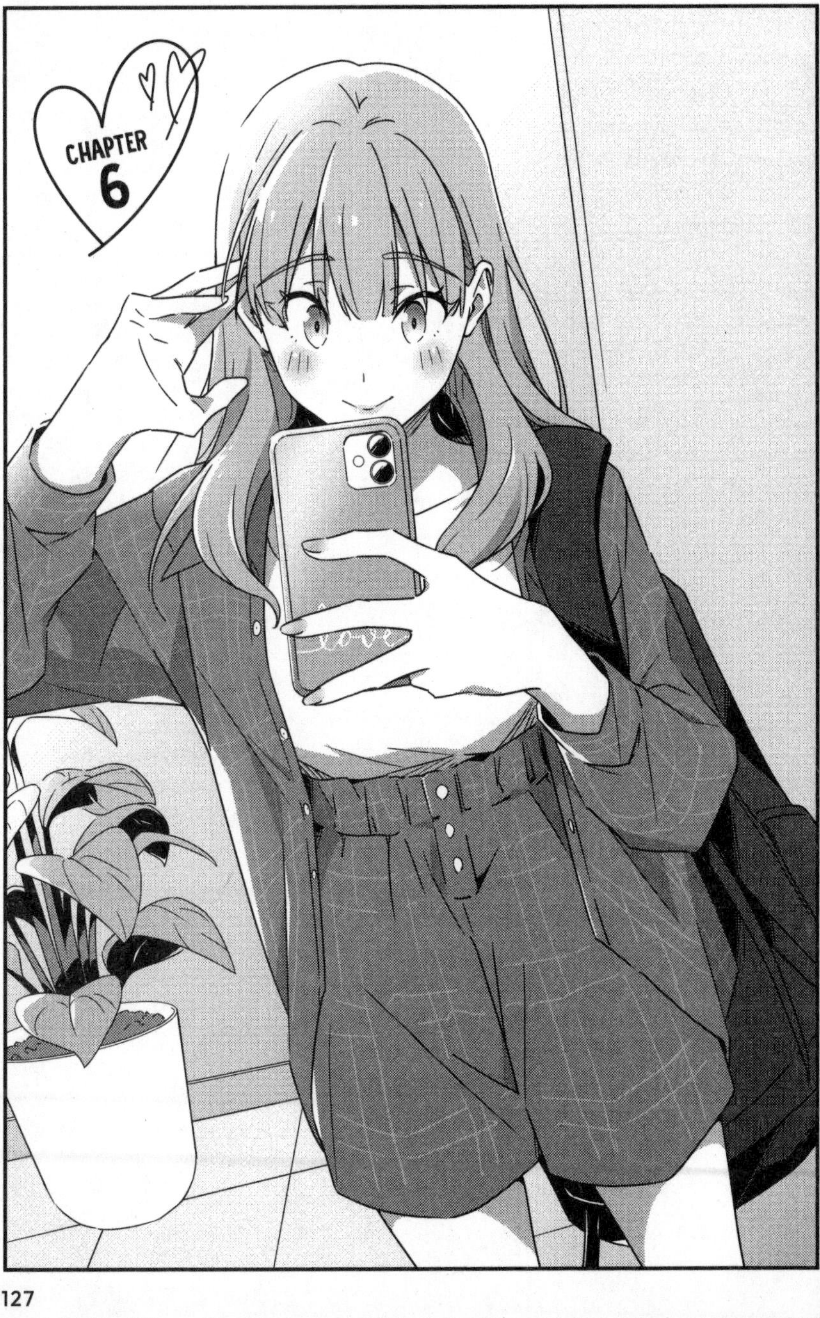
CHAPTER 6
love

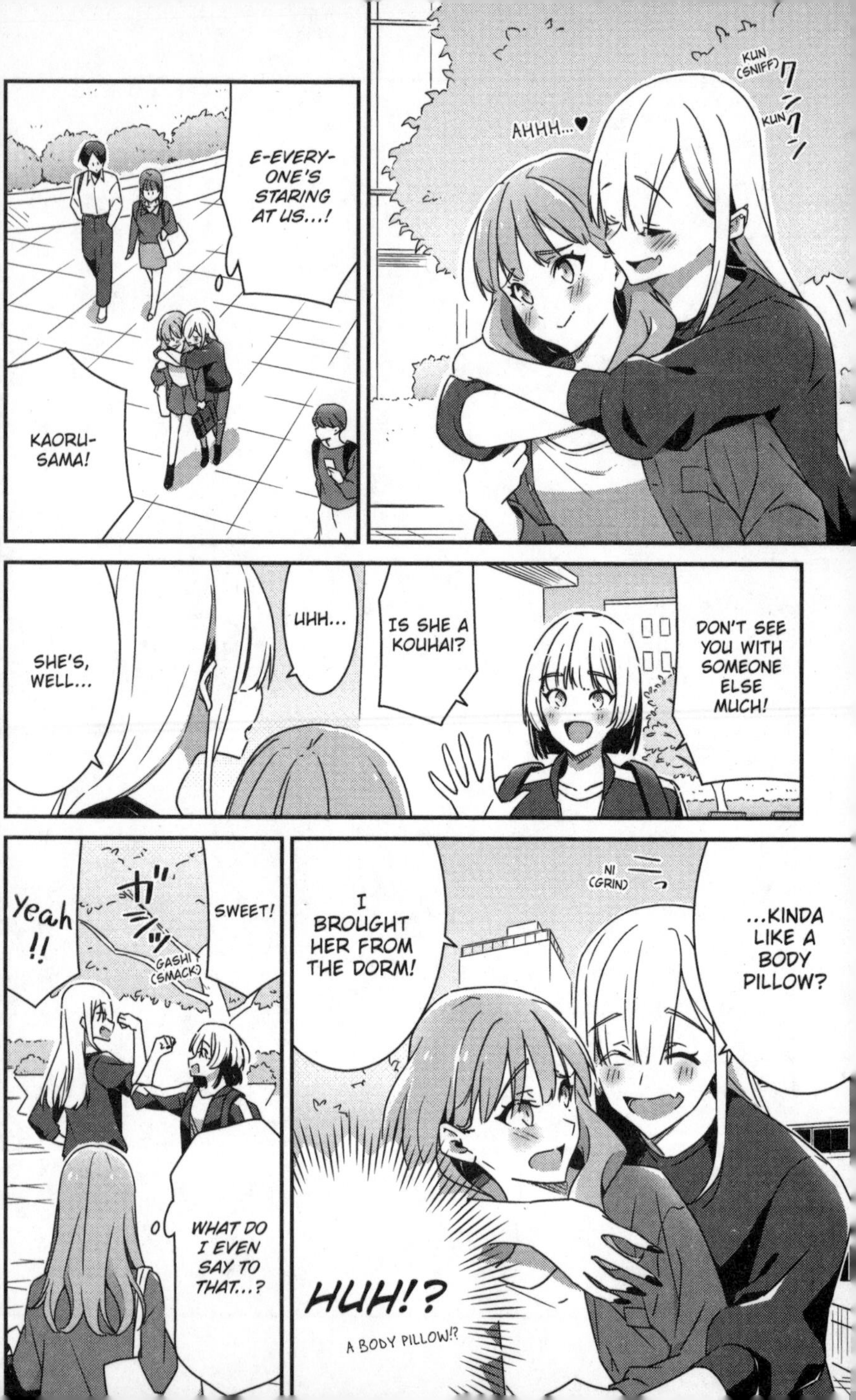
KUN (SNIFF)
KUN
AHHH...♥
E-EVERYONE'S STARING AT US...!
KAORU-SAMA!
DON'T SEE YOU WITH SOMEONE ELSE MUCH!
IS SHE A KOUHAI?
UHH...
SHE'S, WELL...
...KINDA LIKE A BODY PILLOW?
NI (GRIN)
I BROUGHT HER FROM THE DORM!
HUH!?
A BODY PILLOW!?
SWEET!
Yeah!!
GASHI (SMACK)
WHAT DO I EVEN SAY TO THAT...?

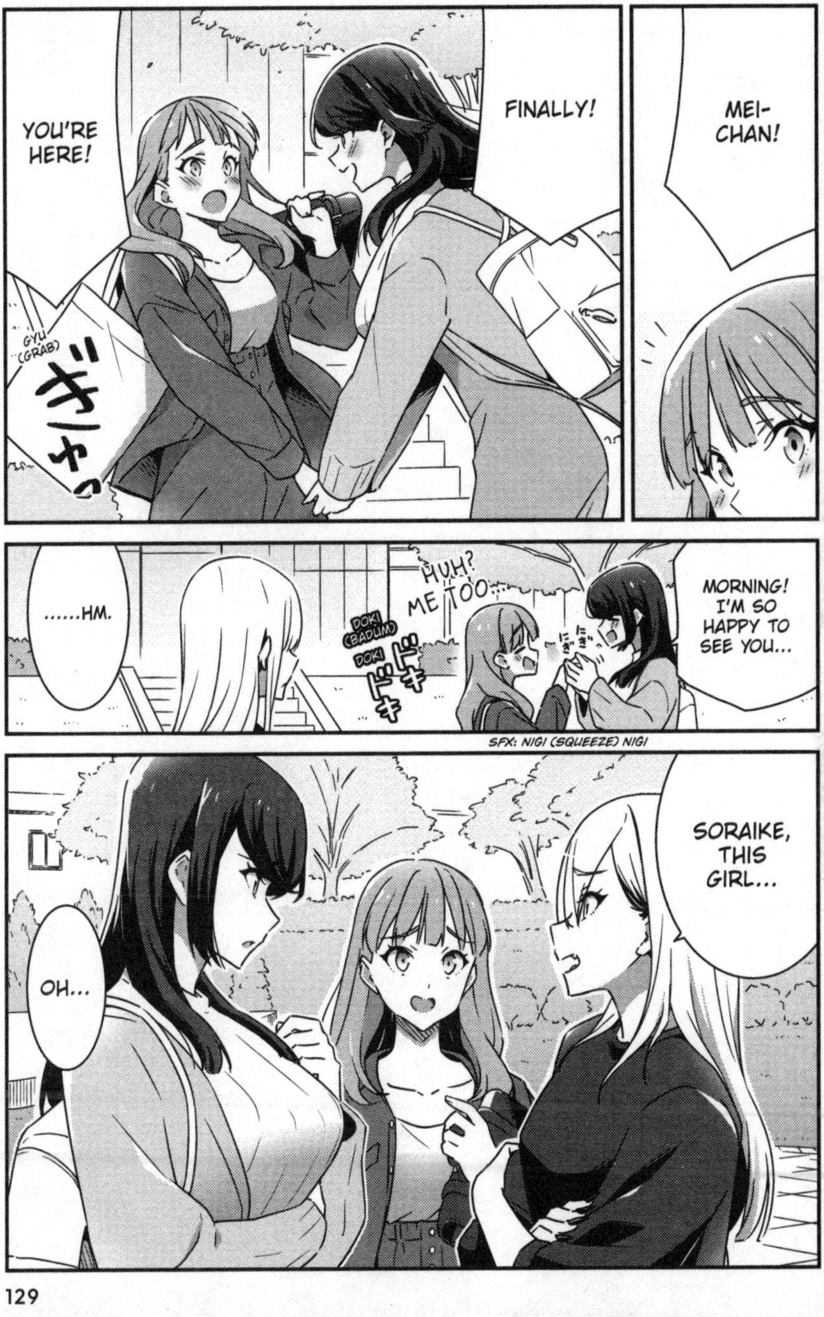
MEI-CHAN!
FINALLY!
YOU'RE HERE!
GYU (GRAB)
ぎゅっ
MORNING! I'M SO HAPPY TO SEE YOU...
HUH? ME TOO...
にぎにぎ
DOKI (BADUM) DOKI
ドキドキ
......HM.
SFX: NIGI (SQUEEZE) NIGI
SORAIKE, THIS GIRL...
OH...

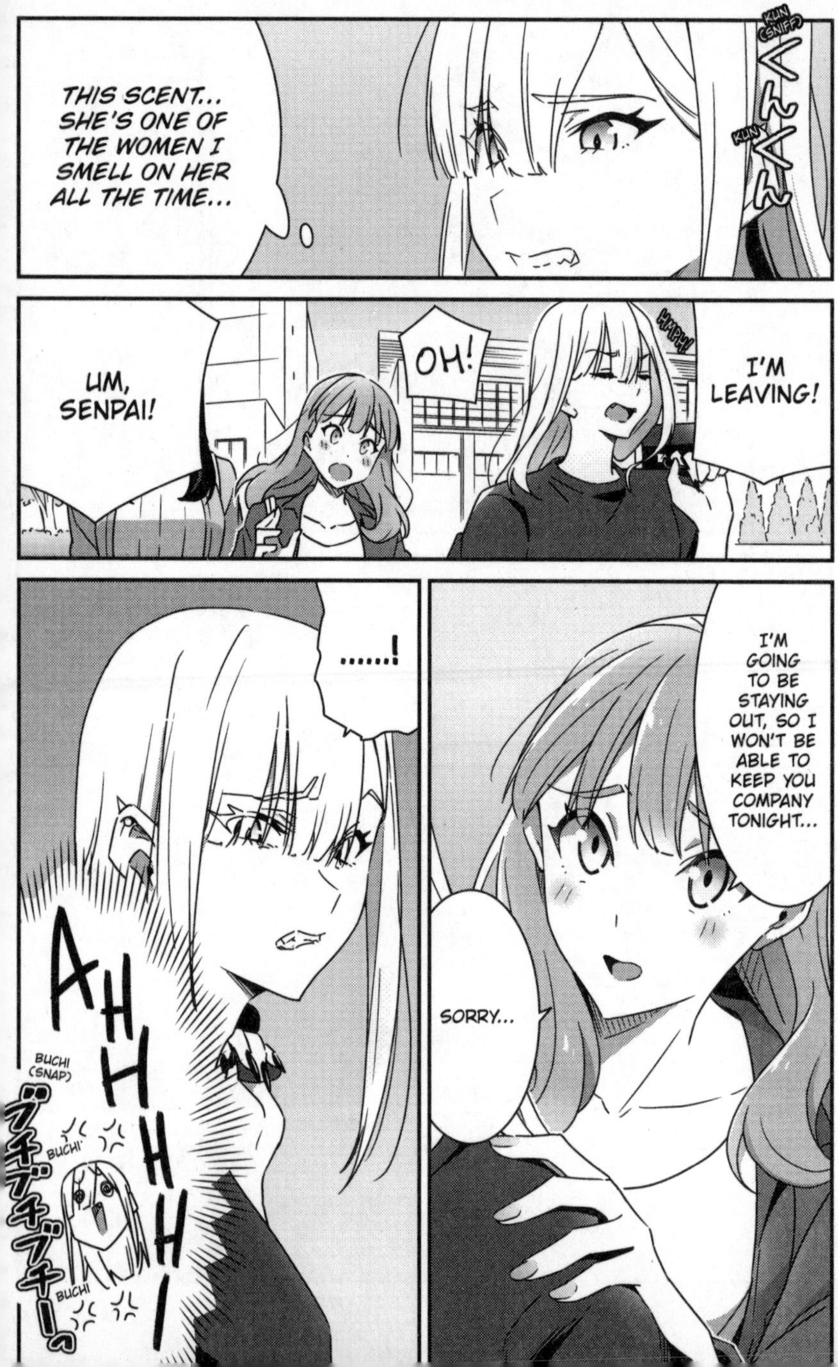
くんくんくん
KUN (SNIFF)
KUN
THIS SCENT... SHE'S ONE OF THE WOMEN I SMELL ON HER ALL THE TIME...
I'M LEAVING!
HMPH!
OH!
UM, SENPAI!
I'M GOING TO BE STAYING OUT, SO I WON'T BE ABLE TO KEEP YOU COMPANY TONIGHT...
SORRY...
......!
AHHHHHH!
ブチブチブチーっ
BUCHI (SNAP)
BUCHI
BUCHI

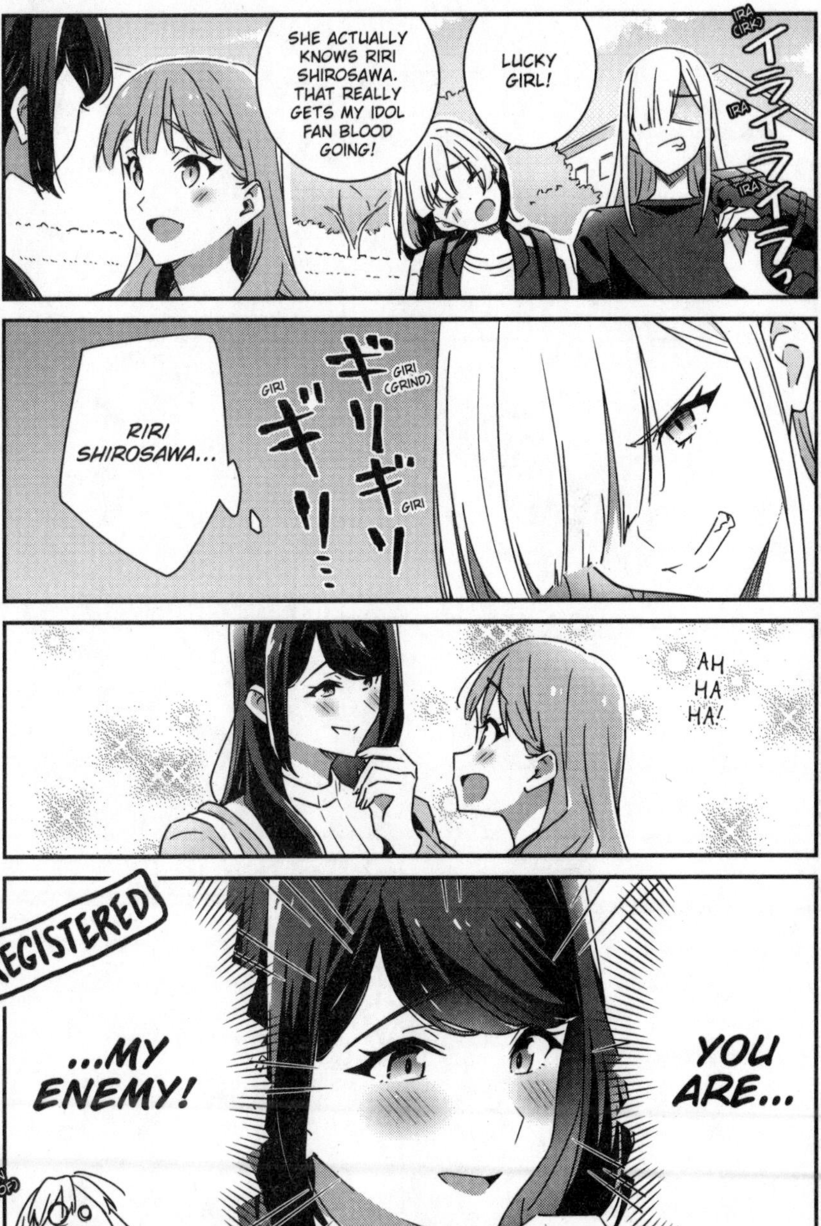
IRA (IRK)
IRA
IRA
LUCKY GIRL!
SHE ACTUALLY KNOWS RIRI SHIROSAWA. THAT REALLY GETS MY IDOL FAN BLOOD GOING!
GIRI (GRIND)
GIRI
GIRI
RIRI SHIROSAWA...
AH HA HA!
YOU ARE...
...MY ENEMY!
REGISTERED
PON (POOF)

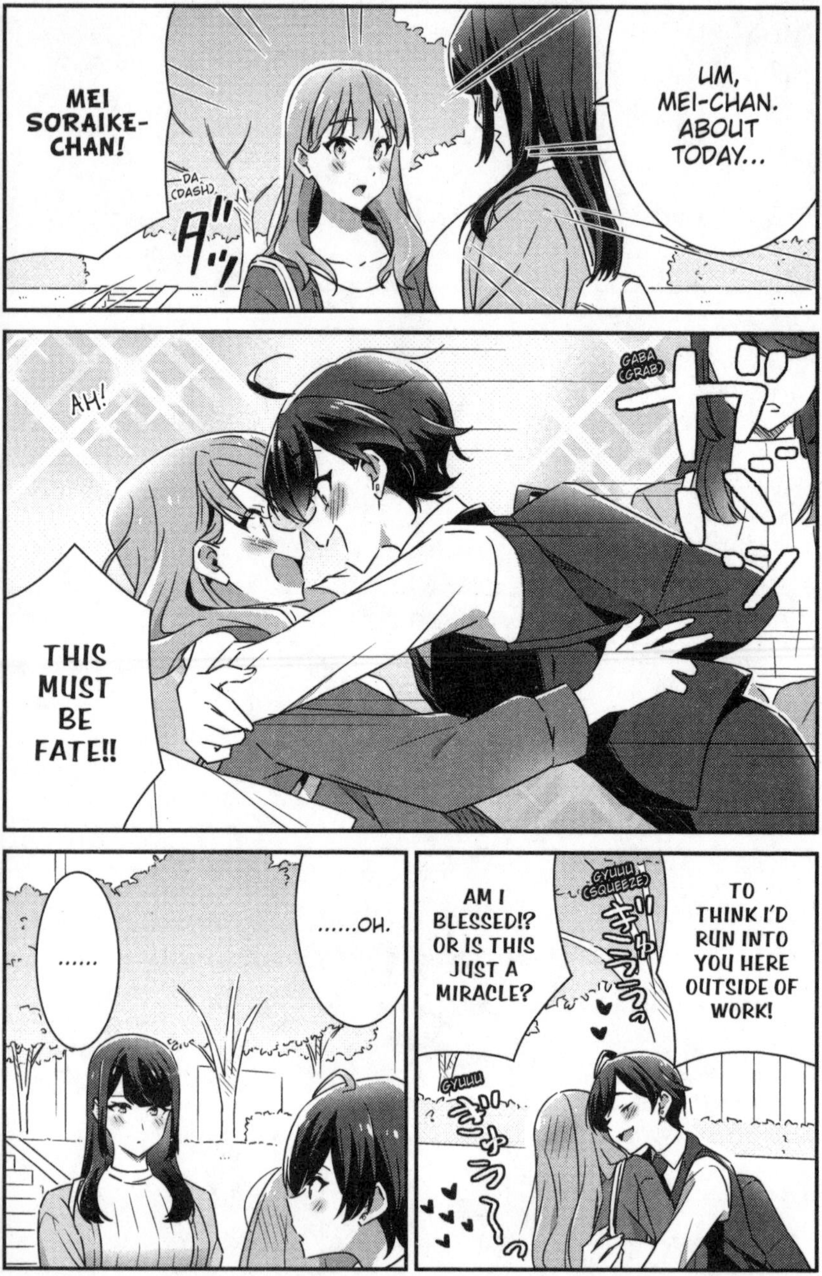
UM, MEI-CHAN. ABOUT TODAY...
MEI SORAIKE-CHAN!
DA (DASH)
GABA (GRAB)
AH!
THIS MUST BE FATE!!
TO THINK I'D RUN INTO YOU HERE OUTSIDE OF WORK!
GYUUU (SQUEEZE)
AM I BLESSED!? OR IS THIS JUST A MIRACLE?
GYUUU
......OH.
......

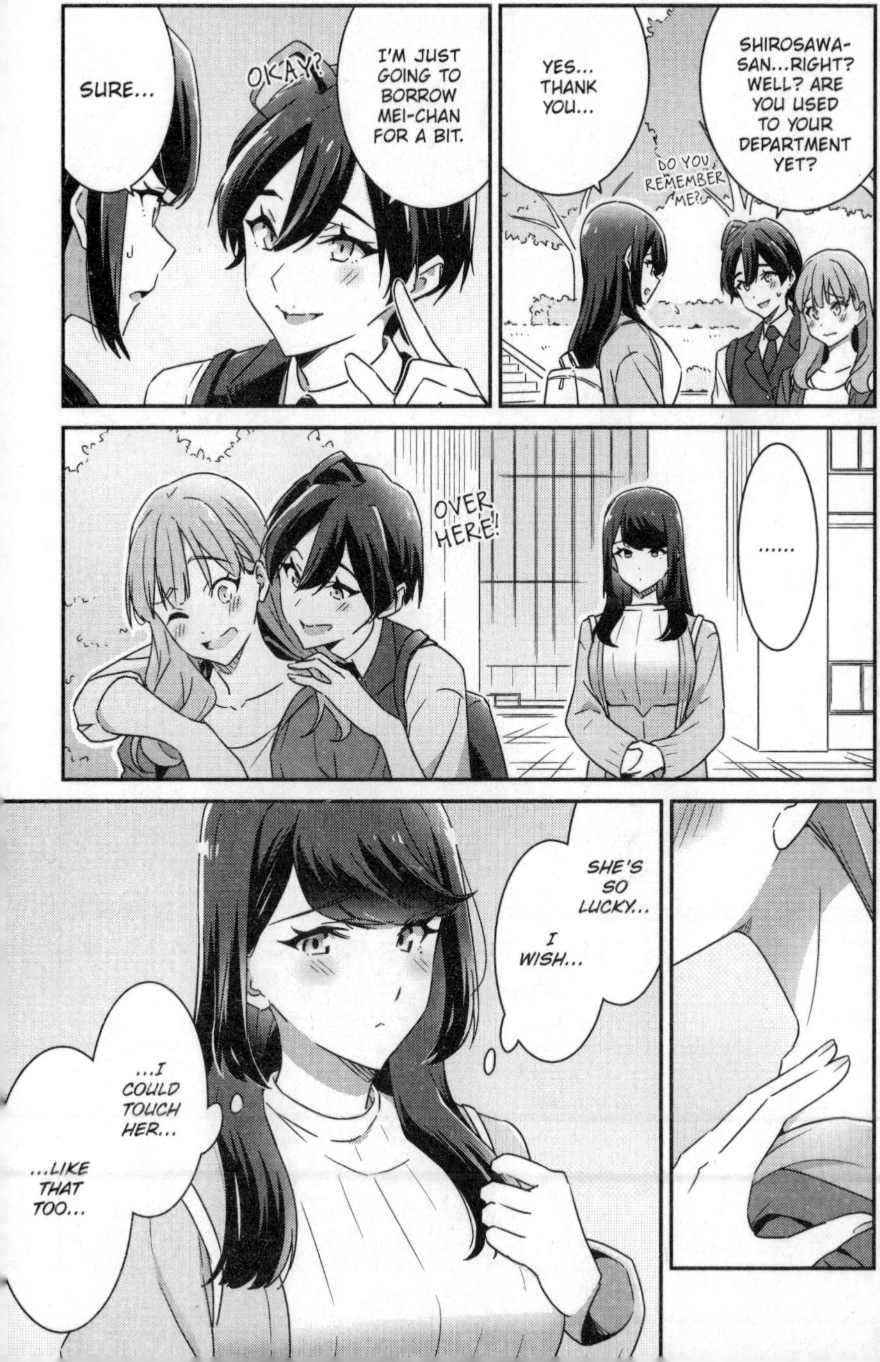
SHIROSAWA-SAN...RIGHT? WELL? ARE YOU USED TO YOUR DEPARTMENT YET?
DO YOU REMEMBER ME?
YES... THANK YOU...
I'M JUST GOING TO BORROW MEI-CHAN FOR A BIT.
OKAY?
SURE...
......
OVER HERE!
SHE'S SO LUCKY...
I WISH...
...I COULD TOUCH HER...
...LIKE THAT TOO...

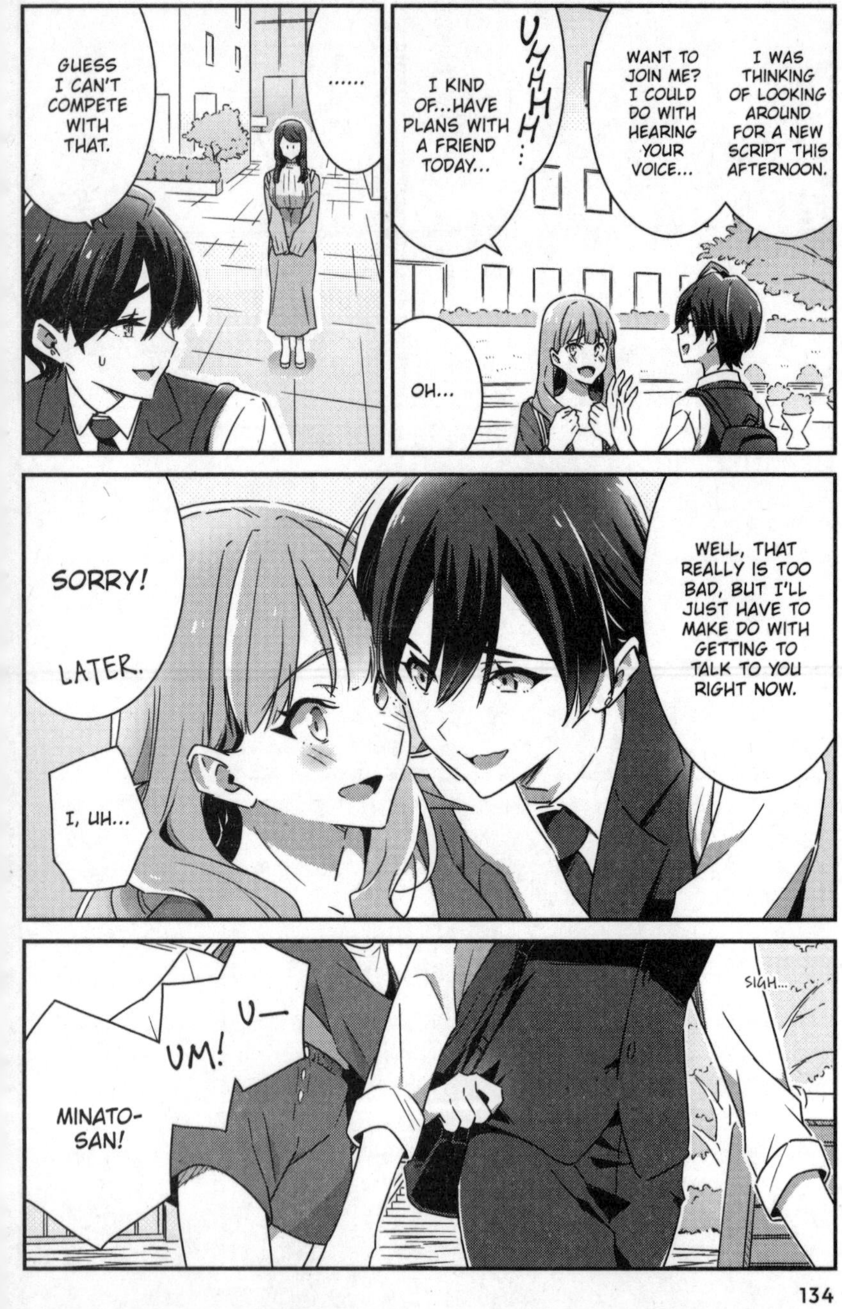
I WAS THINKING OF LOOKING AROUND FOR A NEW SCRIPT THIS AFTERNOON.
WANT TO JOIN ME? I COULD DO WITH HEARING YOUR VOICE...
UHHHH...
I KIND OF...HAVE PLANS WITH A FRIEND TODAY...
OH...
......
GUESS I CAN'T COMPETE WITH THAT.
WELL, THAT REALLY IS TOO BAD, BUT I'LL JUST HAVE TO MAKE DO WITH GETTING TO TALK TO YOU RIGHT NOW.
SORRY!
LATER.
I, UH...
SIGH...
U—
UM!
MINATO-SAN!

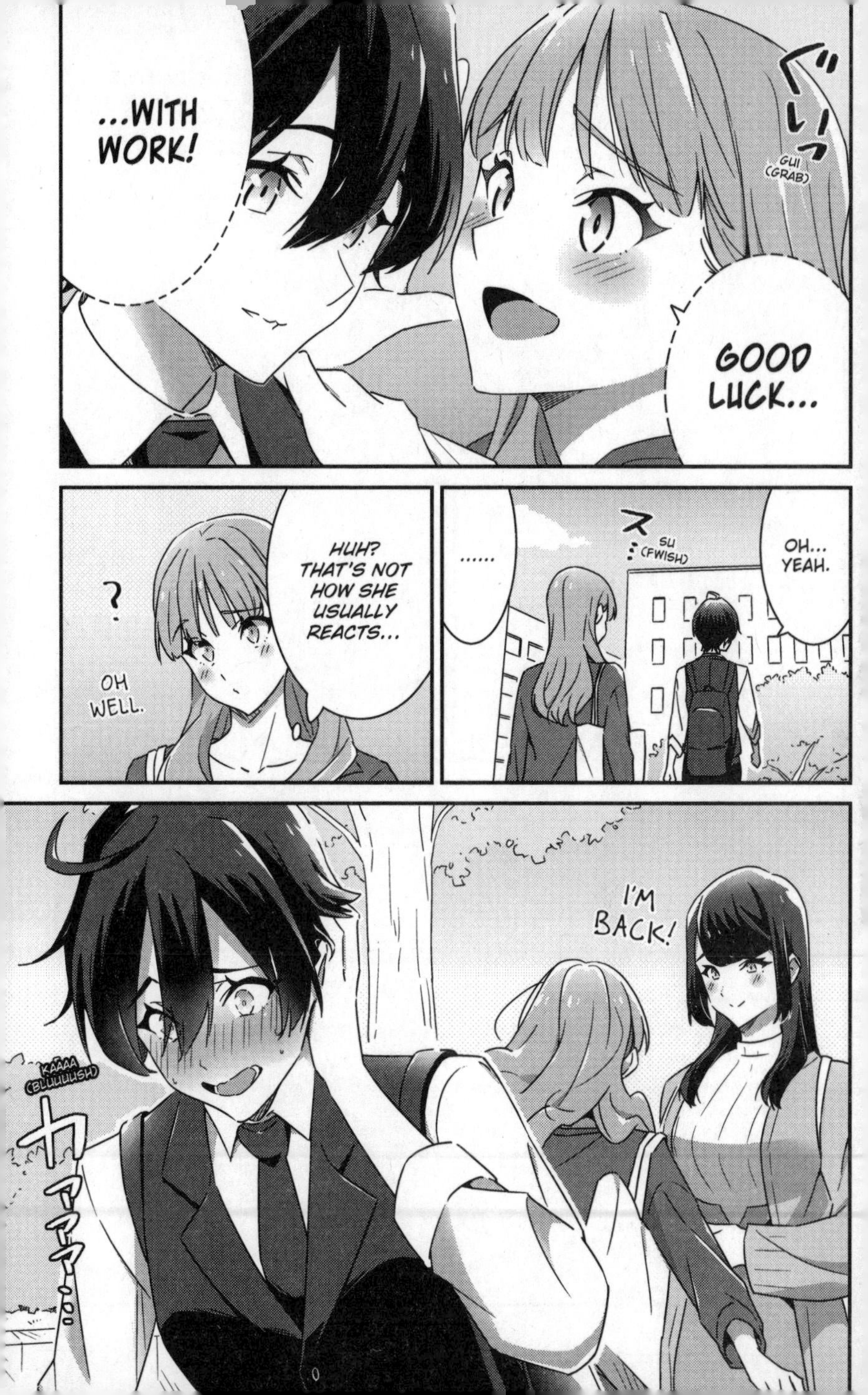
ぐいっ
GUI (GRAB)
GOOD LUCK...
...WITH WORK!
OH... YEAH.
ス
SU (FWISH)
......
HUH? THAT'S NOT HOW SHE USUALLY REACTS...
?
OH WELL.
I'M BACK!
KAAAA (BLUUUUSH)
カァァァ...

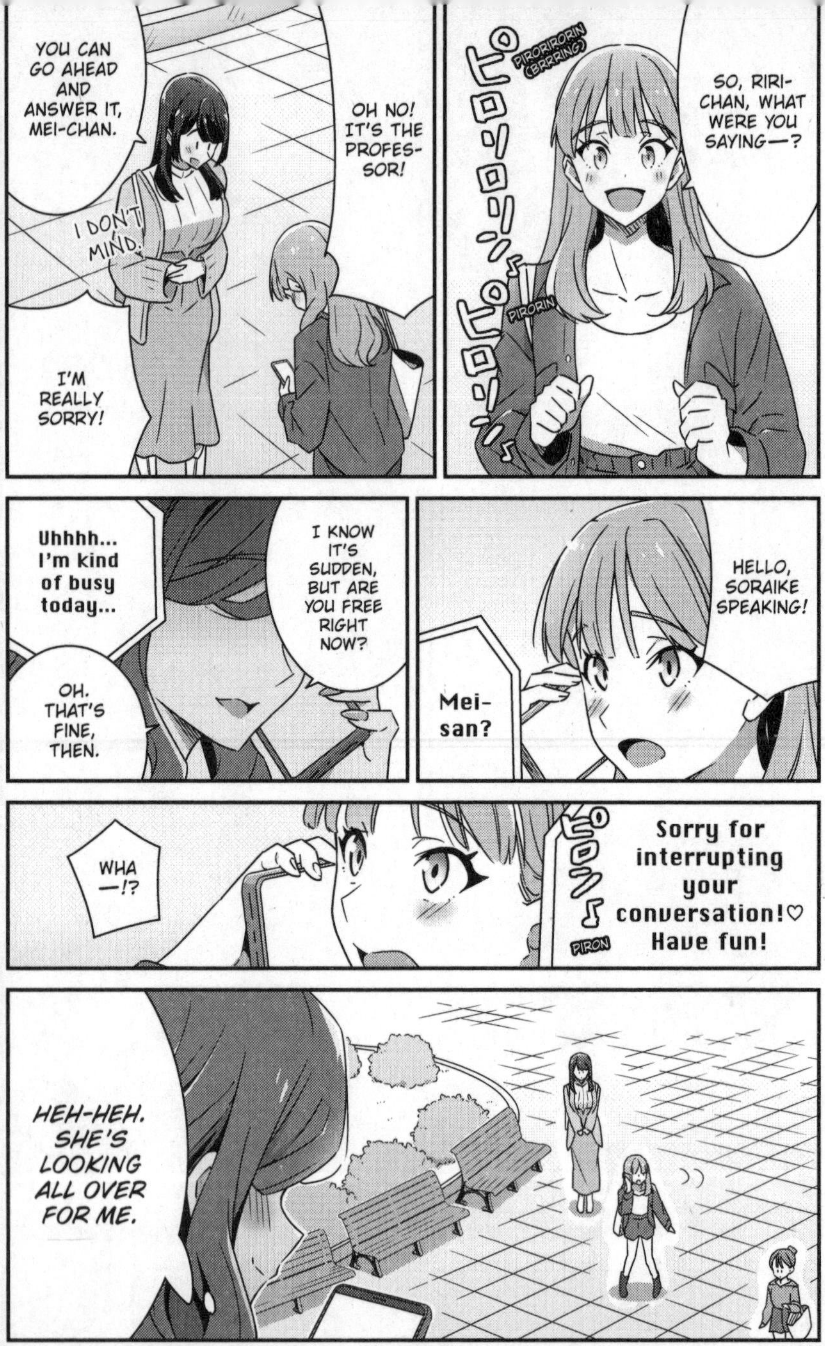

ピロリロリン♪
PIRORIRORIN (BRRRING)
SO, RIRI-CHAN, WHAT WERE YOU SAYING—?
ピロリン♪
PIRORIN
OH NO! IT'S THE PROFESSOR!
YOU CAN GO AHEAD AND ANSWER IT, MEI-CHAN.
I DON'T MIND.
I'M REALLY SORRY!
HELLO, SORAIKE SPEAKING!
Mei-san?
I KNOW IT'S SUDDEN, BUT ARE YOU FREE RIGHT NOW?
Uhhhh... I'm kind of busy today...
OH. THAT'S FINE, THEN.
ピロン♪
PIRON
Sorry for interrupting your conversation!♡ Have fun!
WHA—!?
HEH-HEH. SHE'S LOOKING ALL OVER FOR ME.

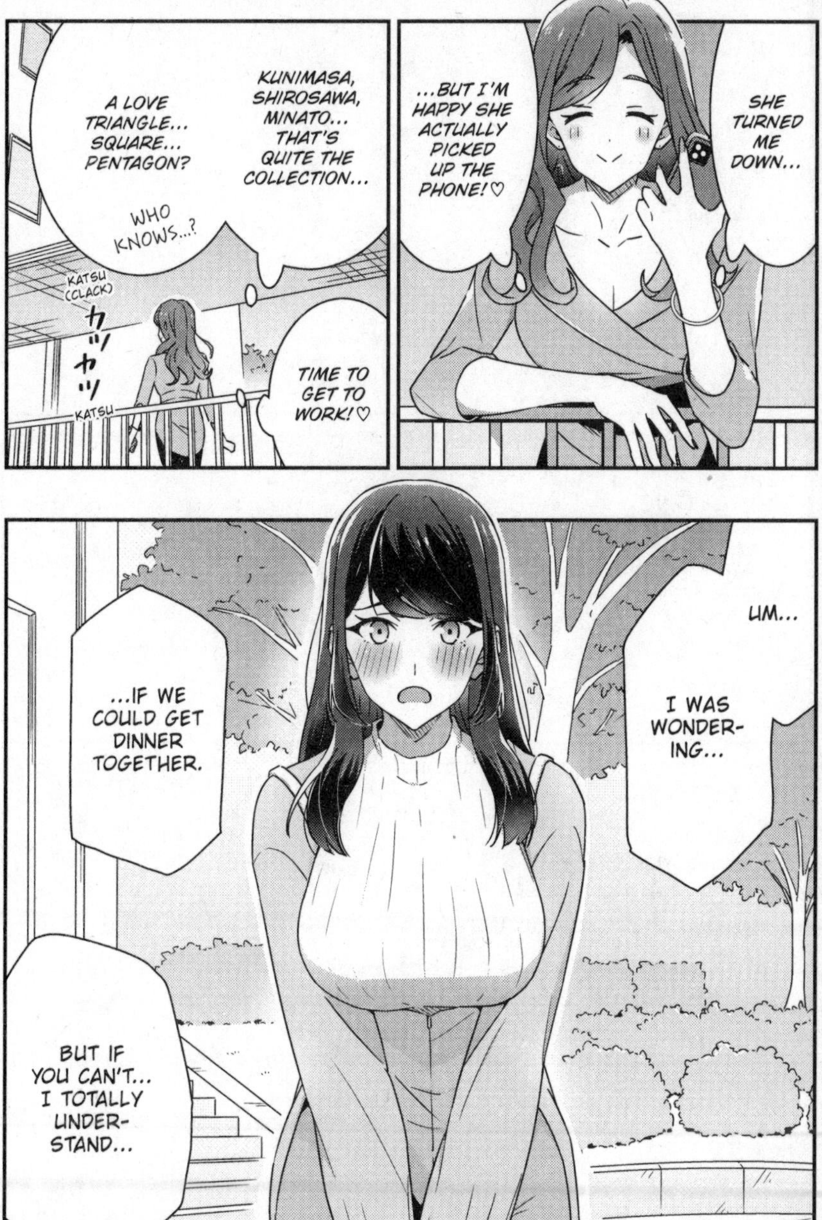
SHE TURNED ME DOWN...
...BUT I'M HAPPY SHE ACTUALLY PICKED UP THE PHONE! ♡
KUNIMASA, SHIROSAWA, MINATO... THAT'S QUITE THE COLLECTION...
A LOVE TRIANGLE... SQUARE... PENTAGON?
WHO KNOWS...?
TIME TO GET TO WORK! ♡
KATSU (CLACK)
カッ
カッ
KATSU
UM...
I WAS WONDER-ING...
...IF WE COULD GET DINNER TOGETHER.
BUT IF YOU CAN'T... I TOTALLY UNDER-STAND...

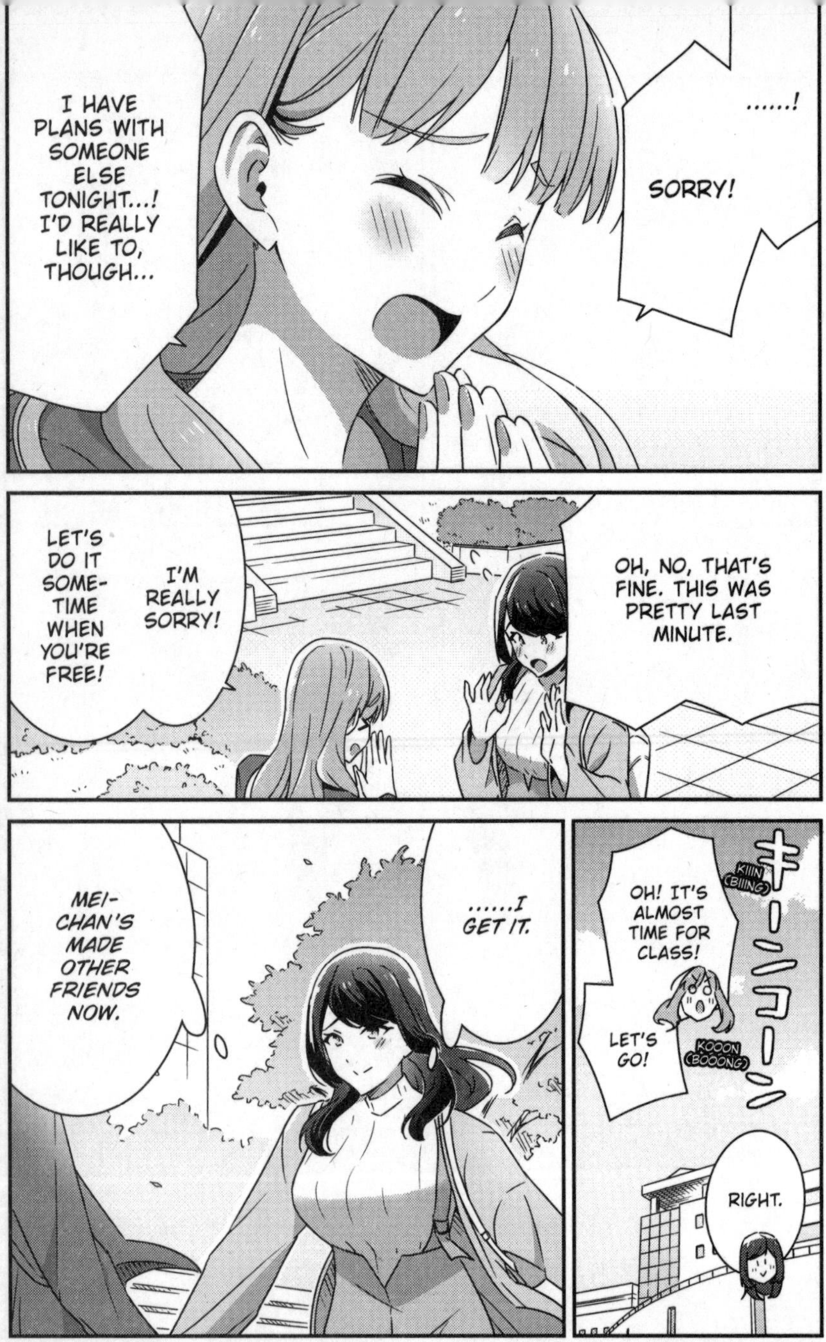
......!
SORRY!
I HAVE PLANS WITH SOMEONE ELSE TONIGHT...! I'D REALLY LIKE TO, THOUGH...
OH, NO, THAT'S FINE. THIS WAS PRETTY LAST MINUTE.
I'M REALLY SORRY!
LET'S DO IT SOME-TIME WHEN YOU'RE FREE!
KIIN (BIIING)
OH! IT'S ALMOST TIME FOR CLASS!
LET'S GO!
KOOON (BOOONG)
RIGHT.
......I GET IT.
MEI-CHAN'S MADE OTHER FRIENDS NOW.

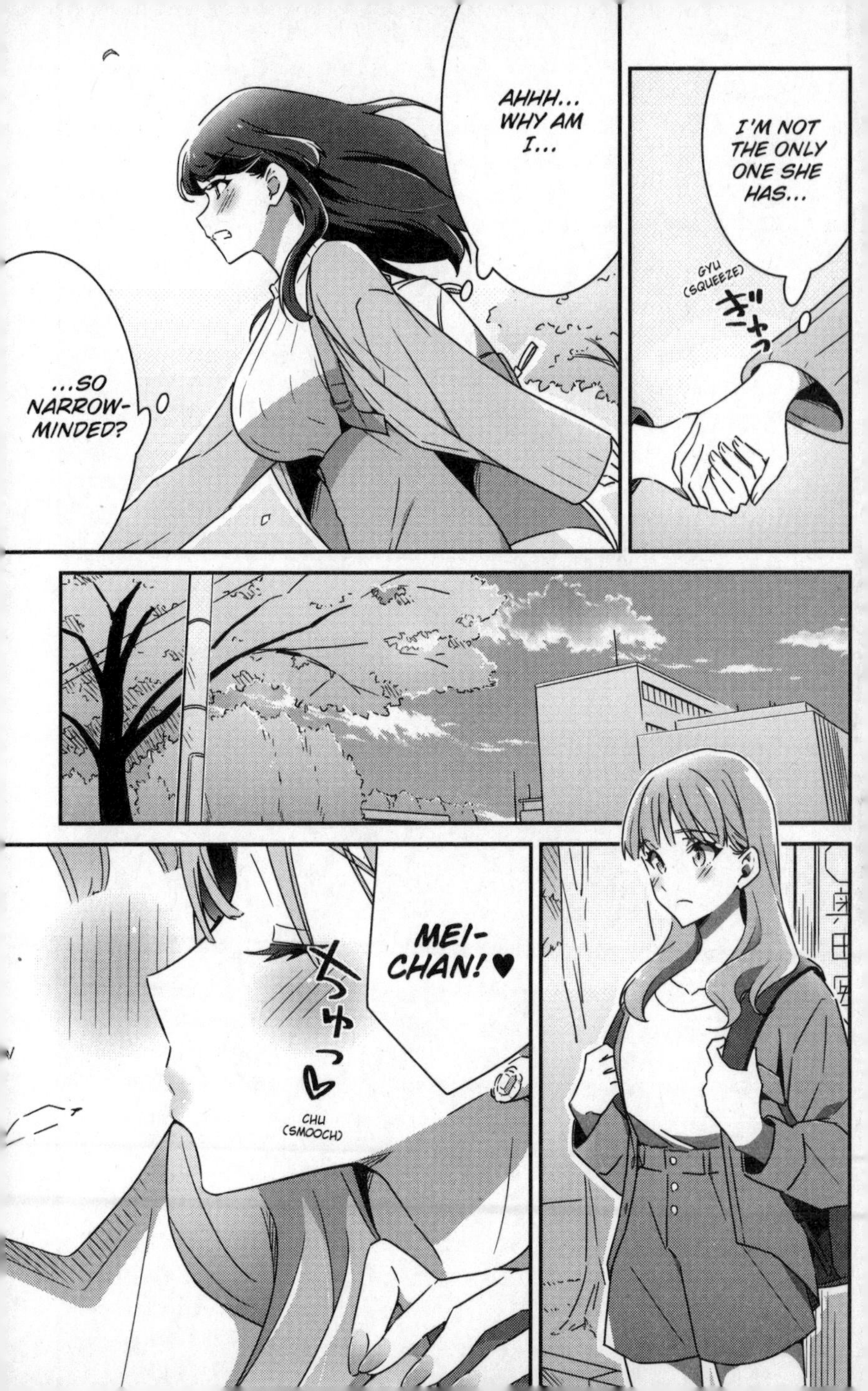
I'M NOT THE ONLY ONE SHE HAS...
ぎゅっ
GYU (SQUEEZE)
AHHH... WHY AM I...
...SO NARROW-MINDED?
MEI-CHAN! ♥
ちゅっ♥
CHU (SMOOCH)

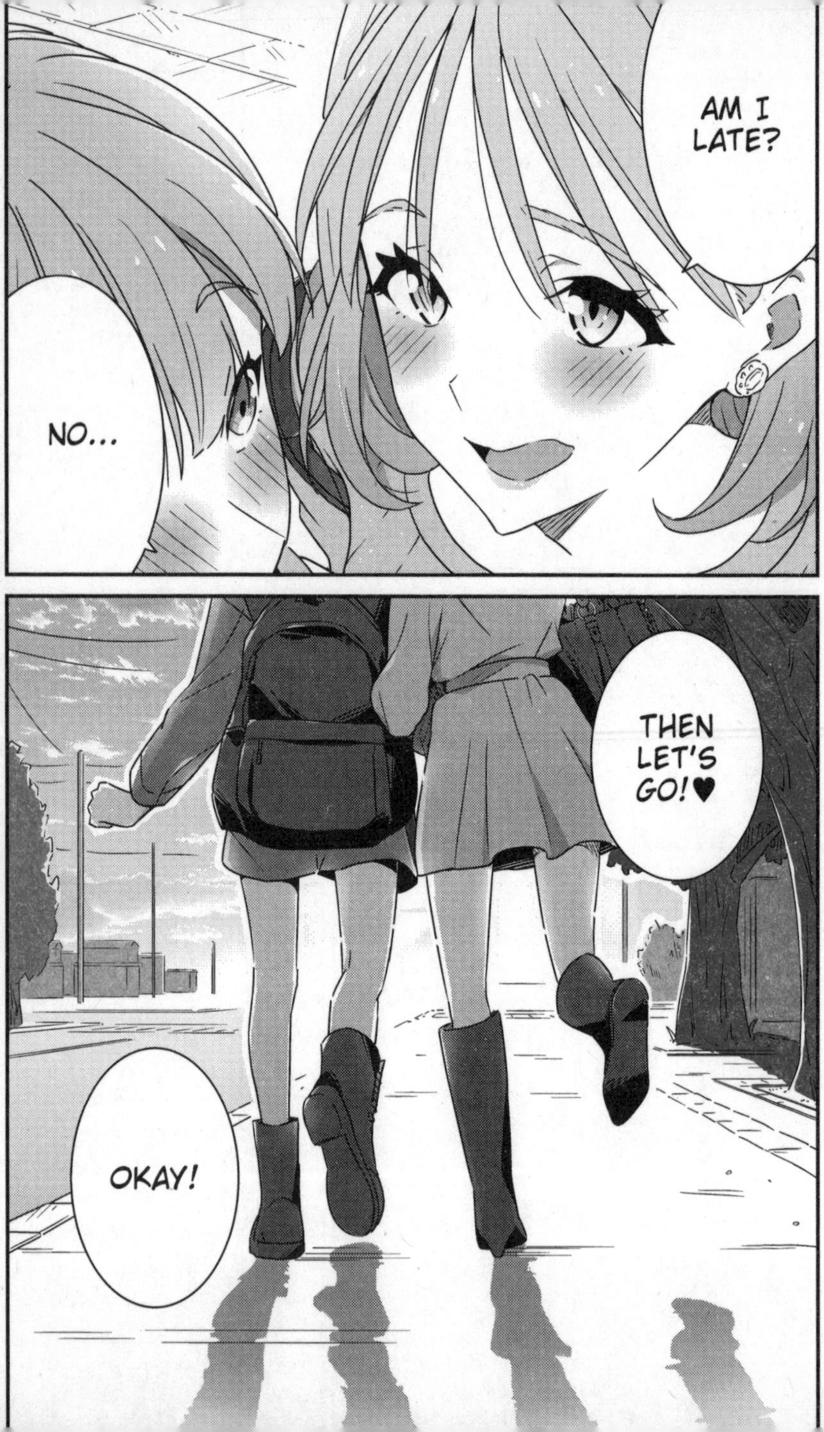
AM I LATE?
NO...
THEN LET'S GO!♥
OKAY!

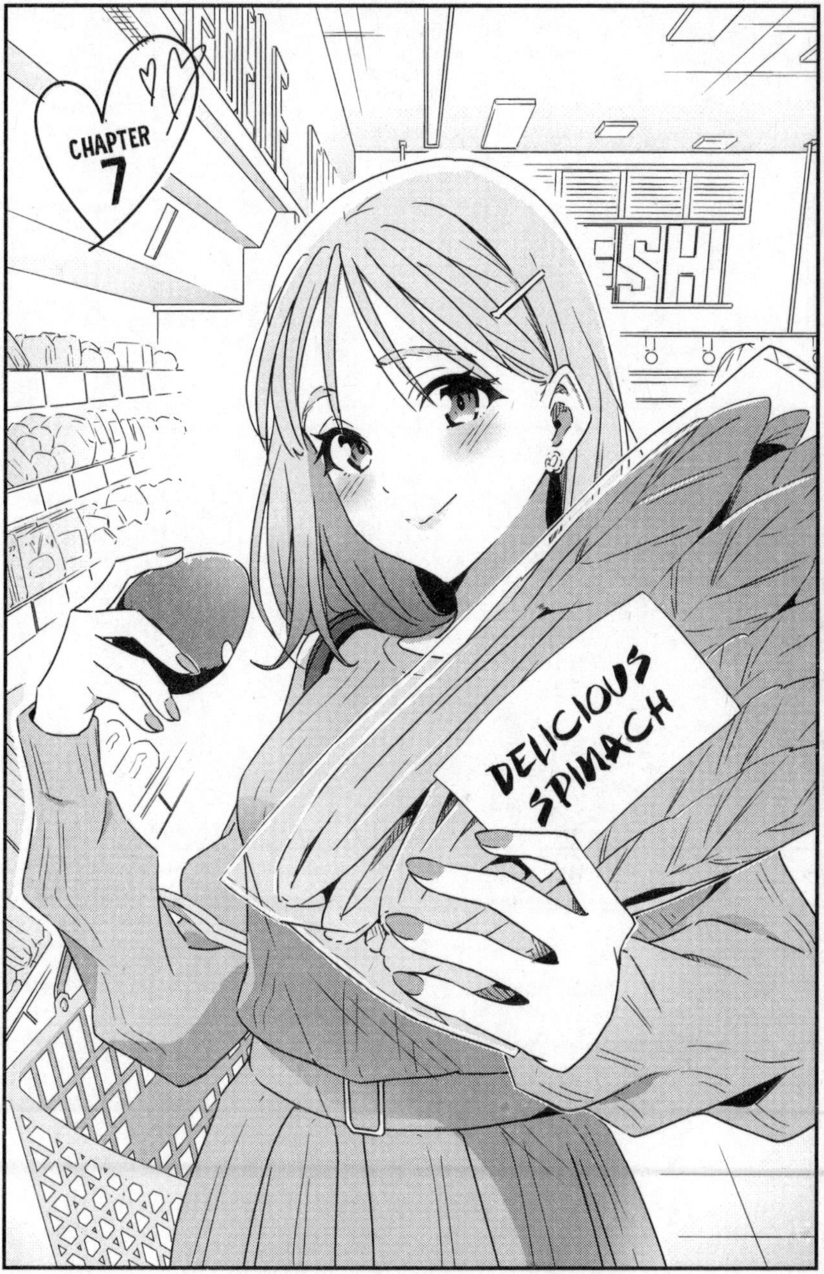
CHAPTER 7
DELICIOUS SPINACH

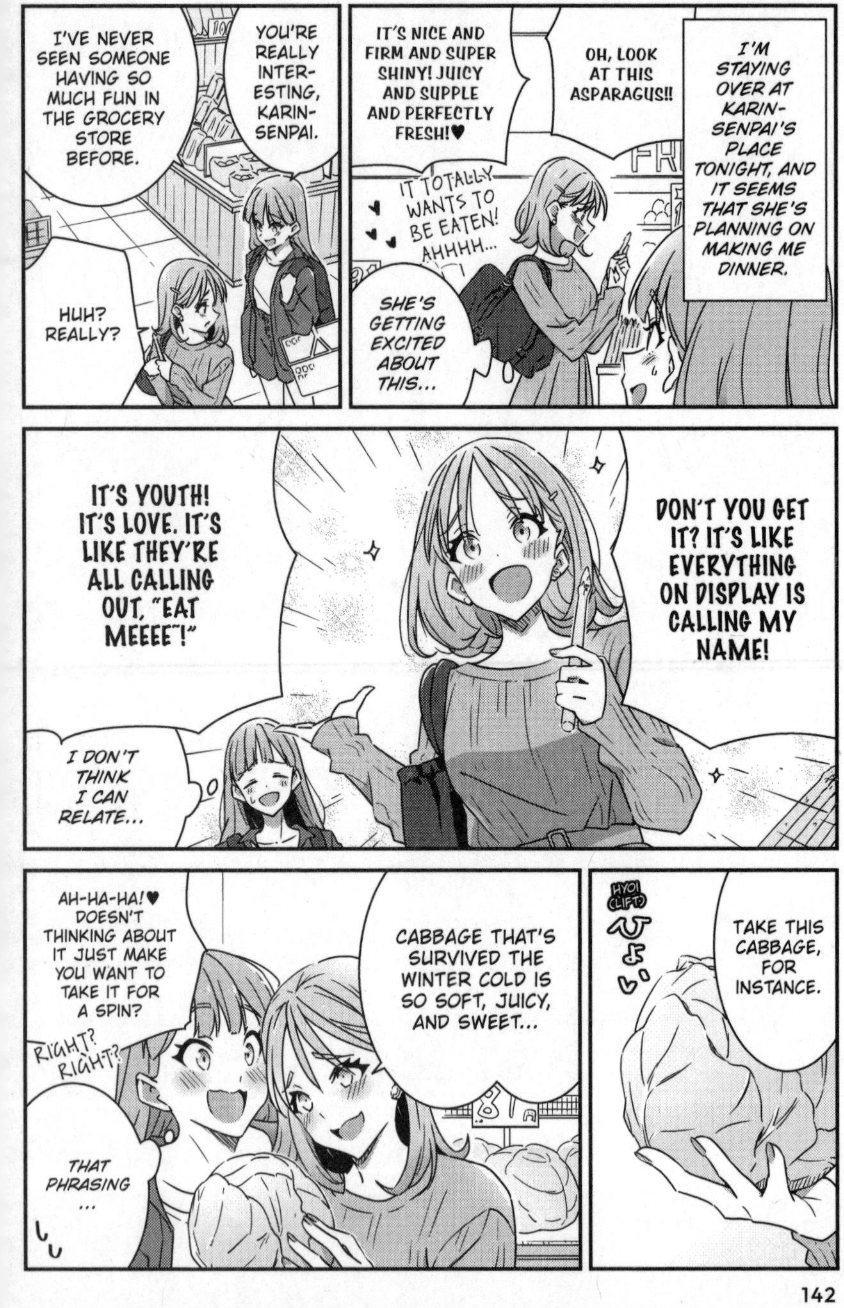
I'M STAYING OVER AT KARIN-SENPAI'S PLACE TONIGHT, AND IT SEEMS THAT SHE'S PLANNING ON MAKING ME DINNER.
OH, LOOK AT THIS ASPARAGUS!!
IT'S NICE AND FIRM AND SUPER SHINY! JUICY AND SUPPLE AND PERFECTLY FRESH!♥
IT TOTALLY WANTS TO BE EATEN! AHHHH...
SHE'S GETTING EXCITED ABOUT THIS...
YOU'RE REALLY INTERESTING, KARIN-SENPAI.
I'VE NEVER SEEN SOMEONE HAVING SO MUCH FUN IN THE GROCERY STORE BEFORE.
HUH? REALLY?
DON'T YOU GET IT? IT'S LIKE EVERYTHING ON DISPLAY IS CALLING MY NAME!
IT'S YOUTH! IT'S LOVE. IT'S LIKE THEY'RE ALL CALLING OUT, "EAT MEEEE~!"
I DON'T THINK I CAN RELATE...
HYOI (LIFT)
TAKE THIS CABBAGE, FOR INSTANCE.
CABBAGE THAT'S SURVIVED THE WINTER COLD IS SO SOFT, JUICY, AND SWEET...
AH-HA-HA!♥ DOESN'T THINKING ABOUT IT JUST MAKE YOU WANT TO TAKE IT FOR A SPIN?
RIGHT? RIGHT?
THAT PHRASING ...

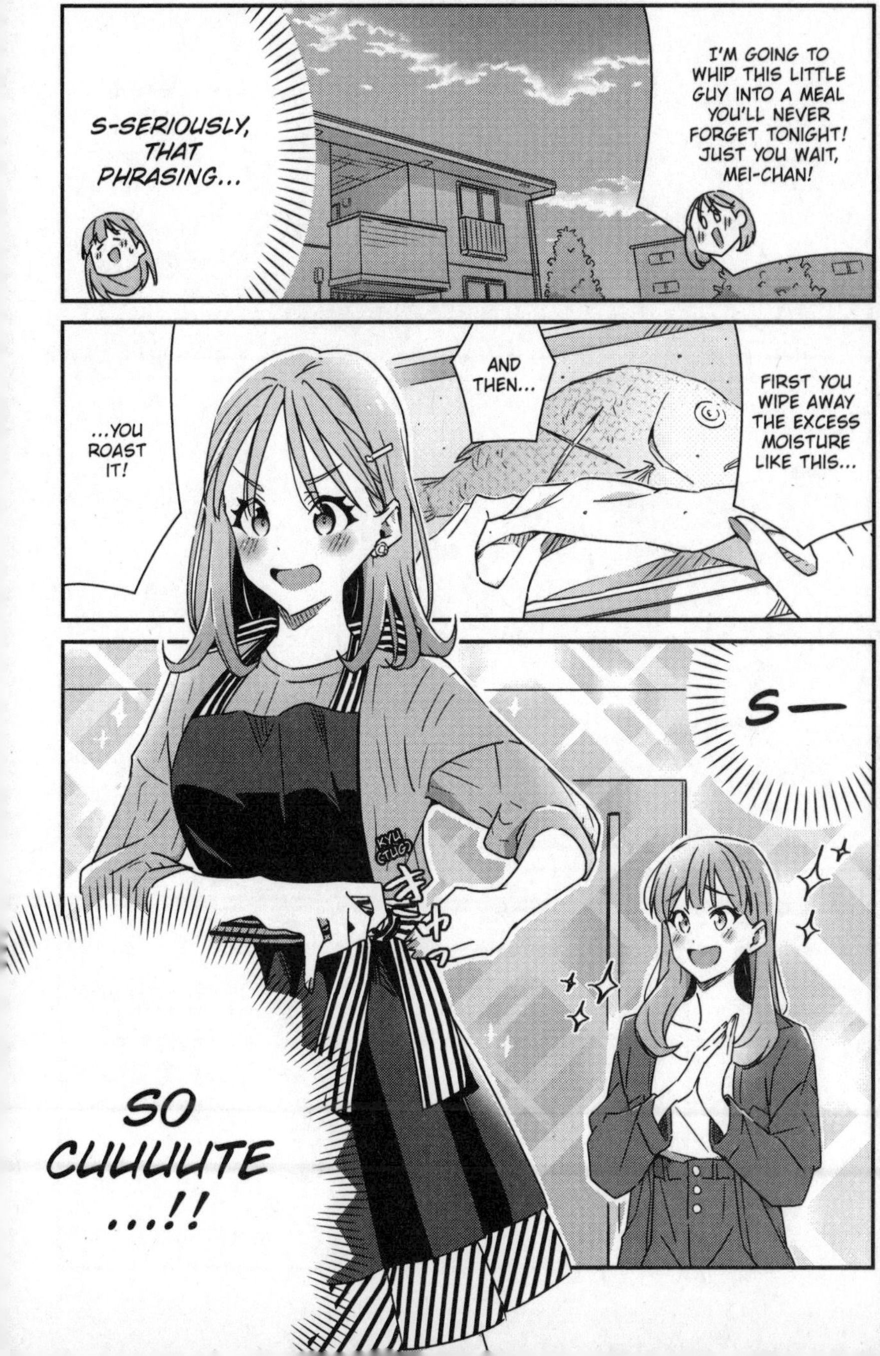
I'M GOING TO WHIP THIS LITTLE GUY INTO A MEAL YOU'LL NEVER FORGET TONIGHT! JUST YOU WAIT, MEI-CHAN!
S-SERIOUSLY, THAT PHRASING...
FIRST YOU WIPE AWAY THE EXCESS MOISTURE LIKE THIS...
AND THEN...
...YOU ROAST IT!
S—
KYU (TUG)
SO CUUUUTE...!!

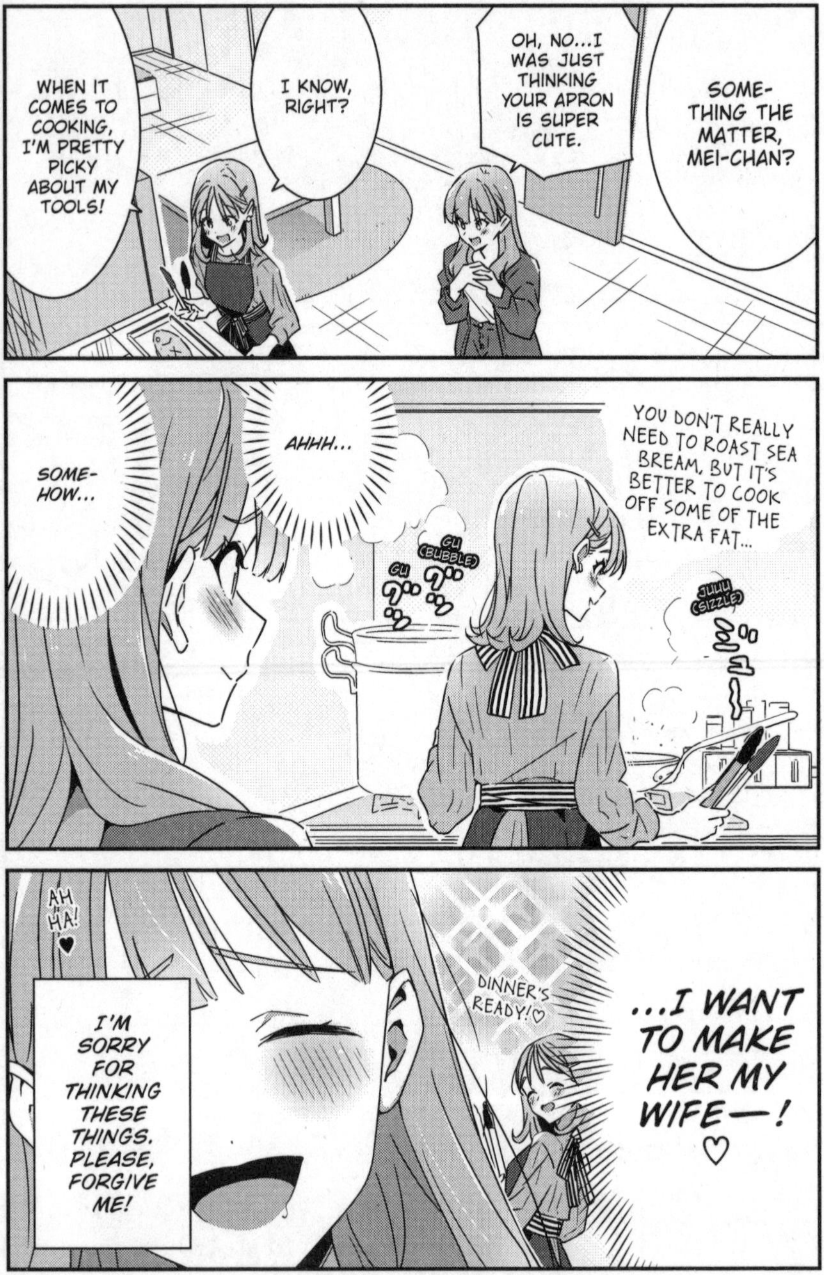
SOME-THING THE MATTER, MEI-CHAN?
OH, NO...I WAS JUST THINKING YOUR APRON IS SUPER CUTE.
I KNOW, RIGHT?
WHEN IT COMES TO COOKING, I'M PRETTY PICKY ABOUT MY TOOLS!
YOU DON'T REALLY NEED TO ROAST SEA BREAM, BUT IT'S BETTER TO COOK OFF SOME OF THE EXTRA FAT...
JUUU (SIZZLE)
GU (BUBBLE)
GU
AHHH...
SOME-HOW...
...I WANT TO MAKE HER MY WIFE—! ♡
DINNER'S READY!♡
AH HA! ♥
I'M SORRY FOR THINKING THESE THINGS. PLEASE, FORGIVE ME!

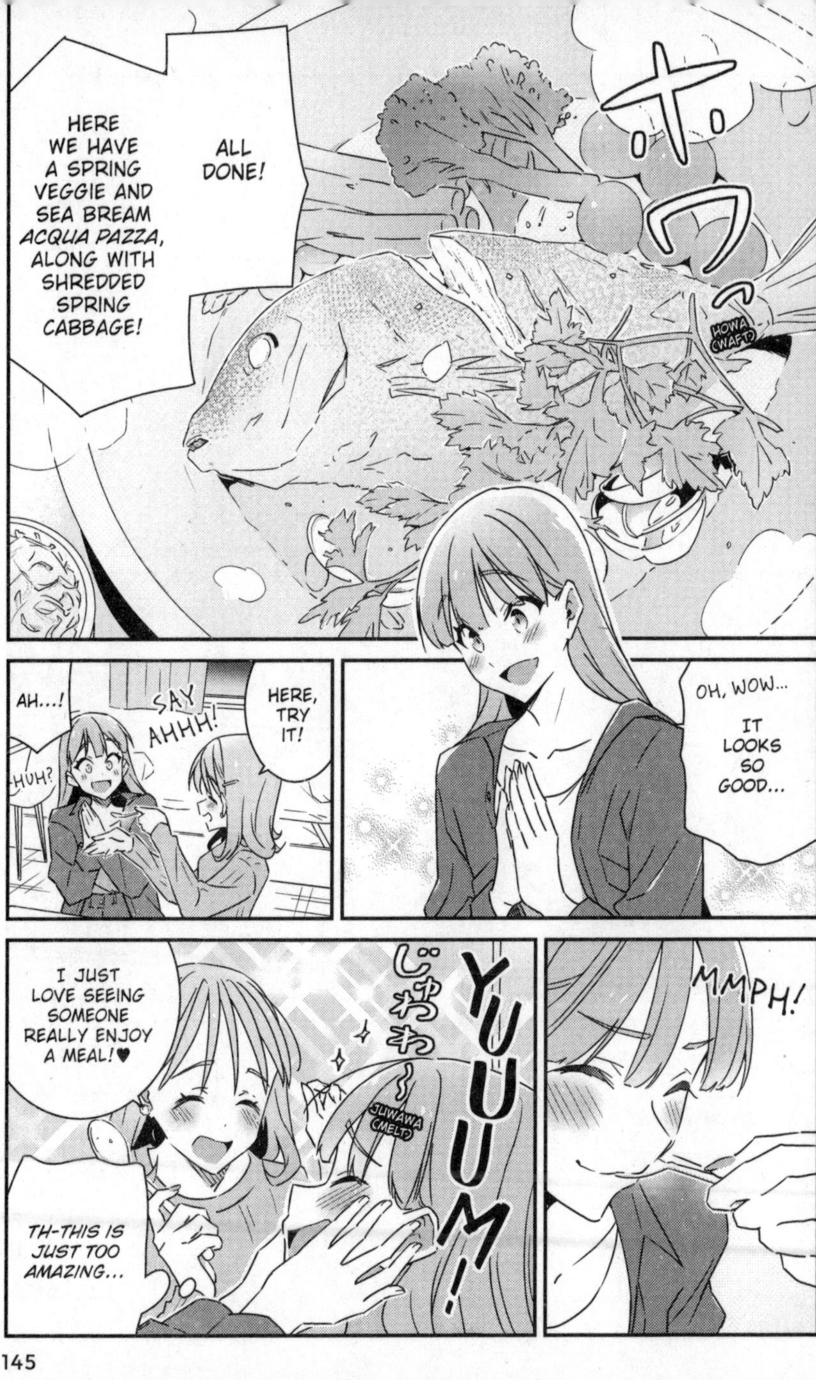
ホワ〜
HOWA (WAFT)
ALL DONE!
HERE WE HAVE A SPRING VEGGIE AND SEA BREAM *ACQUA PAZZA*, ALONG WITH SHREDDED SPRING CABBAGE!
OH, WOW... IT LOOKS SO GOOD...
HERE, TRY IT!
SAY AHHH!
AH...!
HUH?
MMPH!
YUUUUM!
じゅわわ〜
JUWAWA (MELT)
I JUST LOVE SEEING SOMEONE REALLY ENJOY A MEAL!♥
TH-THIS IS JUST TOO AMAZING...

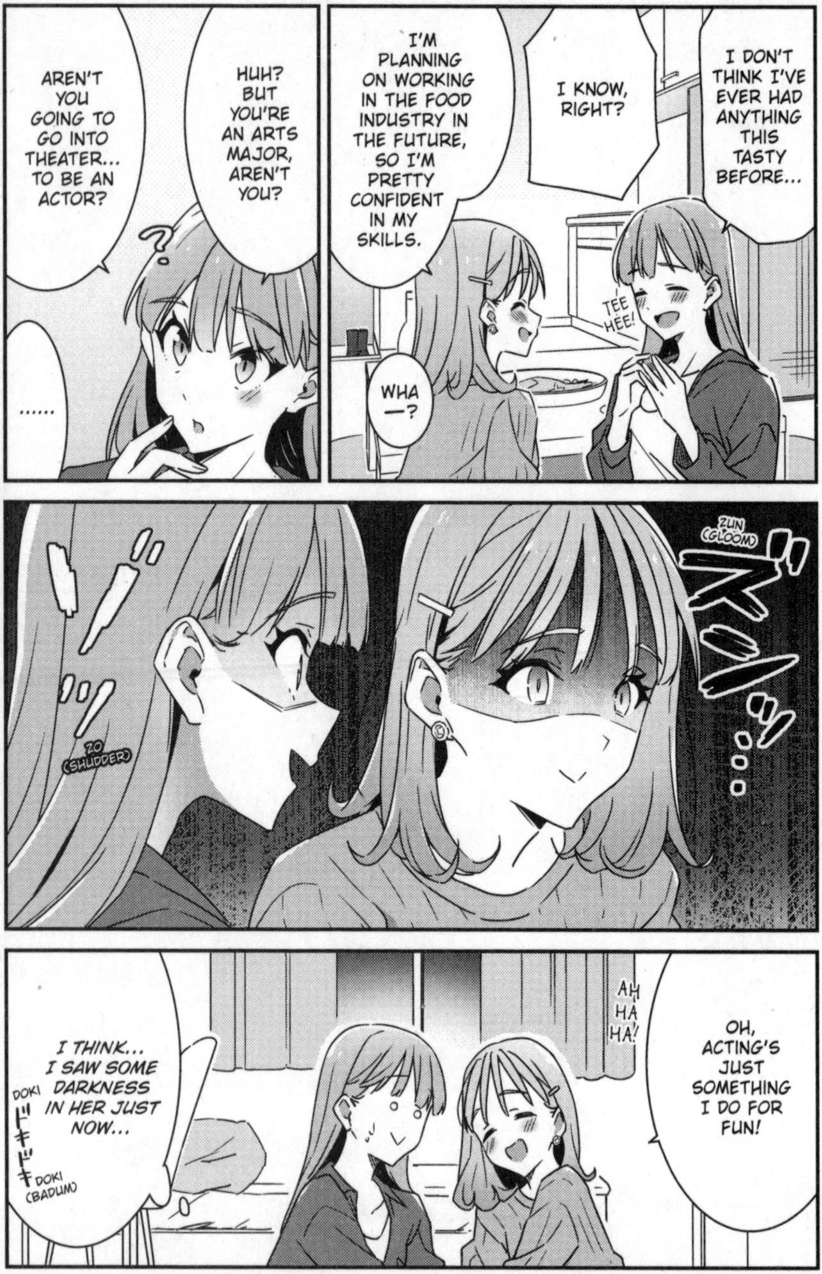
I DON'T THINK I'VE EVER HAD ANYTHING THIS TASTY BEFORE...
TEE HEE!
I KNOW, RIGHT?
I'M PLANNING ON WORKING IN THE FOOD INDUSTRY IN THE FUTURE, SO I'M PRETTY CONFIDENT IN MY SKILLS.
WHA—?
HUH? BUT YOU'RE AN ARTS MAJOR, AREN'T YOU?
AREN'T YOU GOING TO GO INTO THEATER... TO BE AN ACTOR?
......
ZUN (GLOOM)
ZO (SHUDDER)
OH, ACTING'S JUST SOMETHING I DO FOR FUN!
AH HA HA!
I THINK... I SAW SOME DARKNESS IN HER JUST NOW...
DOKI DOKI (BADUM)

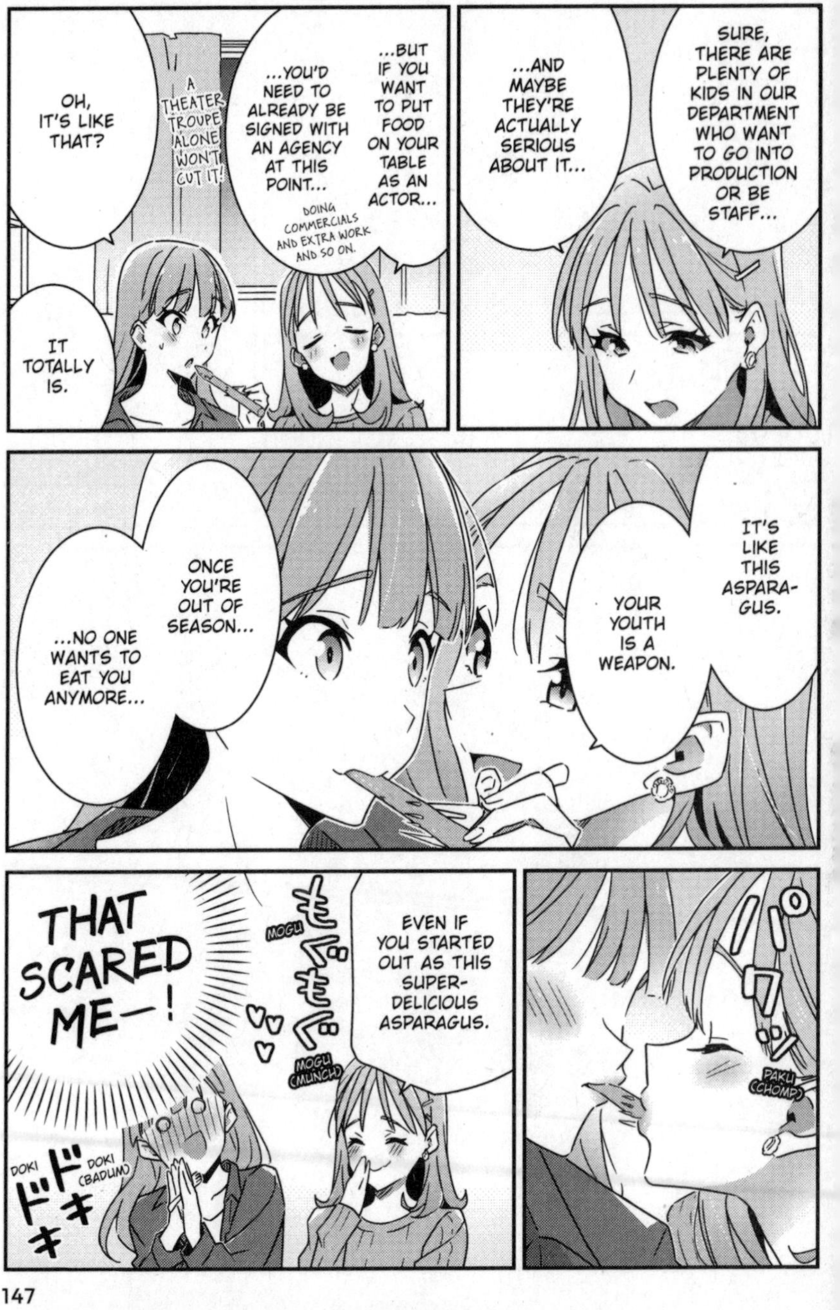
SURE, THERE ARE PLENTY OF KIDS IN OUR DEPARTMENT WHO WANT TO GO INTO PRODUCTION OR BE STAFF...
...AND MAYBE THEY'RE ACTUALLY SERIOUS ABOUT IT...
...BUT IF YOU WANT TO PUT FOOD ON YOUR TABLE AS AN ACTOR...
...YOU'D NEED TO ALREADY BE SIGNED WITH AN AGENCY AT THIS POINT...
DOING COMMERCIALS AND EXTRA WORK AND SO ON.
A THEATER TROUPE ALONE WON'T CUT IT!
OH, IT'S LIKE THAT?
IT TOTALLY IS.
IT'S LIKE THIS ASPARAGUS.
YOUR YOUTH IS A WEAPON.
ONCE YOU'RE OUT OF SEASON...
...NO ONE WANTS TO EAT YOU ANYMORE...
パクッ
PAKU (CHOMP)
EVEN IF YOU STARTED OUT AS THIS SUPER-DELICIOUS ASPARAGUS.
もぐもぐ
MOGU
MOGU (MUNCH)
THAT SCARED ME—!
ドキドキ
DOKI
DOKI (BADUM)

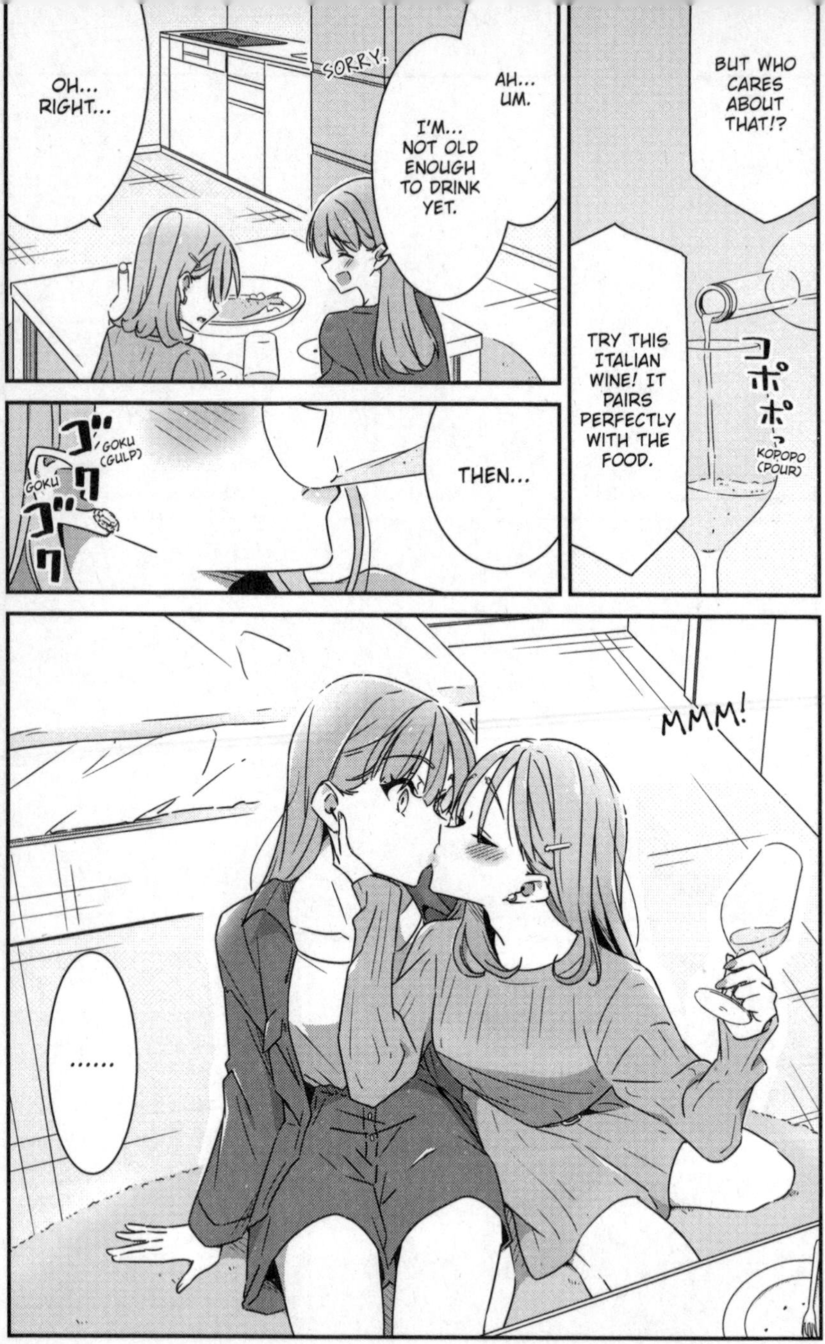
AH... UM.
I'M... NOT OLD ENOUGH TO DRINK YET.
SORRY.
OH... RIGHT...
BUT WHO CARES ABOUT THAT!?
TRY THIS ITALIAN WINE! IT PAIRS PERFECTLY WITH THE FOOD.
コポポッ
KOPOPO (POUR)
THEN...
ゴク
GOKU (GULP)
ゴク
GOKU
MMM!
......

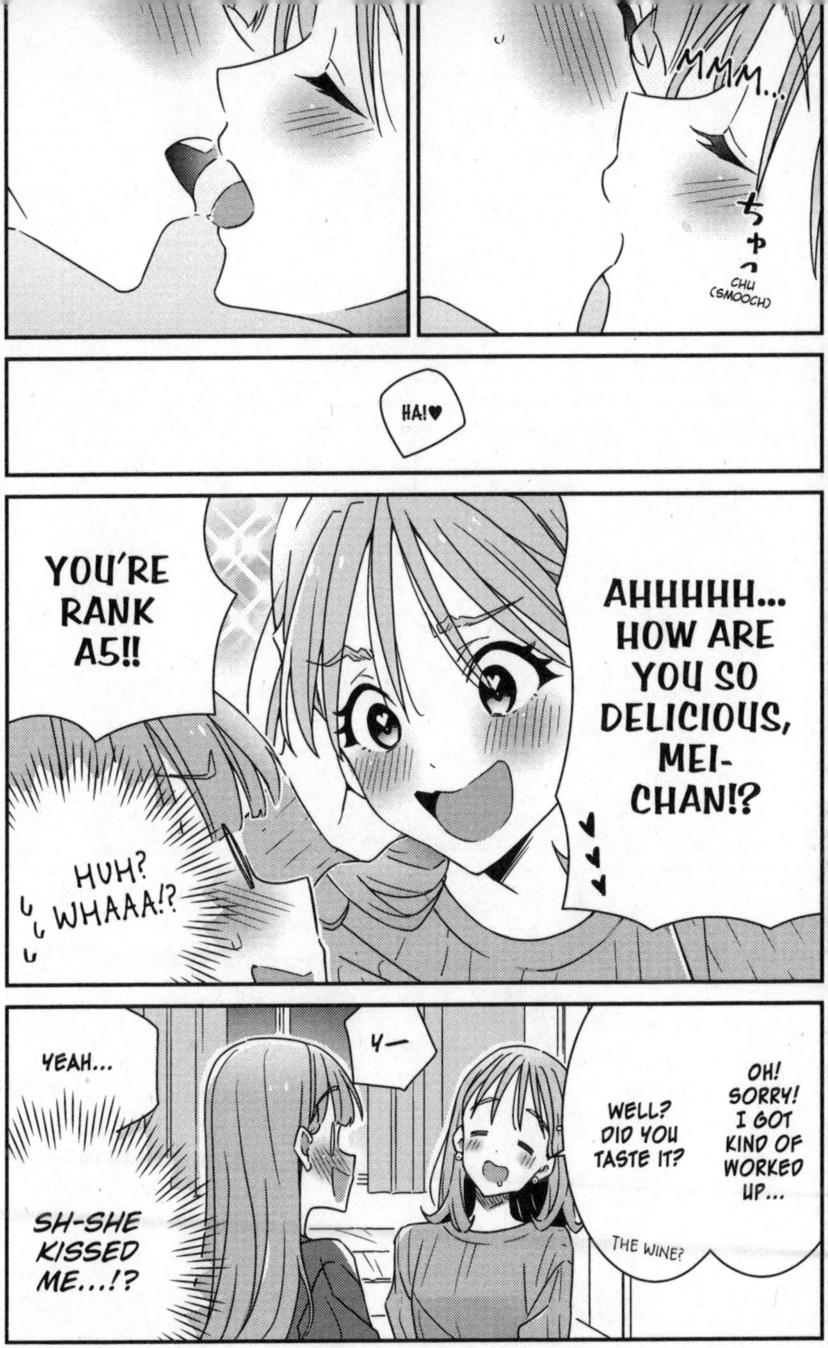
MMM...
ちゅっ
CHU (SMOOCH)
HA!♥
AHHHHH... HOW ARE YOU SO DELICIOUS, MEI-CHAN!?
YOU'RE RANK A5!!
HUH? WHAAA!?
OH! SORRY! I GOT KIND OF WORKED UP...
WELL? DID YOU TASTE IT?
THE WINE?
Y—
YEAH...
SH-SHE KISSED ME...!?

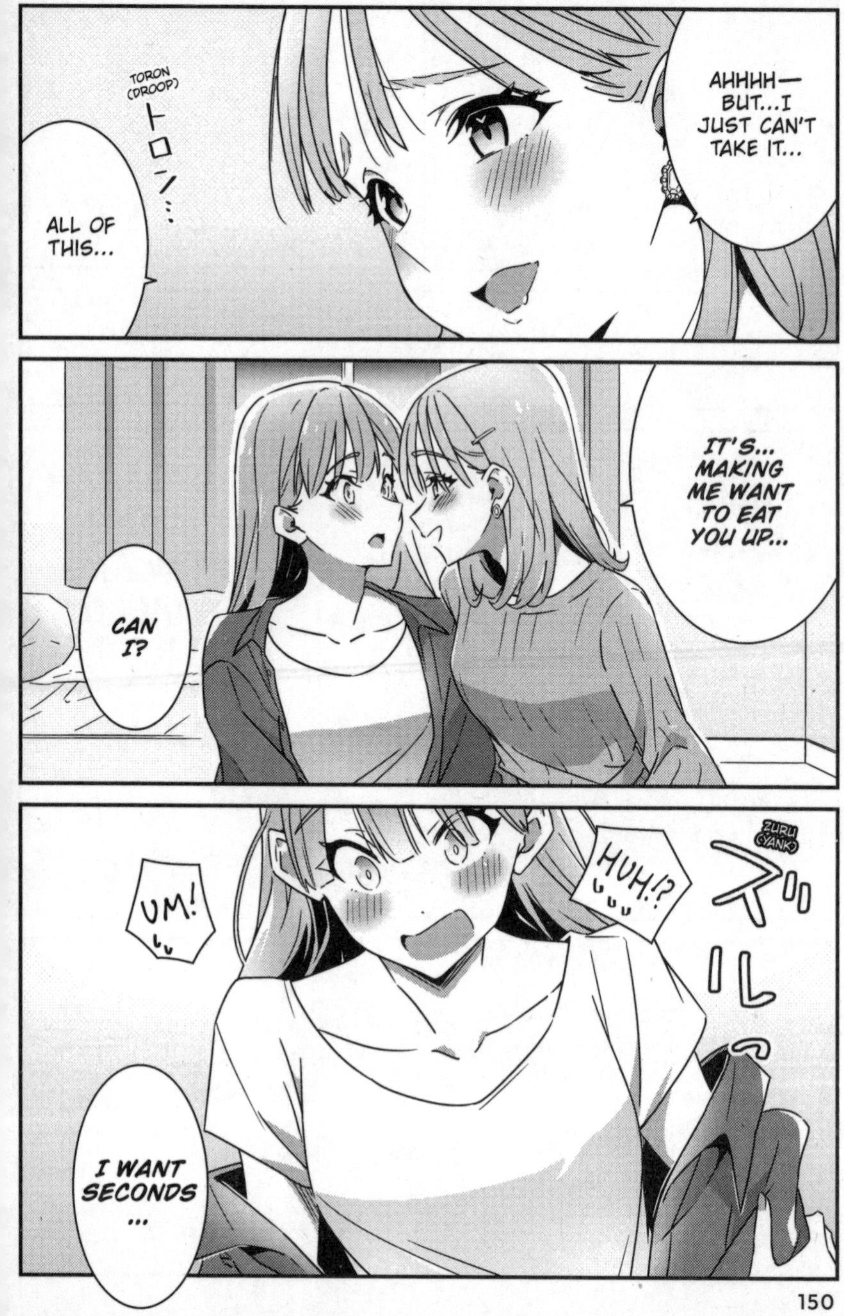
AHHHH— BUT...I JUST CAN'T TAKE IT...
TORON (DROOP)
トロン…
ALL OF THIS...
IT'S... MAKING ME WANT TO EAT YOU UP...
CAN I?
ZURU (YANK)
ズルッ
HUH!?
UM!
I WANT SECONDS ...

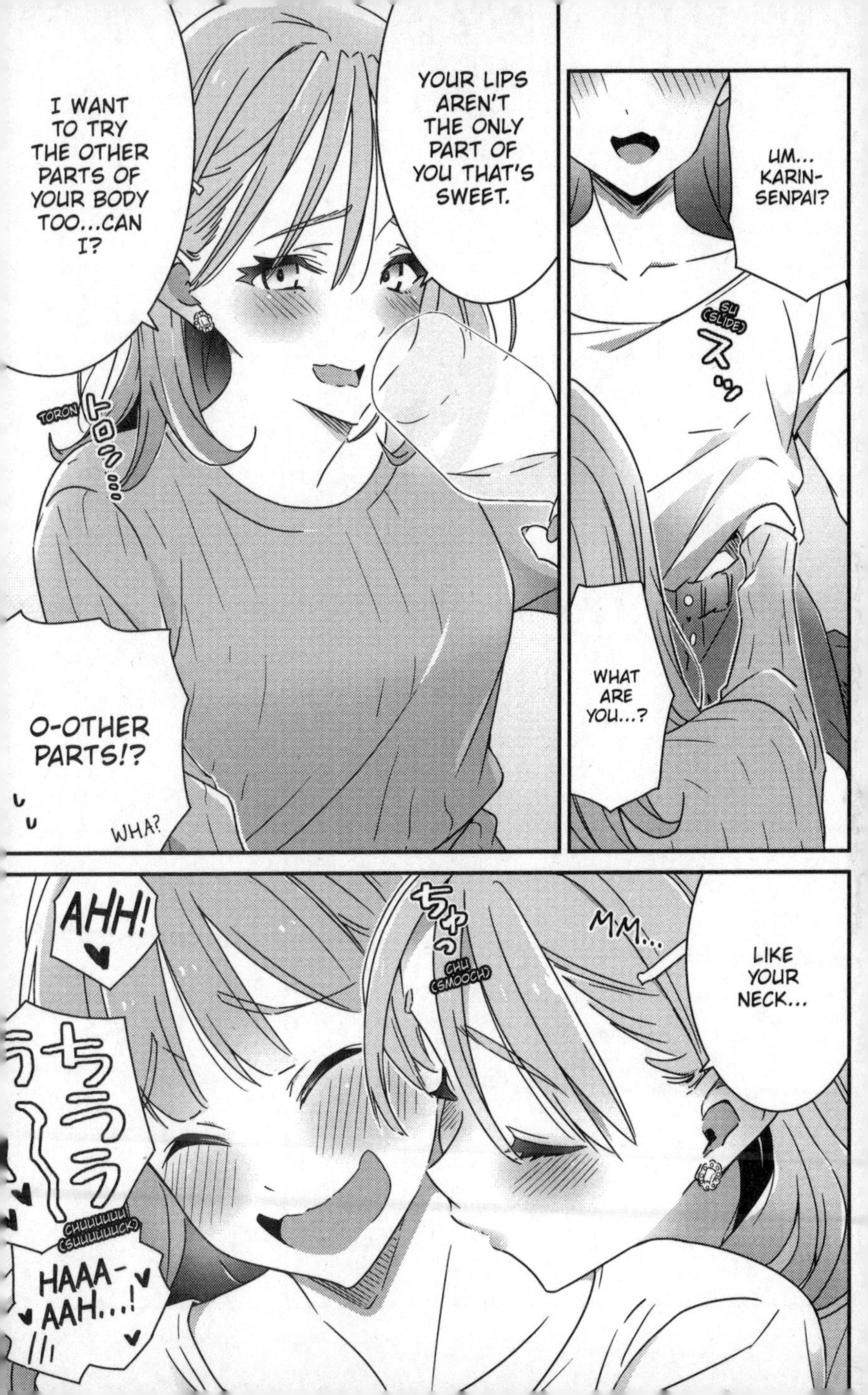
UM... KARIN-SENPAI?
SU (SLIDE)
スッ
WHAT ARE YOU...?
YOUR LIPS AREN'T THE ONLY PART OF YOU THAT'S SWEET.
I WANT TO TRY THE OTHER PARTS OF YOUR BODY TOO...CAN I?
TORON
トロン…
O-OTHER PARTS!?
WHA?
LIKE YOUR NECK...
MM...
ちゅっ
CHU (SMOOCH)
AHH!
CHUUUUUUU (SUUUUUUCK)
HAAA-AAH...!

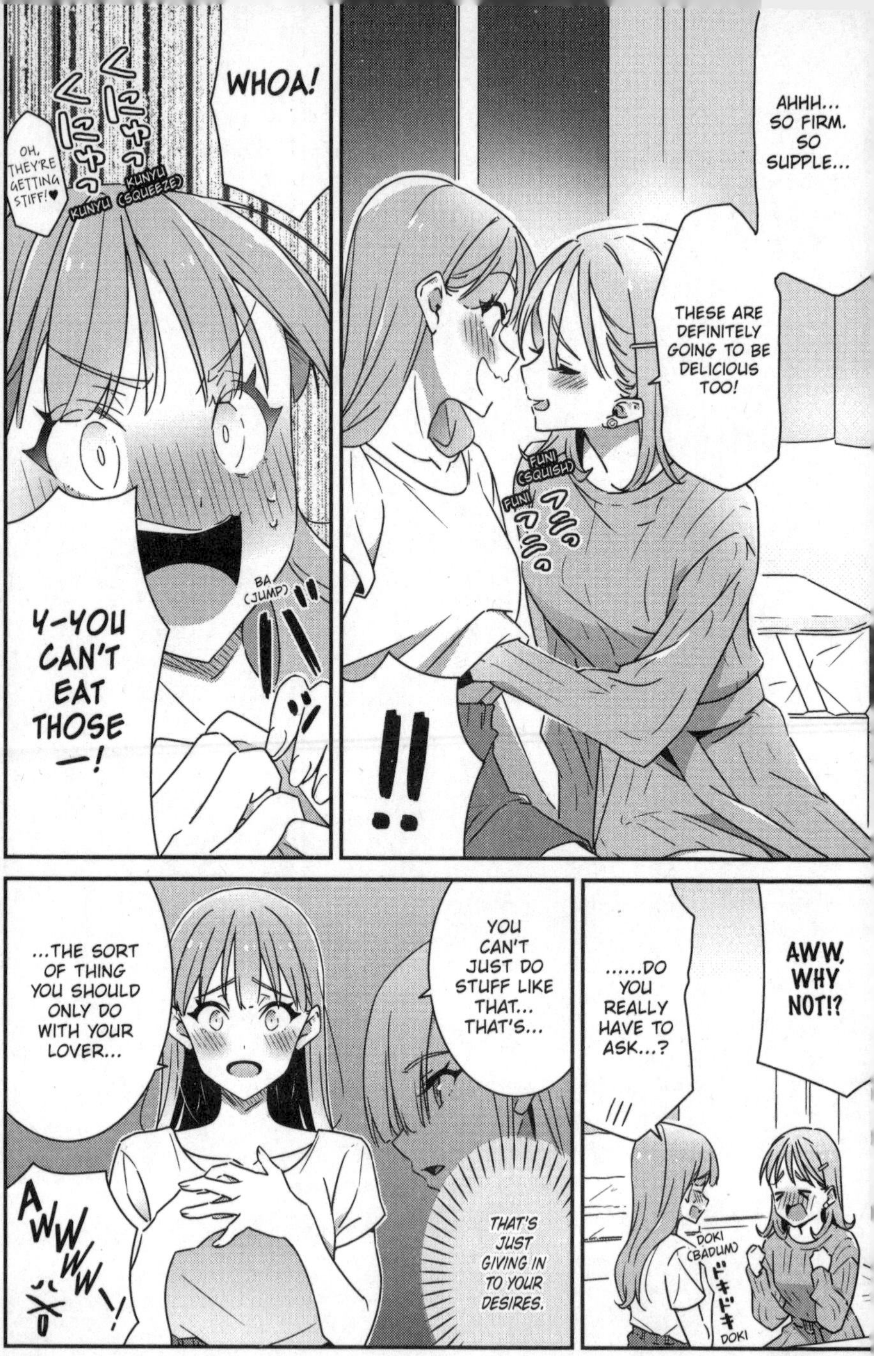
AHHH... SO FIRM. SO SUPPLE...
THESE ARE DEFINITELY GOING TO BE DELICIOUS TOO!
FUNI (SQUISH) FUNI
!!
WHOA!
KUNYU (SQUEEZE) KUNYU
OH, THEY'RE GETTING STIFF!♥
BA (JUMP)
Y-YOU CAN'T EAT THOSE—!
AWW, WHY NOT!?
......DO YOU REALLY HAVE TO ASK...?
DOKI (BADUM)
ドキドキ
DOKI
YOU CAN'T JUST DO STUFF LIKE THAT... THAT'S...
...THE SORT OF THING YOU SHOULD ONLY DO WITH YOUR LOVER...
THAT'S JUST GIVING IN TO YOUR DESIRES.
AWWWWW—!

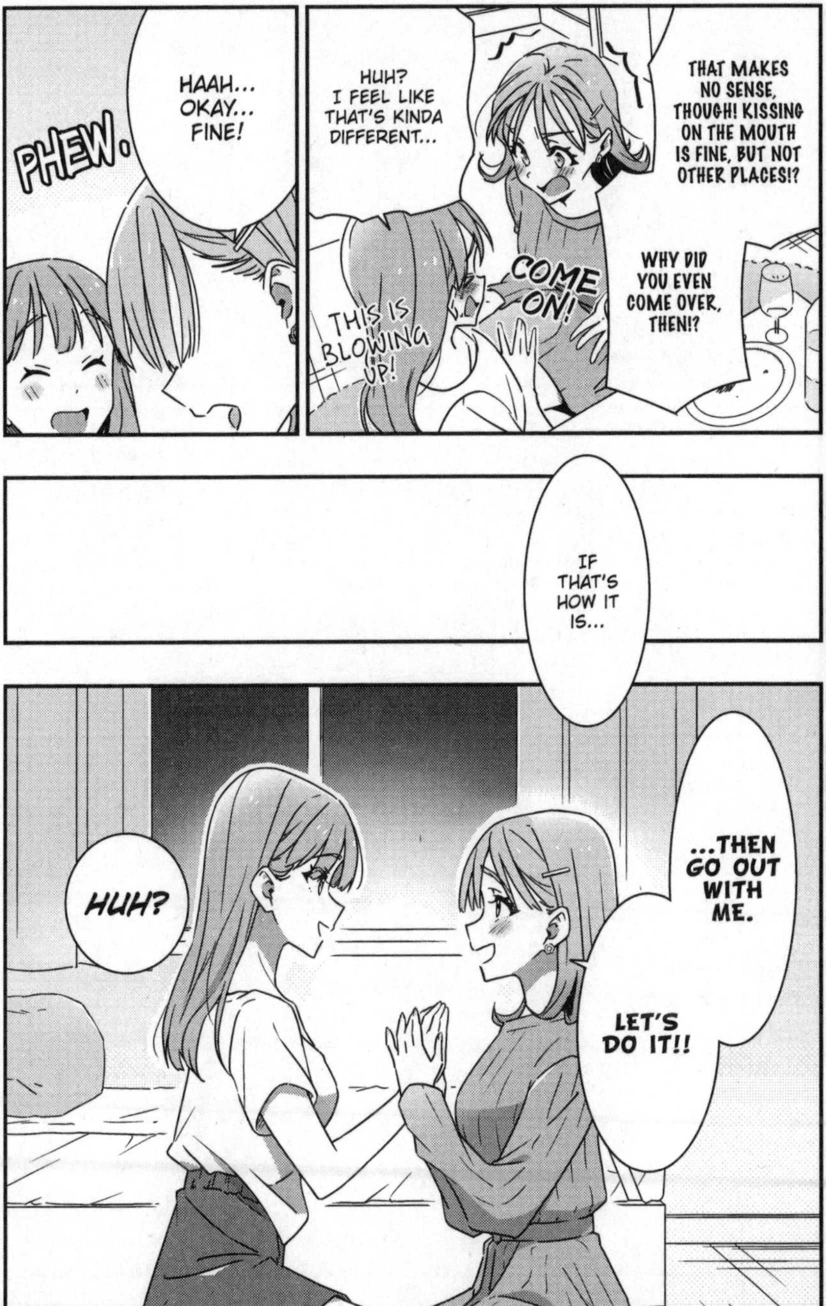
THAT MAKES NO SENSE, THOUGH! KISSING ON THE MOUTH IS FINE, BUT NOT OTHER PLACES!?
HUH? I FEEL LIKE THAT'S KINDA DIFFERENT...
WHY DID YOU EVEN COME OVER, THEN!?
COME ON!
THIS IS BLOWING UP!
HAAH... OKAY... FINE!
PHEW.
IF THAT'S HOW IT IS...
...THEN GO OUT WITH ME.
LET'S DO IT!!
HUH?

...GO OUT WITH HER!?
WORKS FOR ME! I'M SINGLE RIGHT NOW.
CHU (SMOOCH)
AND I REALLY DO LIKE YOU, YOU KNOW!
BWUH?♡
I LIKE YOU. I REALLY DO. I'M IN LOVE WITH YOU! ♡♡
SO PLEASE?
HUH...? THEN...
...I HAVE A GIRL-FRIEND!?
DOES THIS MEAN I'VE COMPLETED MY COLLEGE GOAL!?

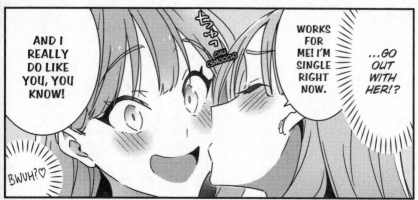

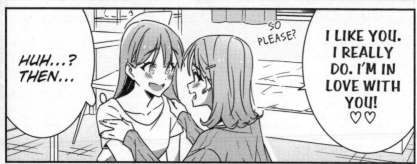

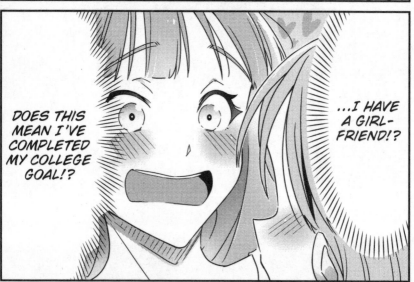

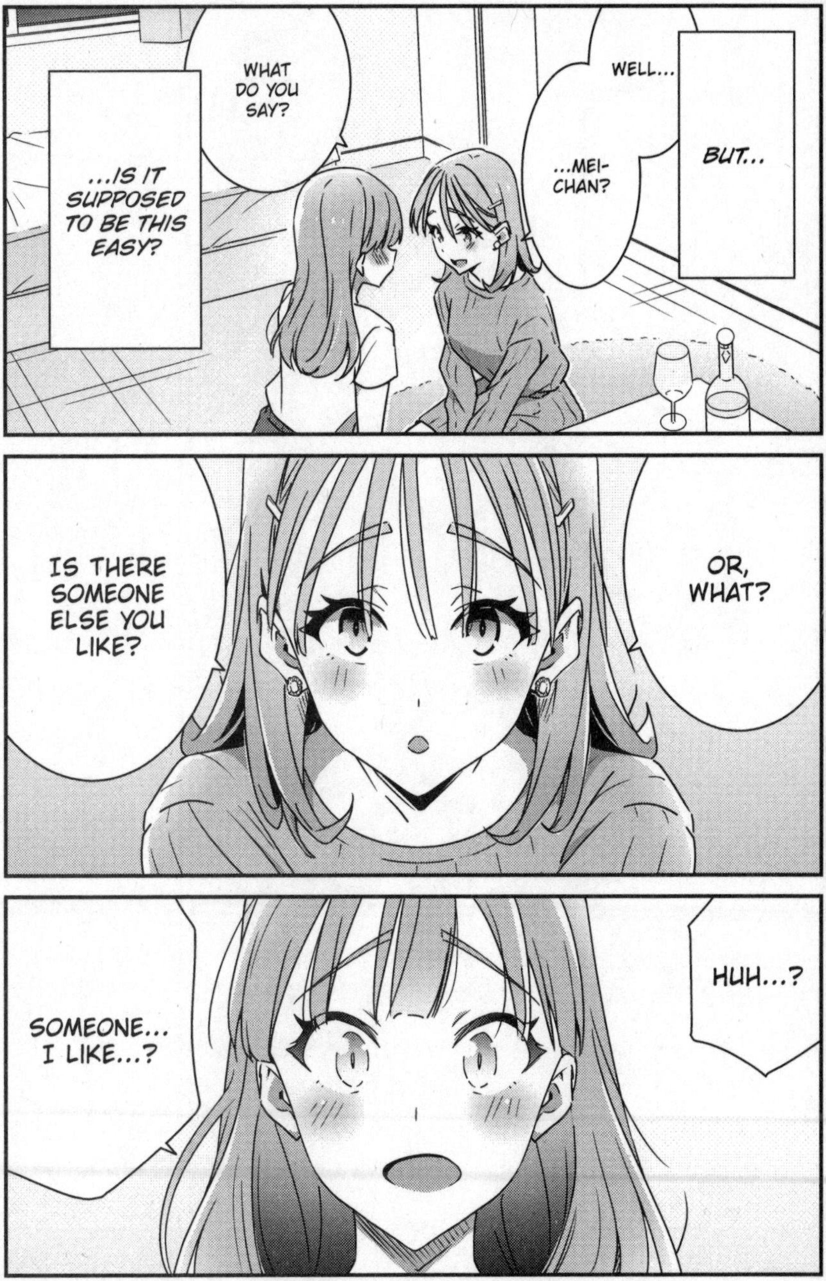
BUT...
WELL...
...MEI-CHAN?
WHAT DO YOU SAY?
...IS IT SUPPOSED TO BE THIS EASY?
OR, WHAT?
IS THERE SOMEONE ELSE YOU LIKE?
HUH...?
SOMEONE... I LIKE...?

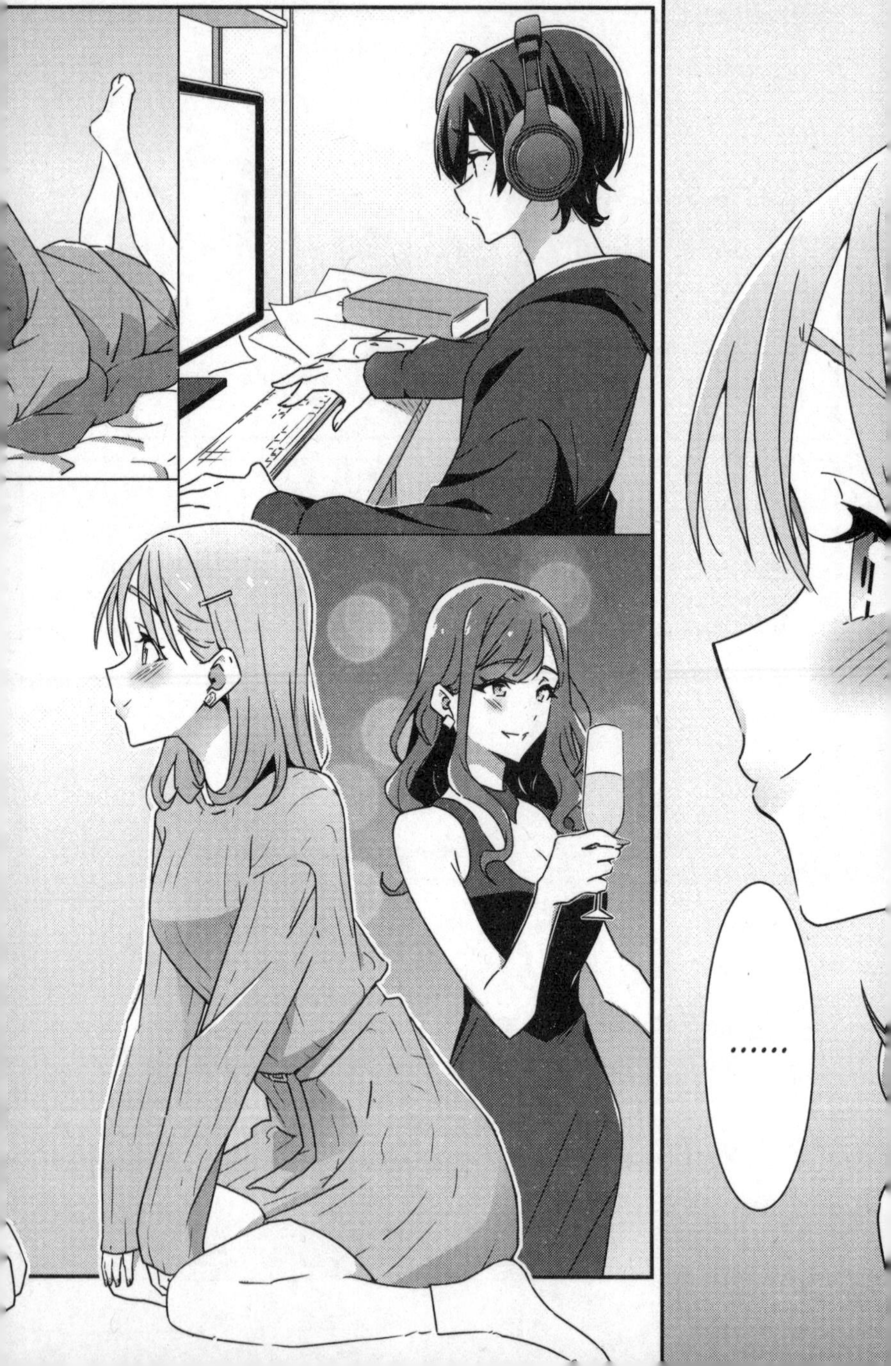
......

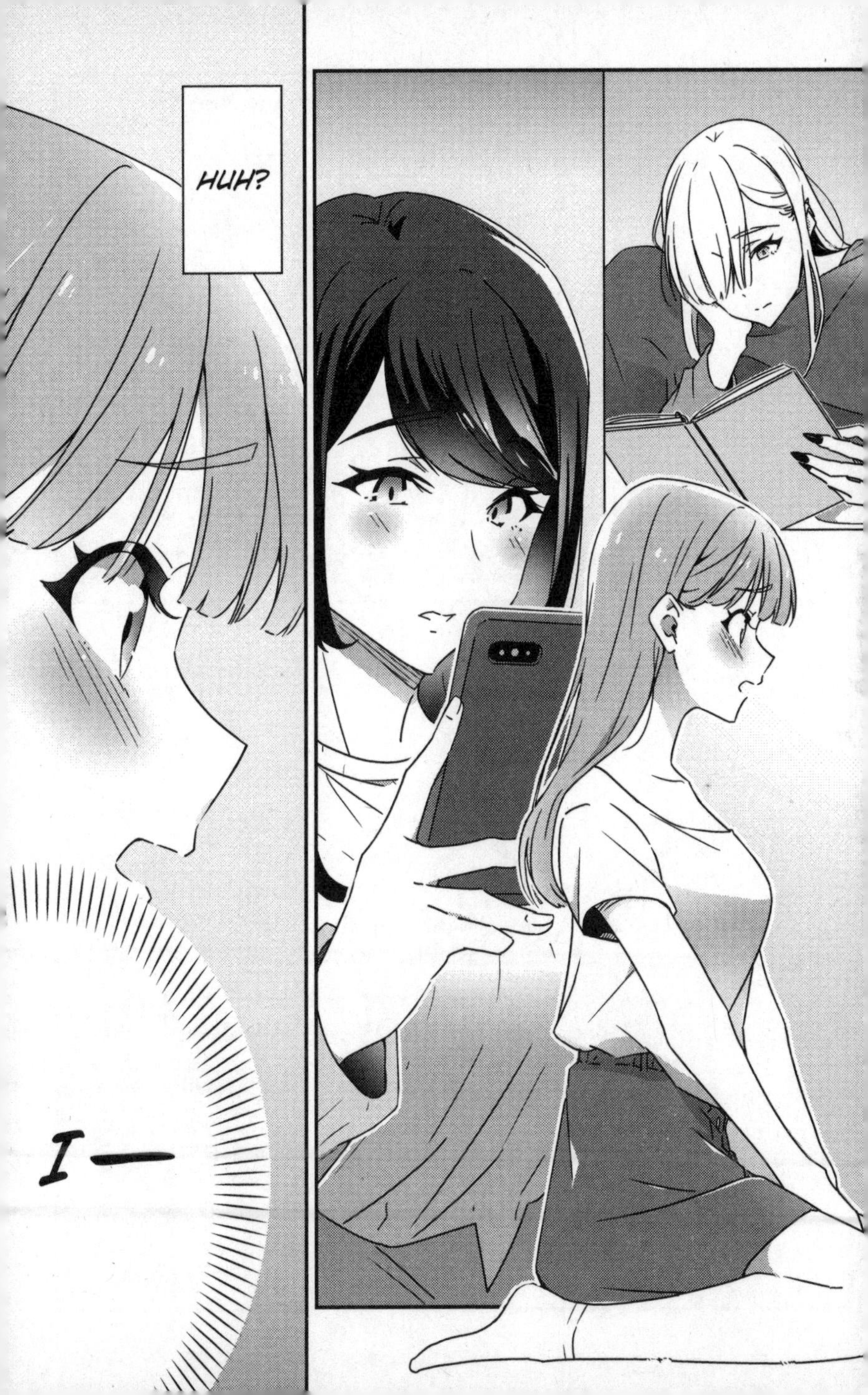
HUH?
I—

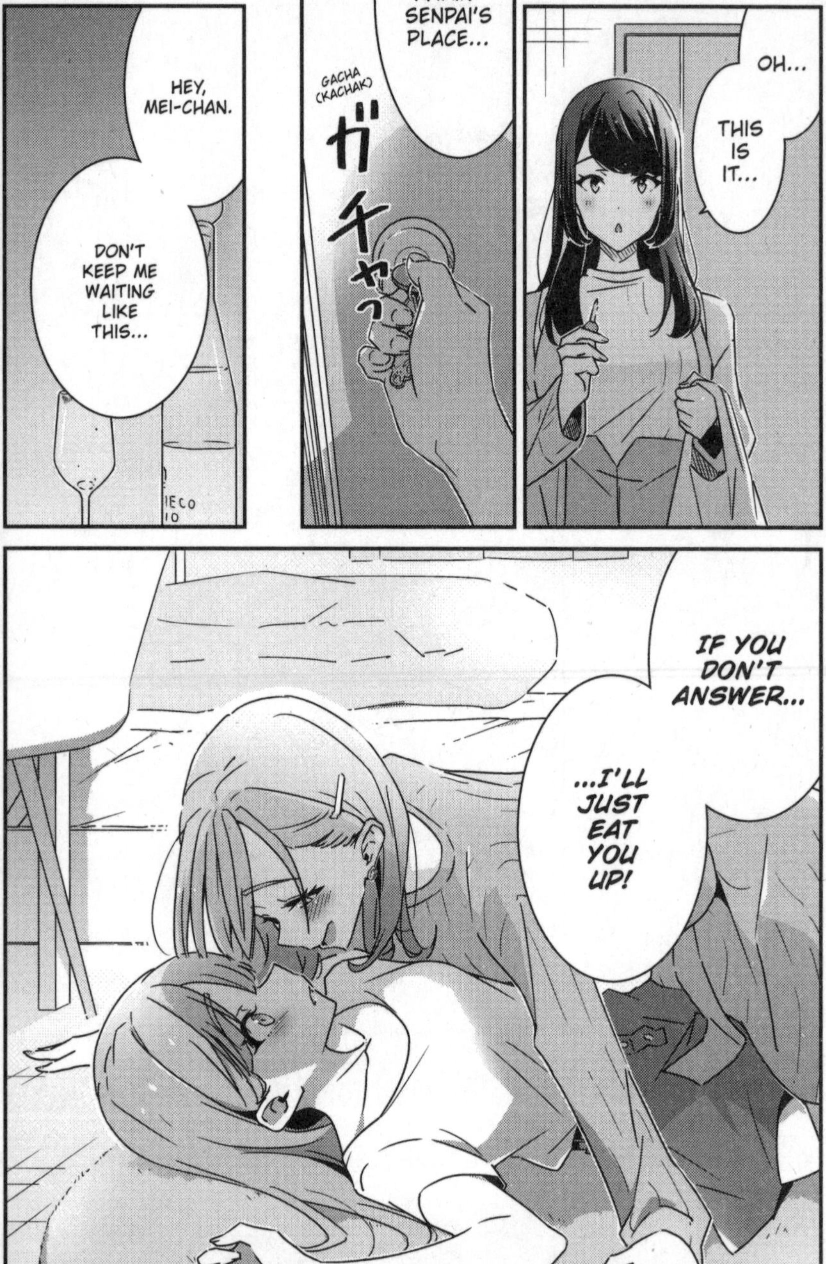
OH...
THIS IS IT...
KARIN-SENPAI'S PLACE...
GACHA (KACHAK)
ガチャッ
HEY, MEI-CHAN.
DON'T KEEP ME WAITING LIKE THIS...
IF YOU DON'T ANSWER...
...I'LL JUST EAT YOU UP!

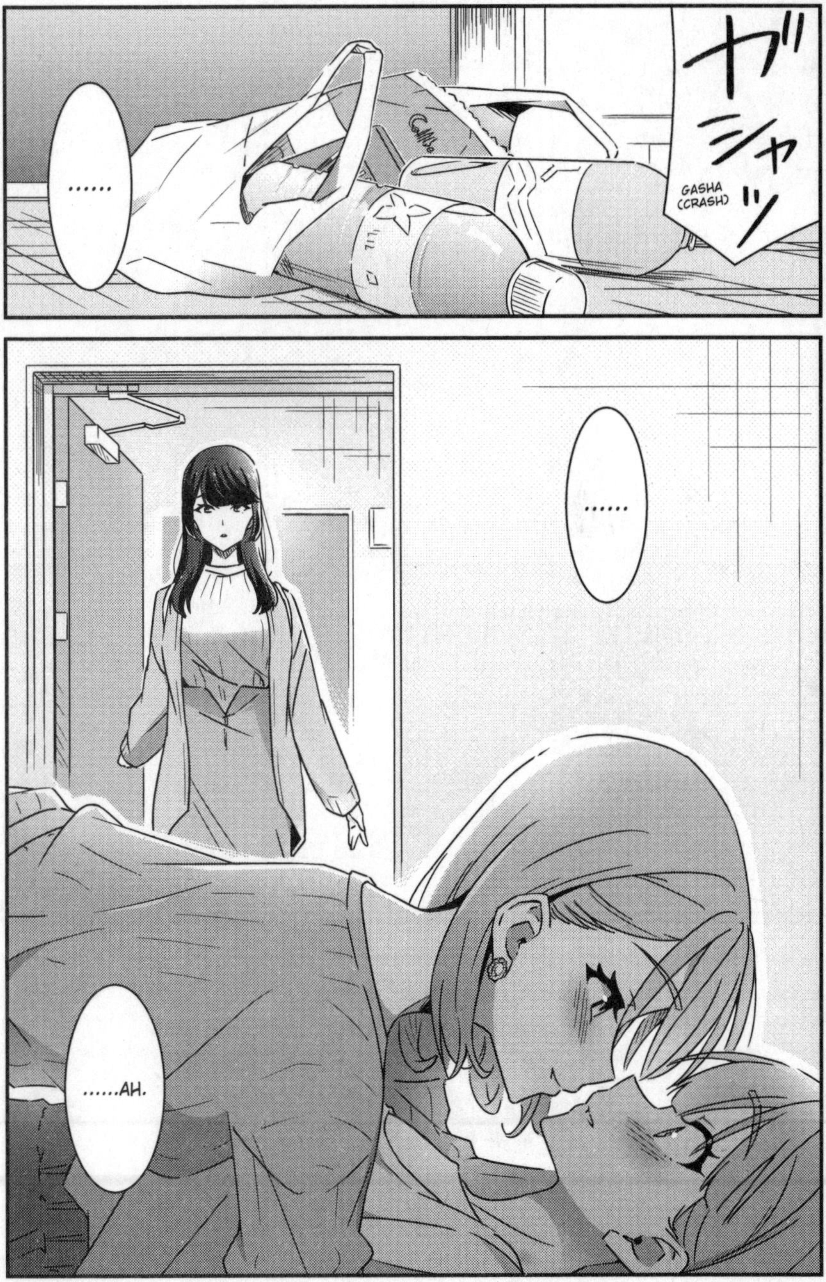
ガシャッ
GASHA (CRASH)
......
......
......AH.

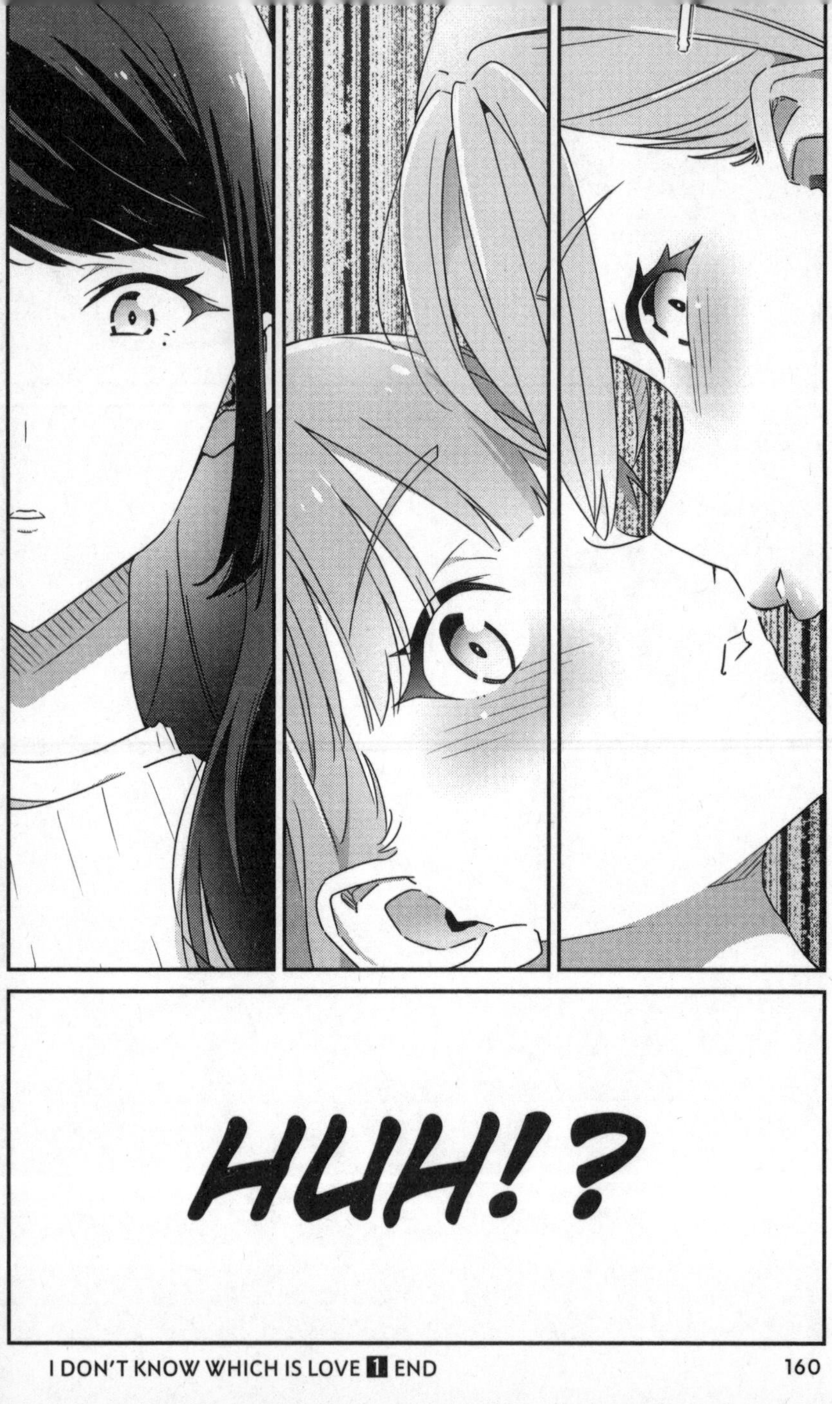
HUH!?

Translation Notes

♥

▼ ▼ ▼ ▼ ▼ ▼ ▼ ▼ ♥ ▼ ▼ ▼ ▼ ▼ ▼ ▼ ▼ ♥ ▼ ▼ ▼ ▼ ▼ ▼ ▼ ▼ ▼

Page 4 - The college Mei attends, **Meigo University**, is based on Meiji University, a private school in central Tokyo that boasts a robust theater department.

Page 9 - Many Japanese universities operate **affiliated high schools**, granting students recommendations to their department of choice and even exempting them from the country's rigorous entrance exams.

Page 15 - A **todomeki** (or *dodomeki*) is a type of supernatural *youkai* monster spoken of in certain collections of ghost stories. Said to appear as a human woman with long arms covered in bird eyes, its name roughly translates to "hundred-eyed demon."

Page 74 - The passage Kaoru reads is from Edgar Allen Poe's *The Black Cat*.

♥

Page 149 - Japanese beef is rated on yield and quality, with the pricy **rank A5** cuts being the highest by both metrics.

♥

Honorifics

♥

▼ ▼ ▼ ▼ ▼ ▼ ▼ ▼ ♥ ▼ ▼ ▼ ▼ ▼ ▼ ▼ ♥ ▼ ▼ ▼ ▼ ▼ ▼ ▼ ▼ ▼

No honorific: Indicates familiarity or closeness; considered rude to use without permission.

-san: The Japanese equivalent of Mr./Mrs./Miss. If a situation calls for politeness, this is the fail-safe honorific.

-chan: An affectionate honorific indicating familiarity used mostly in reference to girls; also used in reference to cute persons or animals regardless of gender.

-senpai: A term commonly used to respectfully refer to upperclassmen in school or seniors at work. Its antonym, used for underclassmen, is *kouhai*.

-sama: Extremely formal and conveys an enormous amount of respect for the addressee.

♥

-(o)nii: Literally means "older brother" but can refer to older unrelated boys.

-(o)nee: Literally means "older sister" but can be used as a term of endearment or respect for an unrelated girl one looks up to.

♥

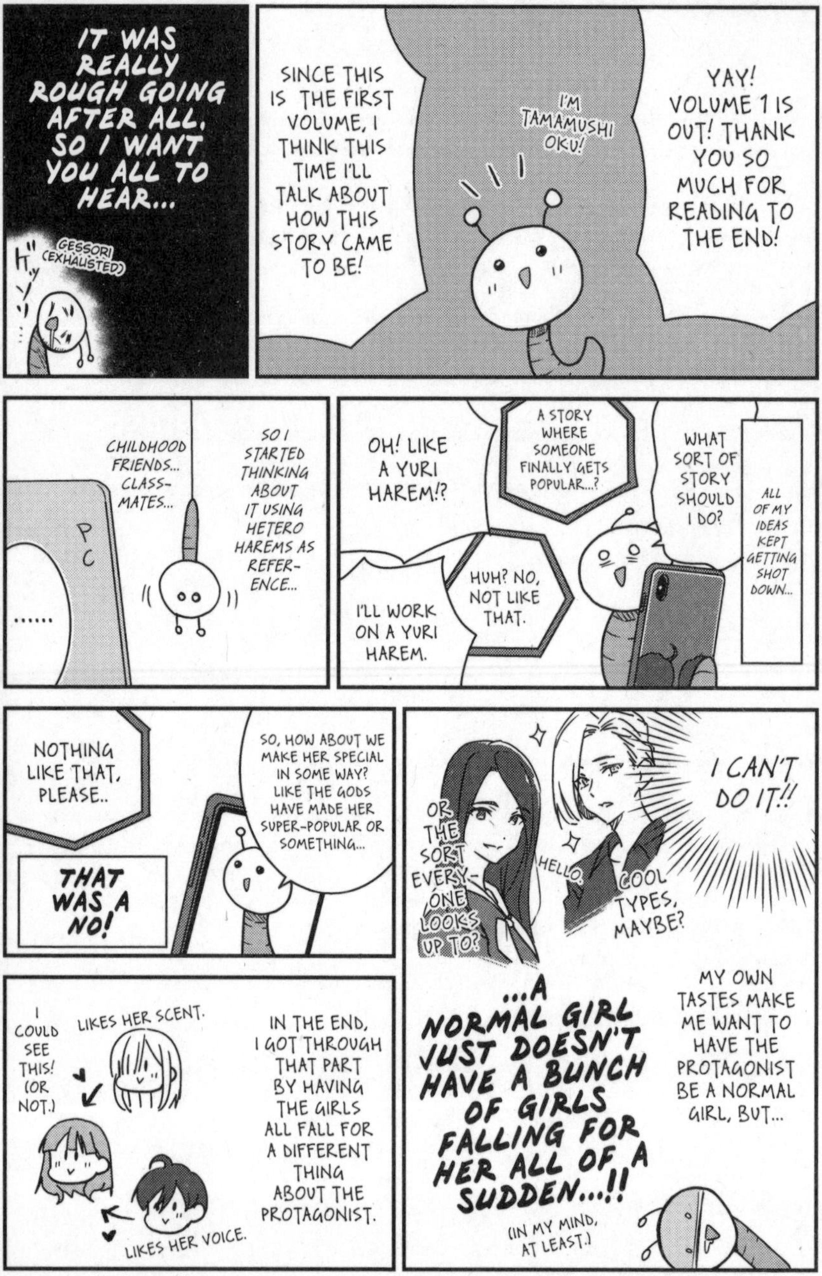

YAY! VOLUME 1 IS OUT! THANK YOU SO MUCH FOR READING TO THE END!
I'M TAMAMUSHI OKU!
SINCE THIS IS THE FIRST VOLUME, I THINK THIS TIME I'LL TALK ABOUT HOW THIS STORY CAME TO BE!
IT WAS REALLY ROUGH GOING AFTER ALL, SO I WANT YOU ALL TO HEAR...
GESSORI (EXHAUSTED)
ALL OF MY IDEAS KEPT GETTING SHOT DOWN...
WHAT SORT OF STORY SHOULD I DO?
A STORY WHERE SOMEONE FINALLY GETS POPULAR...?
OH! LIKE A YURI HAREM!?
HUH? NO, NOT LIKE THAT.
I'LL WORK ON A YURI HAREM.
SO I STARTED THINKING ABOUT IT USING HETERO HAREMS AS REFERENCE...
CHILDHOOD FRIENDS... CLASS-MATES...
PC
......
I CAN'T DO IT!!
COOL TYPES, MAYBE?
HELLO.
OR THE SORT EVERYONE LOOKS UP TO?
MY OWN TASTES MAKE ME WANT TO HAVE THE PROTAGONIST BE A NORMAL GIRL, BUT...
...A NORMAL GIRL JUST DOESN'T HAVE A BUNCH OF GIRLS FALLING FOR HER ALL OF A SUDDEN...!!
(IN MY MIND, AT LEAST.)
SO, HOW ABOUT WE MAKE HER SPECIAL IN SOME WAY? LIKE THE GODS HAVE MADE HER SUPER-POPULAR OR SOMETHING...
NOTHING LIKE THAT, PLEASE..
THAT WAS A NO!
IN THE END, I GOT THROUGH THAT PART BY HAVING THE GIRLS ALL FALL FOR A DIFFERENT THING ABOUT THE PROTAGONIST.
LIKES HER SCENT.
I COULD SEE THIS! (OR NOT.)
LIKES HER VOICE.

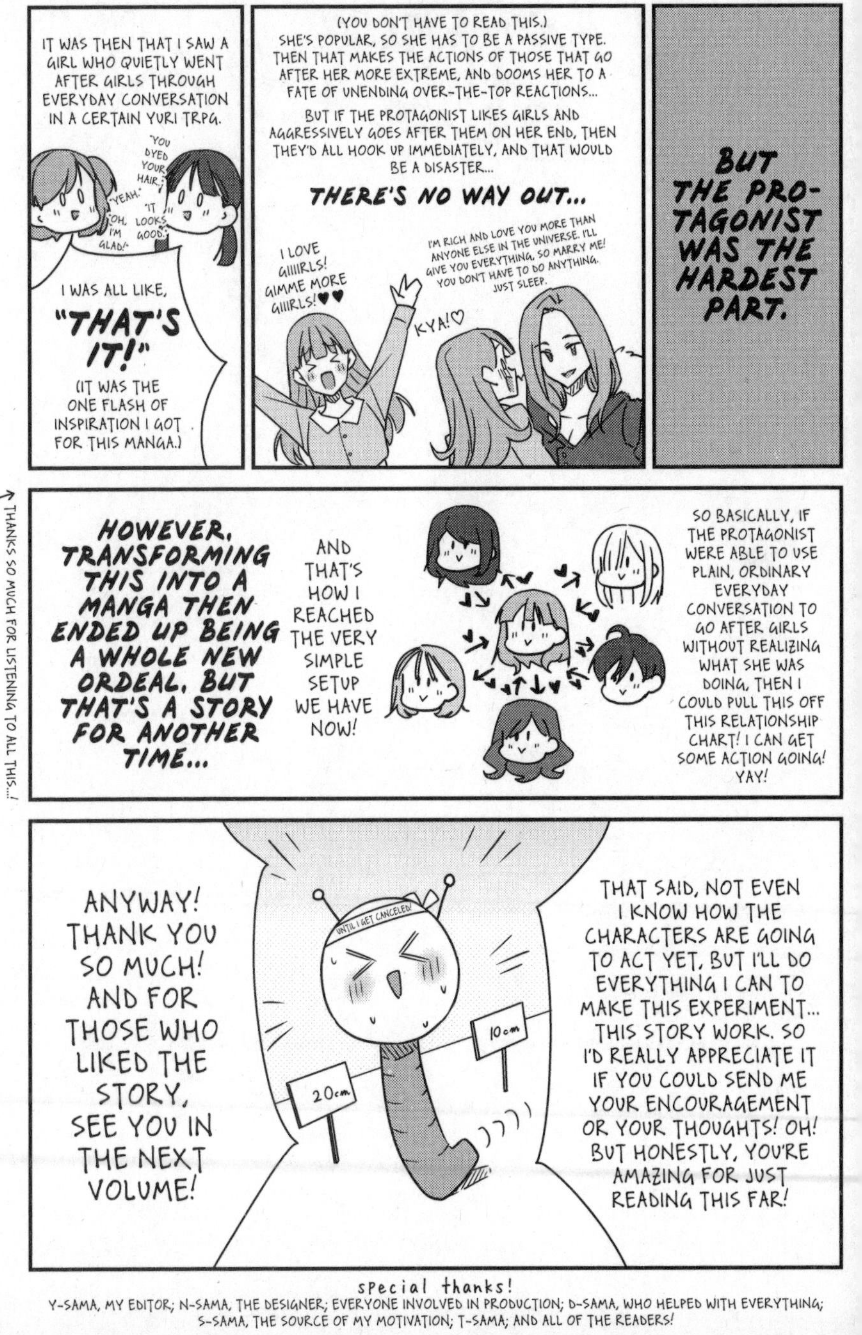
BUT THE PROTAGONIST WAS THE HARDEST PART.
(YOU DON'T HAVE TO READ THIS.) SHE'S POPULAR, SO SHE HAS TO BE A PASSIVE TYPE. THEN THAT MAKES THE ACTIONS OF THOSE THAT GO AFTER HER MORE EXTREME, AND DOOMS HER TO A FATE OF UNENDING OVER-THE-TOP REACTIONS...
BUT IF THE PROTAGONIST LIKES GIRLS AND AGGRESSIVELY GOES AFTER THEM ON HER END, THEN THEY'D ALL HOOK UP IMMEDIATELY, AND THAT WOULD BE A DISASTER...
THERE'S NO WAY OUT...
I'M RICH AND LOVE YOU MORE THAN ANYONE ELSE IN THE UNIVERSE. I'LL GIVE YOU EVERYTHING, SO MARRY ME! YOU DON'T HAVE TO DO ANYTHING. JUST SLEEP.
I LOVE GIIIIRLS! GIMME MORE GIIIRLS!♥♥
KYA!♡
IT WAS THEN THAT I SAW A GIRL WHO QUIETLY WENT AFTER GIRLS THROUGH EVERYDAY CONVERSATION IN A CERTAIN YURI TRPG.
"YOU DYED YOUR HAIR."
"YEAH."
"IT LOOKS GOOD."
"OH, I'M GLAD!"
I WAS ALL LIKE, "THAT'S IT!"
(IT WAS THE ONE FLASH OF INSPIRATION I GOT FOR THIS MANGA.)
SO BASICALLY, IF THE PROTAGONIST WERE ABLE TO USE PLAIN, ORDINARY EVERYDAY CONVERSATION TO GO AFTER GIRLS WITHOUT REALIZING WHAT SHE WAS DOING, THEN I COULD PULL THIS OFF THIS RELATIONSHIP CHART! I CAN GET SOME ACTION GOING! YAY!
AND THAT'S HOW I REACHED THE VERY SIMPLE SETUP WE HAVE NOW!
HOWEVER, TRANSFORMING THIS INTO A MANGA THEN ENDED UP BEING A WHOLE NEW ORDEAL. BUT THAT'S A STORY FOR ANOTHER TIME...
THAT SAID, NOT EVEN I KNOW HOW THE CHARACTERS ARE GOING TO ACT YET, BUT I'LL DO EVERYTHING I CAN TO MAKE THIS EXPERIMENT... THIS STORY WORK. SO I'D REALLY APPRECIATE IT IF YOU COULD SEND ME YOUR ENCOURAGEMENT OR YOUR THOUGHTS! OH! BUT HONESTLY, YOU'RE AMAZING FOR JUST READING THIS FAR!
UNTIL I GET CANCELED!
10cm
20cm
ANYWAY! THANK YOU SO MUCH! AND FOR THOSE WHO LIKED THE STORY, SEE YOU IN THE NEXT VOLUME!

↑ THANKS SO MUCH FOR LISTENING TO ALL THIS...!

special thanks!
Y-SAMA, MY EDITOR; N-SAMA, THE DESIGNER; EVERYONE INVOLVED IN PRODUCTION; D-SAMA, WHO HELPED WITH EVERYTHING; S-SAMA, THE SOURCE OF MY MOTIVATION; T-SAMA; AND ALL OF THE READERS!

I Don't Know Which Is Love

1

Tamamushi Oku

Translation: **LEIGHANN HARVEY** ❖ Lettering: **ELENA PIZARRO**

DORE GA KOI KA GA WAKARANAI Vol. 1
©Oku Tamamushi 2022
First published in Japan in 2022 by KADOKAWA CORPORATION, Tokyo.
English translation rights arranged with KADOKAWA CORPORATION, Tokyo,
through TUTTLE-MORI AGENCY, INC., Tokyo.

English translation © 2023 by Yen Press, LLC

Yen Press
150 West 30th Street, 19th Floor
New York, NY 10001

Visit us at yenpress.com ❤ facebook.com/yenpress ❤ twitter.com/yenpress
❤ yenpress.tumblr.com ❤ instagram.com/yenpress

First Yen Press Edition: August 2023
Edited by Yen Press Editorial: Thomas McAlister, JuYoun Lee
Designed by Yen Press Design: Wendy Chan

Yen Press is an imprint of Yen Press, LLC.
The Yen Press name and logo are trademarks of Yen Press, LLC.

Library of Congress Control Number: 2023938740

ISBNs: 978-1-9753-6985-9 (paperback)
978-1-9753-6986-6 (ebook)

1 3 5 7 9 10 8 6 4 2

WOR

Printed in the United States of America